Practical Strategies for Family-Centered Early Intervention

Early Childhood Intervention Series

Series Editor
M. Jeanne Wilcox, Ph.D.

Working with Parents of Young Children with Disabilities by Elizabeth J. Webster, Ph.D., and Louise M. Ward, M.A.

Pediatric Swallowing and Feeding: Assessment and Management edited by Joan C. Arvedson, Ph.D., and Linda Brodsky, M.D.

Facilitating Hearing and Listening in Young Children by Carol Flexer, Ph.D.

Premature Infants and Their Families: Developmental Interventions by M. Virginia Wyly, Ph.D., with contributions from Jack Allen, M.A., and Janet Wilson, R.N., M.S., N.N.P.

Practical Strategies for Family-Centered Early Intervention by P. J. McWilliam, Ph.D., Pamela J. Winton, Ph.D., and Elizabeth Crais, Ph.D.

Practical Strategies for Family-Centered Early Intervention

Early Childhood Intervention Series

P. J. McWilliam, Ph.D.
Frank Porter Graham Child Development Center,
The University of North Carolina at Chapel Hill
Pamela J. Winton, Ph.D.
Elizabeth R. Crais, Ph.D.
Division of Speech and Hearing Sciences,
The University of North Carolina at Chapel Hill

SINGULAR PUBLISHING GROUP, INC.
SAN DIEGO · LONDON

Singular Publishing Group, Inc.
401 West A Street, Suite 325
San Diego, California 92101-7904

19 Compton Terrace
London N1 2UN, U.K.

Typeset in 10/12 Century by So Cal Graphics
Printed in the United States of America by BookCrafters

Library of Congress Cataloging-in-Publication Data

McWilliam, P. J., 1953–
    Practical strategies for family-centered early intervention / P.J.
McWilliam, Pamela J. Winton & Elizabeth Crais.
      p.   cm. — (Early childhood intervention series)
    Includes bibliographical references and index.
    ISBN 1-879105-94-2
    1. Child psychotherapy.   2. Family psychotherapy.   I. Winton,
Pamela J.   II. Crais, Elizabeth.   III. Title.   IV. Series.
RF504.M38   1996
618.92'8914—dc20
                                       96-25913
                                          CIP

Contents

■

Contents

Foreword

∎

When current social policy regarding at-risk infants and young children is considered in conjunction with advances in theoretical conceptualizations and associated research it is clear that early childhood intervention is emerging as a unique and dynamic area of scientific inquiry across multiple disciplines. The purpose of the Early Childhood Intervention Series is to provide state-of the-art information with respect to interventions focusing on families and their infants and young children who are at risk for or have diagnosed disabilities. As readers will readily recognize, this is no small task; the "art" of effective intervention practices is continually subject to refinement and improvements of existing practices as well as introduction of entirely new ideas and approaches. As is the case with most topics subject to a rapid surge in scholarly attention, new findings and ideas are often steps ahead of their practical application and, in some cases, not easily translated into appropriate practices, creating what many have come to regard as a research as a research-to-practice gap. Books in this series have been designed and prepared with an eye toward reducing this gap and assisting early childhood intervention personnel in becoming consumers of current theoretical and empirical information. The topics in the series are wide ranging, and through explicit examples and discussion, each of the individual books offer a wealth of practical information to assist us all in providing the most effective interventions for families and their infants and young children.

The present volume focuses on families, the critical role they play in the early childhood service delivery process, and the practice of family-centered service design and implementation. All early childhood personnel are aware of the need to practice within a family-centered framework, but the reality of many service systems is at odds (to varying degrees) with principles of family-centered care, a situation that frequently constrains the extent to which early childhood practices are, in truth, family-centered . In this book, Drs. McWilliam, Winton, and Crais demonstrate a keen awareness of such constraints and have packed their pages with practical suggestions for becoming, and staying family-centered in a broad array of service settings. It is this pragmatic focus which distinguishes this volume from others focusing on families and early intervention systems and processes. This book is written from the trenches for those in the trenches and will prove an essential handbook for all personnel charged with serving families and their infants and young children.

Preface

∎

Although much has been written about family-centered service delivery over the past decade, our experiences in training others have indicated that knowledge of family-centered principles alone is not sufficient to ensure that practitioners can effectively translate these principles into their daily work with children and families. Even when professionals wholeheartedly agree with a family-centered approach, the complexity of the situations they encounter in working with families and the numerous administrative barriers they often must work around can make it difficult to implement a family-centered approach. In other words, although most practitioners are aware of family-centered principles, many are still asking, "But what do I do on Monday?" The purpose of this book is to address this important question. In doing so, we have made a concerted effort to steer away from academic writing and, instead, provide practitioners with practical, down-to-earth suggestions for applying family-centered principles in their daily work. Furthermore, the suggestions are not geared toward a specific disipline, but rather are applicable for use by practitioners representing the many professional disciplines that provide services to children from birth to age 5 and the various settings in which they work (home, classroom, hospital, clinic).

In developing an organizational format for this book, we have chosen one that we feel is most closely related to direct service provision. Following a brief overview of family-centered principles and a discussion of the real-world challenges to their implementation, the remaining chapters provide an in-depth look at how family-centered principles can be applied within five aspects of service delivery. We begin with a chapter devoted entirely to discussing the initial contact between a program or professional and a family and suggesting strategies that can be employed to ensure that this first contact reflects a family-centered approach. Succeeding chapters move the reader through a series of steps in the service delivery process that include understanding family priorities, conducting child assessments, developing intervention plans, and day-to-day service delivery.

Although this sequence of activities may seem linear, it is actually circular—repeated over and over again as we work with children and families. For example, although a family will have only one initial contact with a program, within that program each succeeding professional who works with the child and family will have his or her own initial contact. Similarly, the identification of family priorities is an ongoing process, and child assessments and intervention planning are conducted on numerous occasions throughout a family's enrollment in a program. With each new cycle of the sequence, child and family circumstances change, as do the relationships between parents and professionals. As thesee changes occur, so too will the manner in which we interact with families.

Two levels of family-centered service delivery are discussed throughout this book: (a) program policies and procedures and (b) individual interactions with families. The first level deals with organizational structure, rules, and processes that are established at the program or agency level and affect all professionals and families. The second level, although definitely influenced by program procedures and policies, focuses on aspects of service delivery over which individual practitioners have more control. These include all one-to-one interactions that a professional has with each family served. Although there is some overlap between program policies and individual interactions, the distinction between these two levels of service delivery seems important for two reasons. First, in our experiences in working with early intervention programs, changes in program policies and practices usually take far more time to achieve than changes at the level of the individual practitioner. Second, although some professionals may work in settings where there is little support for family-centered practices, they can still be family-centered in aspects of service delivery where they have control. In fact, the apparent strength of influence individual practitioners have in achieving the outcomes of a family-centered approach led us to emphasize this level of service delivery.

In each chapter, examples from real life are included to illustrate the translation of family-centered principles to everyday practice. Many of the examples come from our own experiences in early intervention; others are based on true stories told to us by parents and professionals we have been privileged to meet and talk with in our roles as instructors. Each chapter also includes strategies for effective communication with families because, although communication skills are critical to the successful implementation of a family-centered approach, few practitioners receive adequate preservice training in this area of skill development. Rather than just providing general principles or rules for communicating with families, each chapter includes suggestions for specific words that professionals might use in their conversations with parents.

The final chapter of the book deals with the issue of change. If there is one thing we have learned in training others, it is that moving from child-focused early intervention to a family-centered approach isn't easy—

even for those who are highly motivated to do so. Service systems and individual programs are steeped in traditions that often run counter to a family-centered approach, and it may be difficult to get all members of the team on board when it comes to organizational or procedural changes. Even for the individual professional, overcoming comfortable habits and long-standing beliefs can be challenging, and new skills may be needed to achieve the desired results of a family-centered approach. Although not professing to have all the answers, the last chapter discusses the process of change and provides some practical suggestions and resources for clinicians who want to implement some of the ideas presented in this book.

**For Don
Who forged our alliance**

■ CHAPTER 1

Family-Centered Practices In Early Intervention

The field of early intervention has undergone many changes over the past decade. A major event for the field was the passage of U.S. Public Law 99-457 (Education of the Handicapped Amendments of 1986), which mandated free and appropriate public education for preschoolers with disabilities (ages 3–5 years). The same law provided financial incentives to states providing services to infants and toddlers (birth to 3 years) at risk for or demonstrating developmental delays.

Although the concepts embedded within the legislation preceded its passage, the law itself created a sense of urgency within the field to create services where none existed and to make changes in existing services to ensure that they were in compliance with the new regulations. Among the changes spurred by the new legislation, unprecedented training efforts have been undertaken to ensure that a sufficient number of qualified professionals are available to staff our nation's early intervention programs. This has included the training of new professionals, as well as the retooling of professionals already working in the field.

Although P.L. 99-457 and its subsequent reauthorization (Individuals with Disabilities Education Act Amendments of 1991) provide guidelines and regulations for many aspects of early intervention services, this book addresses only one—a family-centered approach to service delivery. The importance of this one aspect, however, should not be underestimated, as it is the philosophical basis for all regulations contained in Part H of the law that covers services to infants and toddlers. Furthermore, this book is not about the law. It is about the philosophical approach embraced by the regulations, and we propose here, at the outset of our writing, that a family-centered approach to service delivery should not be restricted to those working with children from birth to 3 years of age. The book should also serve as a guide for programs and individuals serving preschoolers and, although not covered in this text, it is our belief that a family-centered approach is a sound approach for the provision of human services across the lifespan.

■ PRINCIPLES OF A FAMILY-CENTERED APPROACH

The origins of a family-centered approach can be found in the ecological and social systems perspectives of Brofenbrenner (1975) and Hobbs et al. (1984). Carl Dunst and his colleagues (Dunst, 1985; Dunst, Trivette, & Deal, 1988, 1994) have elaborated on this earlier work and were instrumental in promoting the adoption of family-centered principles by early interventionists. The terms "empowerment" and "enablement" were introduced to the field of early intervention in their 1988 book, *Enabling and Empowering Families.* At about the same time, preliminary guidelines for implementing family-centered care were issued in a publication by the Association for the Care of Children's Health (Shelton, Jeppson, & Johnson, 1987). These works and others that followed have contributed to the rethinking and reshaping of services to young children with disabilities and their families. Although there are some variations in definitions of family-centered practices, we present here the principles of family-centered practice that most would agree on.

Family-Centered Principles

- Viewing the family as the unit of service delivery
- Recognizing child and family strengths
- Responding to family-identified priorities
- Individualizing service delivery
- Responding to the changing priorities of families
- Supporting family values and lifestyles

Viewing the Family as the Unit of Service Delivery

Historically, early intervention efforts have focused exclusively on the young child who is at risk for or demonstrates developmental delays. The work of early intervention professionals was to identify the factors associated with the risk of eventual or continued developmental delay and to design and implement interventions aimed at alleviating the impact of these factors on the child's future development. Much work went into the development of assessment instruments and curricula that were appropriate for infants and preschoolers, many of which are still in use today.

The importance of the family in the life of the young child was not forgotten even in the earliest days of early intervention. The classic statement, *"Parents are the first and most important teachers of their children,"* was made to a great number of parents by early intervention professionals in the past and, no doubt, is still heard by many parents today. Although recognizing the critical role of the parent in child development, this phrase and others similar to it imparted to parents the philosophical basis for parent training. Early intervention professionals were considered to be the experts in identifying the needs of the child and determining appropriate intervention strategies to ensure developmental progress. Parents received training and continued guidance from professionals to appropriately implement these same interventions with their children. Thus, even when working with parents, the focus of early intervention was on the child (Turnbull & Winton, 1984).

A family-centered approach looks beyond the child to include the entire family as the unit of intervention. This approach recognizes that the well-being of each family member has an impact on every other member of the family. For example, if one or both of the parents are worried about family finances, this is likely to affect the quality of interactions with their child, which, in turn, may affect the child's developmental progress. Similarly, conducting interventions with their child with special needs may result in parents having less time available for meeting their own needs or less time to spend with other children in the family (Turnbull & Turnbull, 1985). Given this perspective, a family-centered approach supports the policy of recognizing and responding to the needs of each family member rather than only the needs of the child with a disability. Helping a parent find housing, employment, or tuition waivers to complete a college degree are viewed as being equally valid to locating adaptive equipment for a child or providing speech-language therapy.

The ultimate outcome of a family-centered approach is to enhance the well-being of the family as a whole. This includes minimizing stress, maintaining or enhancing relationships within the family, and enabling the family to as closely as possible follow the lifestyle that they would have chosen for themselves if their child did not have special needs. One of the advantages of a family-centered approach is that this outcome may be achieved by intervening in a variety of ways. Unlike traditional child-focused approaches, success isn't solely dependent on the developmental progress of the child. Furthermore, differences in values, beliefs, and preferred lifestyles among families participating in early intervention means that the definition of success will be different for each family.

Recognizing Child and Family Strengths

Although we have mentioned child and family needs in previous paragraphs, an important principle of a family-centered approach is the recognition of child and family strengths. In fact, in the reauthorization of early intervention legislation, the amendments to Part H replaced the term "family needs" with "family resources, concerns, and priorities." This change is more than a matter of semantics, it represents the conviction that we should view all children and families as capable and competent. When truly believed and acted upon, this positive orientation yields quite different results from deficit-oriented approaches.

It is usually easy to recognize and acknowledge family strengths when working with parents or guardians whose values and beliefs are comparable to our own and who have the knowledge, skills, and resources to accomplish what they set out to do. It can be far more difficult to recognize the strengths of families who are less knowledgeable, whose skills and resources are limited, and whose values are different from our own. Nevertheless, these families are also capable and competent. Given appropriate information, skill training, and adequate support, such families can demonstrate their abilities and act upon their priorities in an effective manner. Even prior to such interventions, the strengths of less privileged families are visible. For example, providing food, shelter, and clothing for a family on an extremely limited income, keeping children safe in dangerous neighborhoods, finding jobs with a limited education, and using public transportation all require considerable skill and knowledge of community resources.

Recognizing and acknowledging family strengths is only the first task in taking a positive approach. To complete the job, these same strengths must be used and expanded upon in the development and implementation of intervention plans. This means helping parents to recognize their own strengths and abilities, encouraging them to use and build upon their existing knowledge and skills, and assisting them in locating and using resources that they need. Not only is such an approach likely to enhance parents' self-esteem and self-confidence, but it also lends itself to the acquisition of skills and knowledge that can be used by the family in the future. As summarized by Dunst, Trivette, & Mott (1994), "the goal of intervention must *not* be seen as 'doing for people' but rather the strengthening of functioning in ways that make families less and not more dependent upon professionals for help" (p. 117).

A positive approach also involves recognizing child strengths. Because most early intervention professionals are trained to recognize and ameliorate developmental deficits, they tend to focus their efforts on those aspects of development in which children demonstrate their greatest delays. Parents are also concerned about delays in their children's development and usually appreciate the information and help they receive. All too often, however, children's strengths are overlooked or underappreciated in the process. Just as all families have strengths, so do all children. Greater emphasis on a child's areas of strength can bolster a parent's pride—pride in their child's accomplishments and also pride in what they have done for their child. In addition, when a child's strengths are fully recognized, they can be put to good use in intervention.

As shall be shown in the chapters that follow, recognizing child and family strengths cannot be reduced to a simple one-time procedure. Instead, this aspect of a family-centered approach should permeate all phases of service delivery, from the very first time we meet a child and family until the time that they leave our services. Furthermore, acknowledging child and family strengths may be accomplished through a variety of methods, perhaps the most important of which are the little things we say and do that communicate genuine respect for children and families and sincere appreciation of even their smallest successes. Each of the chapters in this book include specific strategies for acknowledging and building on child and family strengths.

Responding to Family Priorities

The identification of family priorities is critical to implementing a family-centered approach. Family priorities consist of what parents or guardians consider important for their child and for their entire family, and each family's priorities will be different. The purpose of identifying family priorities is to ensure that interventions are designed and implemented to help families accomplish what is important to them, rather than what professionals think should be important to them.

As shall be pointed out, the process of identifying family priorities is continuous and requires skills that professionals may or may not have learned in their preservice training. The professional is responsible for providing a structure that allows families to clearly communicate what it is that is important to them, while at the same time sharing their information and expertise in order that families may make fully-informed decisions about the priorities or goals that they select. Most important, professionals must maintain a nonjudgmental stance in sharing their expertise and responding to what parents or guardians identify as priorities for their children and their entire family. This can be difficult when a professional's training or personal beliefs are in conflict with what the family decides is most important.

Individualizing Service Delivery

Because each family's priorities are unique, responding to family priorities requires an individually tailored plan of services. The availability of service options from which to choose and flexibility within each service option is, therefore, critical. A family-centered approach also requires a more comprehensive menu of services, in that, services should go beyond meeting the needs of the child to include the priorities of the family as a whole. This is not to say that early intervention programs must offer all possible child and family services—for, indeed, they cannot. It does mean, however, that early intervention professionals are responsible for knowing about the variety of services and resources available in their communities and assisting families in accessing those that would help them accomplish their priorities (Dunst & Trivette, 1994; Shelton & Stepanek, 1994).

In short, a family-centered approach recognizes that "One size does *not* fit all." Each family is unique and services must be individually tailored to ensure a "best fit" between available service options and the priorities of the family. Furthermore, it is the family that ultimately determines what the "best fit" is.

Responding to Changes in Family Priorities

Family priorities are not static, but ever-changing. Consequently, services or intervention strategies that are appropriate one week, may not be appropriate the following week or several months later. The hospitalization of a family member, change in a parent's job or work schedule, the birth of a sibling, or an upcoming family vacation can result in a change of family priorities. Obtaining new information about their child or information about alternative intervention strategies can, likewise, change parents' priorities. And sometimes parents just change their mind about what is important for their child and family. Changes in priorities may be temporary or permanent, and, in some cases, no reason for a change may be given. The important thing, however, is that professionals be aware of changes in family priorities and willing to adjust services and intervention plans to accommodate any changes that may occur. As shall be shown throughout this book, keeping abreast of family priorities and ensuring that interventions are responsive to changes in priorities requires more than the traditional once-a-year meeting of professionals and parents to develop an individualized family service plan (IFSP) or individualized education plan (IEP). It requires the development of a trusting relationship and continuous communication between professionals and parents.

Supporting Family Lifestyles

The birth of a child—any child—has a big impact on a family's lifestyle. The daily routines of every other family member will be disrupted to some extent. Each change is followed by a process of adaptation and accommodation as new routines are developed or adjustments to old routines are made. The initial disruption may be even greater when a child is born with special needs or a disability is later discovered, and the process of adaptation may involve some dramatic changes in the way a family conducts its daily living (e.g., Morton, 1985; Wikler, 1981). Many of these changes will have already taken place before an early intervention professional ever has a first contact with the family.

The changes a family makes are directed toward achieving an equilibrium—at least a minimum level of comfort for all members of the family (Gallimore, Weisner, Kaufman, & Bernheimer, 1989). More important, the direction of these changes usually reflects the family's values, beliefs, and priorities. This includes the family's preferred pace of life, how family members want to spend their time, and the level of importance they attribute to various aspects of each routine of the day.

The goal of a family-centered approach is not to disrupt family routines even further, but rather to support families in achieving the balance that they want. Methods for accomplishing this are described throughout this book. They include letting parents function as parents rather than as therapists, assessing child needs within the context of family life, developing interventions that fit comfortably within existing family routines, and building or strengthening the family's existing support systems (e.g., church, civic groups, extended family, friends, and neighbors) rather than replacing them with professional services.

■ FROM THEORY TO PRACTICE

Although many may agree with the principles of a family-centered approach, incorporating these principles into our daily work with children and families is not always easy. There are a number of difficulties that may be faced in trying to adopt this approach (McWilliam, 1993). While not wishing to dwell on the negative, it is perhaps best that we briefly address some of these issues up front.

Philosophy Versus Procedure

First and foremost, family-centered service provision is a philosophy. It is based on a set of deeply held values and beliefs about relationships between children and their families, relationships between professionals and parents, and the role of community services as a whole in ensuring the well-being of children with developmental disabilities and their families. There are no step-by-step procedures for implementing a family-centered approach, but rather the basic principles of the approach must be applied individually to each situation encountered in working with children and their families. The uncertainty involved in individually applying the principles can cause discomfort for some professionals, especially for those who are just beginning to use a family-centered approach.

One reason there can be no clear-cut set of procedures is that the nature of early intervention services varies considerably from state to state, from community to community, and from agency to agency. Differences in population density, the administrative organization of services, and the availability and distribution of resources within states and across the nation give rise to a plethora of ways in which early intervention services are delivered. There are classroom-based programs, home-based programs, inclusive and noninclusive programs, clinic-based services, and consultative services. In some places, a single program may handle services to a family from the initial referral until the time the child goes to public school. Whereas, in other places, services may be scattered across a number of programs and agencies, and numerous transitions may occur over a period of a few years. A single set of procedures couldn't possibly be developed that would be appropriate and effective for all these situations.

Another reason for the lack of specific procedures is the diversity among families participating in early intervention. Not only do families vary in terms of their priorities for themselves and their children, but also in the manner in which they prefer to interact with agencies and professionals. For example, some parents freely discuss their feelings with professionals and readily provide information about intimate aspects of their personal lives. In contrast, other parents may prefer to keep personal matters and their feelings to themselves, or perhaps only share such information with close friends or relatives. Furthermore, parents' preferences may change over time. The parent who at first prefers not to divulge personal information may, over time, warm up to professionals and develop more intimate relationships. In the same manner, parents who are initially quite open with professionals about personal matters may desire more privacy at a later time. Once again, when it comes to translating family-centered principles into practice, "One size does **not** fit all." The key to success is understanding the unique preferences of each family and ensuring that the services offered by programs are flexible enough to allow professionals to be responsive to each family's preferences and priorities.

Established Traditions

Although the federal regulations governing early intervention services are relatively new, early intervention has a long history in the United States (Safer & Hamilton, 1993; Shonkoff & Meisels, 1990). An even longer history exists for special education services to school-aged youth, human services in general, and medical and allied health services. Each history has given rise to a set of beliefs about the purposes of service delivery, the scope of services, and the manner in which services should be offered. The influence of these established traditions on early intervention should not be underestimated. They have exerted significant influence in shaping the organizational structure of services; policies and procedures for payments; the training, certification, and licensing of professionals; and regulations and monitoring practices related to quality assurance.

Some traditions are inconsistent with a family-centered approach to service delivery. This is especially true when traditions are based on a medical model or child-focused approach to providing services. For example, regulations related to the payment of services (e.g., Medicaid and private health insurance) are renowned for being inconsistent with family-centered practices (Fox, Wicks, McManus, & Newacheck, 1992). All too often, reimbursement policies only allow for billing of service hours spent in direct contact with the target child; so time spent collaborating with other professionals or talking to the child's parents (e.g., IFSP and IEP meetings) are not reimbursed.

Thus, a professional or team of professionals may encounter any number of administrative roadblocks when trying to be family-centered. This is not to say it can't be done. It just means that the desired level of support for implementing family-centered practices may not always be present (Bailey, McWilliam, & Winton, 1992). Administrative roadblocks may need to be worked around. Furthermore, changes in early intervention are occurring at a rapid rate, and perhaps new traditions will eventually be established that will be more consistent with a family-centered approach.

A Team Effort

Children and families participating in early intervention often receive services from multiple agencies or programs. Even when services are provided within a single program, professionals from several disciplines are typically involved with a child and family. Recognizing the confusing patchwork of early intervention services that exists in many communities, Part H of the Individuals with Disabilities Education Act Amendments of 1991 (IDEA) mandates that a service coordinator be identified for each child and family receiving services. The purpose of the service coordinator is to ensure that services needed from the various professionals, programs, and agencies in the community to meet each family's unique concerns and priorities are secured.

No doubt the role of a service coordinator is important, but the existence of a service coordinator, alone, is not sufficient to ensure a family-centered approach to service delivery. In fact, recent research (Harbin, 1996) has shown that many families don't even know who their service coordinator is. Ideally, the entire service system and each professional who is a part of it would share a common philosophy of family-centered care and provide services accordingly (Bruder & Bologna, 1993). Although efforts are underway to infuse family-centered approaches into the training of professionals across the various disciplines, this work is far from complete. Consequently, professionals within a program may be divided in their beliefs about how best to work with children and families, and those individuals attempting to implement family-centered practices may not have the support of other team members and may even encounter active resistance.

New Role Expectations

The educational backgrounds of early interventionists are diverse. Not only do academic training programs vary in terms of the specific discipline content covered, but also in the amount of course work related to early intervention and working with families. In fact, surveys of university programs (Bailey, Palsha, & Simeonsson, 1991; Bailey, Simeonsson, Yoder, & Huntington, 1991; Crais & Leonard, 1990; Hanson & Lovett, 1992) have shown that the majority of professionals who enter the field of early intervention will have had little course work related specifically to early intervention and even less in the area of working with families. Furthermore, many university programs have indicated that they are unlikely to add these content areas to their curricula, in that they are already having difficulty fitting in existing content requirements for professional certification or licensing (Bailey et al., 1991).

Although the formal preparation of many professionals may remain unchanged, the roles and expectations for early interventionists across all disciplines are expanding (Bailey, 1989; Brown & Rule, 1993; Fenichel & Eggbeer, 1991). Full implementation of a family-centered approach will therefore require not only a retooling of our current early intervention workforce, but also the continual training and reorientation of new professionals as they enter the field. In addition, implementation will require that many practitioners be willing to assume roles and responsibilities that have traditionally not been a part of their profession and to acquire new skills that enable them to do so.

In part, this book is written in response to the challenges described above. First, it is intended to serve as a resource for those wishing to acquire knowledge and skills related to family-centered service provision. Second, it is designed to be useful to professionals from all discipline backgrounds rather than taking a single-discipline perspective. Third, this book recognizes the numerous barriers to family-centered care that early interventionists face every day, such as the lack of time and the interference of organizational policies and structures. Fourth, and most important, this book does not attempt to provide a single, idealistic model with step-by-step instructions for providing family-centered services. Instead, the chapters that follow provide practical strategies for implementing family-centered principles in the many and varied settings where early intervention takes place. The diverse characteristics of families participating in early intervention are also recognized, and strategies are suggested throughout the book on how to individualize family-centered practices to accommodate these differences.

■ REFERENCES

Bailey, D. B. (1989). Issues and directions in preparing professionals to work with young handicapped children and their families. In J .J. Gallagher, P. L. Trohanis, & R. M. Clifford (Eds.), *Policy implementation and P.L. 99-457: Planning for young children with special needs* (pp. 97–132). Baltimore: Paul H. Brookes.

Bailey, D. B., McWilliam, P. J., & Winton, P. J. (1992). Building family-centered practices in early intervention: A team-based model of change. *Infants and Young Children, 5*(1), 73–82.

Bailey, D. B., Palsha, S. A., & Simeonsson, R. J. (1991). Professional skills, concerns, and perceived importance of work with families in early intervention. *Exceptional Children, 58*(2), 156–165.

Bailey, D. B., Simeonsson, R. J., Yoder, D. E., & Huntington, G. S. (1991). Preparing professionals to serve infants and toddlers with handicaps and their families: An integrative analysis across eight disciplines. *Exceptional Children, 57,* 26–35.

Bronfenbrenner U. (1975). Is early intervention effective? In B. Friedlander, G. Sterritt, & G. Kirk (Eds.), *Exceptional infant: Vol. 3. Assessment and intervention.* New York:Brunner/Mazel.

Brown, W., & Rule, S. (1993). Personnel and disciplines in early intervention. In W. Brown, S.K. Thurman, & L.F. Pearl (Eds.), *Family-centered early intervention with infants and toddlers: Innovative cross-disciplinary perspectives,* (pp. 246–268). Baltimore: Paul H. Brookes.

Bruder, M. B., & Bologna, T. (1993). Collaboration and service coordination for effective early intervention. In W. Brown, S. K. Thurman, & L. F. Pearl (Eds.), *Family-centered early intervention with infants and toddlers: Innovative cross-disciplinary perspectives* (pp. 103–127). Baltimore: Paul H. Brookes.

Crais, E., & Leonard, R. (1990). P.L. 99-457: Are speech-language pathologists prepared for the challenge? *ASHA, 32*(4), 57–61.

Dunst, C. J. (1985). Rethinking early intervention. *Analysis and Intervention in Developmental Disabilities, 5,* 165–201.

Dunst, C. J., & Trivette, C. M. (1994). Aims and principles of family support programs. In C. J. Dunst, C. M. Trivette, & A. G. Deal (Eds.), *Supporting and strengthening families: Vol. 1. Methods, strategies, and practices* (pp. 30–48). Cambridge, MA: Brookline Books.

Dunst, C. J., Trivette, C. M., & Deal, A. G. (1988). *Enabling and empowering families: Principles and guidelines for practice.* Cambridge, MA: Brookline Books.

Dunst, C. J., Trivette, C. M., & Deal, A. G. (1994). *Supporting and strengthening families. Vol. 1. Methods, strategies, and practices.* Cambridge, MA: Brookline Books.

Dunst, C. J., Trivette, C. M., & Mott, D. W. (1994). Strengths-based family-centered intervention practices. In C. J. Dunst, C. M. Trivette, & A. G. Deal (Eds.), *Supporting and strengthening families: Vol. 1. Methods, strategies, and practices* (pp.115–131). Cambridge, MA: Brookline Books.

Education of the Handicapped Act Amendments of 1986, Pub. L. No. 99-457. (October 8, 1986.) Title 20, U.S.C. §1400 et seq. U.S. *Statues at Large, 100,* 1145–1177.

Fenichel, E. S., & Eggbeer, L. (1991). Preparing practitioners to work with infants, toddlers, and their families: Four essential elements of training. *Infants and Young Children, 4*(2), 56–62.

Fox, H. B., Wicks, L. B., McManus, M. A., & Newacheck, P. W. (1992). Public and private health insurance for early intervention services. *Journal of Early Intervention, 16,* 109–122.

Gallimore, R., Weisner, T. S., Kaufman, S. Z., & Bernheimer, L. P. (1989). The social construction of ecocultural niches: Family accommodation of developmentally delayed children. *American Journal on Mental Retardation*, *94*(3), 216–230.

Hanson, M. J., & Lovett, D. (1992). Personnel preparation for early interventionists: A cross-disciplinary survey. *Journal of Early Intervention*, *16*, 123–135.

Harbin G. (1996). The challenge of collaboration. *Infants and Young Children*, *8*(3), 68–76.

Hobbs, N., Dokecki, P. R., Hoover-Dempsey, K. V., Moroney, R. M., Shayne, M. W., & Weeks, K. H. (1984). *Strengthening families*. San Francisco: Jossey Bass.

Individuals with Disabilities Education Act Amendments of 1991, Publ. No. 102-119. (October, 7, 1991.) Title 20, U.S.C. §1400 et seq. *U.S. Statutes at Large, 105*, 587–608.

McWilliam, P. J. (1993). Real-world challenges to achieving quality. In P. J. McWilliam & D. B. Bailey, *Working together with children and families: Case studies in early intervention* (pp. 21–32). Baltimore, MD: Paul. H. Brookes.

Morton, K. (1985). Identifying the enemy: A parent's complaint. In H. R. Turnbull & A. P. Turnbull (Eds.), *Parents speak out: Then and now* (2nd ed., pp. 143–147). Col-umbus, OH: Charles E. Merrill Publishing Co.

Safer, N. D. & Hamilton, J. L. (1993). Legislative context for early intervention services. In W. Brown, S. K. Thurman, & L. F. Pearl (Eds.), *Family-centered early intervention with infants and toddlers: Innovative cross-disciplinary perspectives* (pp. 1–19). Baltimore: Paul H. Brookes.

Shonkoff, J. P., & Meisels, S. J. (1990). Early childhood intervention: The evolution of a concept. In S. J. Meisels & J. P. Shonkoff (Eds.), *Handbook of early childhood intervention* (pp. 3–31). Cambridge, MA: Cambridge University Press.

Shelton, T. L., Jeppson, E. S., & Johnson, B. H. (1987). *Family-centered care for children with special health care needs*. Washington, D.C.: Association for the Care of Children's Health.

Shelton, T. L., & Stepanek, S. S. (1994). *Family-centered care for children needing specialized health and developmental services* (3rd ed.). Bethesda, MD: Association for the Care of Children's Health.

Turnbull, H. R., & Turnbull, A. P. (1985) *Parents speak out: Then and now* (2nd ed.). Columbus, OH: Charles E. Merrill Publishing Co.

Turnbull, A. P., & Winton, P. J. (1984). Parent involvement policy and practice: Current research and implications for families of young, severely handicapped children. In J. Blacher (Ed.), *Severely handicapped young children and their families: Research in review*. Orlando, FL: Academic Press.

Wikler, L. (1981). Chronic stresses of families of mentally retarded children. *Family Relations, 30*, 281–288.

■ RESOURCES

Family-Centered Practices

Title:	*Family-Centered Care for Children Needing Specialized Health and Developmental Services*
Authors:	Terri L. Shelton and Jennifer Smith Stepanek

Date: 1994 (3rd ed.)
Ordering Info: Association for the Care of Children's Health
                  7910 Woodmont Avenue, Suite 300
                  Bethesda, MD 20814
                  (301) 654-6549

Title: *Working Together with Children and Families:*
                  Case Studies in Early Intervention
Authors: P. J. McWilliam and Donald B. Bailey
Date: 1993
Ordering Info.:   Paul H. Brookes Publishing Co.
                  P.O. Box 10624
                  Baltimore, MD 21285-0624
                  1-800-638-3775
                  FAX: (410)-337-8539

Title: *Heart-to-Heart* (Videotape)
Author: Tacy Fullerton
Date: 1992
Ordering Info: Robin Sims
                  Developmental Disabilities Council
                  275 East Main Street
                  Frankfort, KY 40621
                  1-800-928-6583
Cost: $10.00 (when purchased, may be freely reproduced)

Title: *Family-Centered Care* (Videotape)
Authors: Association for the Care of Children's Health
Date: 1988
Ordering Info: Association for the Care of Children's Health (ACCH)
                  7910 Woodmont Avenue, Suite 300
                  Bethesda, MD 20814-3015
                  (301) 654-6549
Cost: $85.00 plus shipping/handling
                  (Discount for ACCH members)

CHAPTER 2

First Encounters with Families

In the development of any relationship, there is always a first meeting or contact during which first impressions are made by both parties. As we know from our own personal relationships, first impressions are important and can have a lasting effect on subsequent interactions. When families first enter our programs or begin working with a new professional within a program, the manner in which first contacts are handled set the stage for the development of parent–professional relationships. In this chapter, we explore the many factors that influence how first encounters with families are conducted and the impressions that are formed on both sides of the relationship. We also provide guidelines for using these initial contacts as a springboard for the development of parent–professional relationships that are consistent with a family-centered approach to service delivery.

■ FACTORS INFLUENCING FIRST ENCOUNTERS

On the surface, referral and program entry seems so straightforward. A call is made, the parents complete the necessary paperwork, eligibility is determined, appropriate services are decided upon, and services are begun. This view, however, does not take into consideration the human relationship factors involved in the process. The perceptions of professionals by parents and vice versa are determined by a host of variables on both sides of the relationship. Among these are past experiences, values, expectations, and personal interaction styles.

Family Perspectives

Past Experiences

Each family has a unique story to tell of their experiences related to the identification of their child's delays or disabilities and their initial encounters with professionals. Some families are eager to tell their stories, while others are not. Regardless of whether or not we are privileged to hear about a family's previous experiences, they are likely to influence how the family relates to us during our initial contacts with them. Stories about parents' first encounters with early intervention professionals are found in the books listed in the resource section at the end of this chapter. Among these stories are numerous accounts of the pain and anger parents felt when the communication of initial diagnoses was handled insensitively. As Ann Oster (1984) points out these experiences can have a strong and lasting impact.

> I am still angry five and a half years later at the professionals who were too insensitive or unskilled or human to give me what I needed. I am still mad at the doctor who said, when Nick was three days old, that I was in an awfully good mood for someone with such a sick baby. I am mad at the nurse who last week told another mother, who called at 11:30 at night to check on her 2 lb. 3oz. son before she went to sleep, that she would have to call back in an hour, after rounds. The reason that these incidents are worth recalling here is not to prove, like other people, professionals make mistakes, but because cumulatively their impact on families is profound. (p. 29)

Hurtful experiences with professionals may make a family reluctant to open up to the next professional they meet and can even give rise to defensive posturing. Although reluctance or defensiveness may be a natural reaction on the part of a parent, the next professional is unlikely to understand the source of the parent's reactions and may form faulty impressions.

Families also come to our programs with varying levels of understanding their children's disabilities, abilities in coping with the knowledge of their children's differences, and skills for facilitating their children's development. As a result, families' reasons for seeking services from our programs may be quite diverse. Some may be looking for a diagnosis, some for emotional support, some for very specific services, and some may not be certain why they have come to us. Still others may approach us on recommendation or even coercion by other professionals or agencies. These variations among families will affect the approach they take with us during initial contacts and their reactions to the things we say and do.

Family Values and Expectations

From the family's perspective, the first contact with a service agency or individual professional usually represents a request for help or assistance. For some parents this comes easy, but for others it may be quite difficult. Cultural and ethnic heritage, individual family history, and personal values all may influence a parent's reaction to asking others for help. For example, parents who place a high value on self-reliance may find it humiliating to ask others for assistance and may subsequently lose some confidence in their ability to parent their child.

Seeking assistance from an early intervention program may also be influenced by the values of others in the family's social support network. If, for example, a parent's spouse, close friend, or respected relative has not recognized the child's disability or has expressed implicit or explicit opposition to early intervention services, seeking help may be perceived as a potential threat to continued support by significant others. The opposite may also be true, wherein a parent does not want services but feels compelled to seek them out because of pressure from others in their social network.

Finally, parents may differ in their initial expectations of what your program has to offer and the potential influence it will have on their child and themselves. Parents may expect that the program will provide them with knowledge about their child's disability and prognosis, advice on dealing with a specific aspect of the child's skill development (e.g., feeding, toilet training, tantrums), a sounding board for their feelings or concerns related to their child, or a specific type of service (e.g., physical therapy, child care). Then again, there may be parents who expect that your program has little to offer them or that the program may even be disruptive to their lives. The expectations parents hold for a program are determined by their perception of their child's disability, their concerns and priorities for their child and family, their history of interactions with human service agencies, what friends or relatives have told them, and what other professionals have told them about their child's needs and what your program will do for them.

Personal Characteristics

A parent's style of interaction undoubtedly influences the professional's perception of them. Parents may be talkative and open or quiet and withdrawn. They may be assertive or passive, articulate or obtuse, friendly or defensive. The parent's style of interaction during initial contacts may be typical of them or it may be a style assumed by the parent as a result of any one or more of the factors just discussed. The professional has no way of knowing the meaning of a parent's style of interaction during first encounters. Nevertheless, the professional will respond to the parent's style and form impressions of the parent based on these interactions. After all, we are all human.

Professional Perspectives

Past Experiences

Professionals' own backgrounds will, likewise, influence their initial perceptions of families during initial contacts and, subsequently, their behavior. Professionals bring with them the influences of their professional training, their philosophy of service provision and accompanying role definitions, their history of working with children and families, and their own personal values and beliefs.

Along with the teaching of theory, knowledge, and specific skills, our professional training includes infusion of our role as a service provider. Role definitions imparted to students may vary from one professional discipline to another and from one training program to another within a specific discipline. For good or bad, each of us comes away from our formal professional training with a conceptualization of our responsibilities, duties, and goals as a professional in our field of specialization. This includes a philosophy of our role in working with families.

Accumulated experiences in working with families may further influence our role definitions as service providers and our perceptions of the families we meet. Being human, we have a tendency to interpret the actions of others and assign intent. When we meet new families, we try to understand why they act the way they do and may draw on our experiences with other families to explain their behavior. Consequently, we may draw conclusions about what a family wants, how they are coping, or their level of competence based on their apparent similarity to other parents we have worked with in the past. Sometimes our initial assumptions will be valid, but they are just as likely to be wrong. If we then act on false assumptions, the relationship between parents and professionals may be jeopardized.

In addition to our professional training and work experiences, our own personal backgrounds play a role in our initial perceptions of parents. Our ethnic or cultural heritage and the unique values and beliefs ingrained in each of us by our own families shape our sense of priorities. All too often, we are unaware of the strong influence our own value systems can have on our assessment and judgment of others. For example, when we perceive parents as similar to ourselves, we may assume that they share our values and priorities and may act on this assumption. On the other hand, when we meet parents whose values are greatly different from our own, it is easy to mistake differences for deficits and we may become judgmental or try to influence them in the direction of our own values.

Personal Characteristics

Personal interaction styles are as varied among professionals as they are among parents. Some of us are open, talkative, and humorous; others are more conservative, shy, and serious. Although there are no absolute right or wrong styles of communicating with parents, parents will, nevertheless, form impressions of the type of person we are based on our style of communication and they will respond accordingly. Their level of comfort with the style we use will, in large part, determine the amount of time it takes to establish rapport with a family. Thus, it may take more time to establish rapport with some families than with others. The ability to be flexible in our style to accommodate the apparent needs of a family can go a long way in establishing a trusting relationship. For example, if a family is expressing sadness over the prospect of their child being developmentally delayed, a compassionate style would be far more suitable than a more business-like style of interacting. We are not suggesting that any professional undergo a personality change, but rather that professionals be sensitive to what a family might need from them and adapt their interactions accordingly.

In summary, the histories of both professionals and families can significantly influence the interactions that take place during initial contacts. On the basis of these interactions, parents and professionals may form rapid impressions of one another, and these impressions are likely to influence subsequent interactions. Professionals cannot be expected to know all of the factors that influence the behavior of parents during initial encounters. In fact, they are likely to know nothing at all or only what has been told to them by professionals who have previously worked with the family—information that may, itself, be based on faulty impressions. What a professional can be expected to know, however, is that numerous factors can influence a parent's behavior, and professionals should guard against making hasty and unwarranted assumptions about families during first contacts.

■ GUIDELINES FOR PRACTICE

The importance of implementing a family-centered approach in our first contacts with families should not be underestimated. The impressions and expectations formed by families during this time set the stage for all future contacts and phases of service delivery. It is during this time that we convey our philosophy, not only through our words but also through our actions. If we are to convey a philosophy consistent with a family-centered approach, our actions and words should communicate a respect for the unique lifestyle and values of each family and a willingness to adapt our services to meet the priorities established by the family.

FIRST ENCOUNTERS
Outcomes for Working with Families

- ■ To convey to families that we respect them and their children
- ■ To offer immediate assistance if it is wanted
- ■ To give families control over entry into services
- ■ To let families know who you are and what you do
- ■ To understand families' major areas of concern

Referrals

Prior to the first contact with a family, events have taken place in the referral process that may influence the parents' reactions to your program and their interactions with staff members. Often these events are out of our direct control. How is it that a family knows about your program? Who recommends that the family seek services from your program and how is this recommendation handled? What information about your program do families have before they have direct contact with members of your staff? In all likelihood, you will never know the answers to all of these questions. Even so, you may be able to exert some influence over this aspect of the referral process through ongoing communication with the professionals and community agencies who frequently refer families to your program.

Ideally, families should feel in control of the referral process—that they have a real choice as to whether they request services from your program or they do not. This can be accomplished by communicating to referral sources that you prefer families to refer themselves to your program as opposed to having professionals make referrals for them. In other words, you could request that other agencies and professionals encourage families to make the first phone call to your program. In addition to this request, it may be helpful to prepare a brochure or other written information describing your program's philosophy and services and ask that referral sources give these materials to families who may be interested in your program. By doing so, families can make informed decisions as to whether or not they are interested in contacting you for more information.

The First Phone Call

Making the initial phone call to a program can be anxiety-producing for many families. This is especially true for families who suspect or have only recently discovered that their child has special needs. For most families, contacting an early intervention program or specialist is entering unknown and perhaps frightening territory. For some it may even represent a giving up of hope that their child is "normal." Some parents have told stories of holding onto a phone number for weeks or months before "getting up the nerve" to make the first call to a program. There may be similar trepidation by parents whose children are making a transition from one program to another. It should be noted, however, that not all families will have these feelings. Some may be very eager to pick up the phone and call.

When a parent does make the phone call, what do they encounter on the other end of the line? In many programs, the person who picks up the phone is a secretary or receptionist. Are they friendly and receptive in answering these first calls? Do they portray the program and its staff as a warm and receptive audience for parents to voice their concerns? We seldom think of such details, but they can have an effect on families. For example, the mother an infant who had a severe hearing impairment described what happened when she finally got up the nerve to call a program. "South Hampton School for the Deaf," announced the business-like receptionist who answered her phone call. "May I help you?" asked the receptionist. "The word 'DEAF' shot through my heart like an arrow," said the mother. "I just hung up the phone—I couldn't speak." Similar greetings such as "Winchester Mental Retardation Services," spoken in a flat, institutional voice can have the same effect. Along the same lines, a small group of veteran parents once requested that an early intervention program change or discontinue use of its business stationery that was embossed with the words "Kenworth Center—Serving the Mentally Retarded of Wilson County." "Families of infants and toddlers don't want those words printed on letters and envelopes that come to their mailboxes," the parents explained. "It has a gut-wrenching effect and we feel as though it stigmatizes our children."

Following the initial greeting, what is said to parents and what action is taken? Is someone available for the families to talk to about their concerns, what the program has to offer, or the application process? Chances are that the secretary or receptionist takes down their name and phone number and tells them that a staff member will call them back. They may or may not be given the name of a staff member or a time when their phone call will be returned. Thus, the parent is immediately put in an inferior position, albeit unintentional on the part of the program. Control is in the hands of the professionals.

Being responsive to these first phone calls can do much to foster our goals of conveying respect for the family, giving the parent a sense of control, offering immediate assistance, and providing them with information about the program. Perhaps a staff member can be designated as being "on call" to take referral phone calls and spend time talking to the families about their concerns and provide them with information about the program. With guidance from the professional staff, a sensitive secretary may even be able to do this. If this can't be done, providing parents with a staff member's name and a specific time when he or she will return their call shows respect. Offering parents choices is an even better idea. For example, parents can be asked: "Would you like to talk to someone now or would you prefer me to send you some written information about our program first?" Whatever action is taken, the key to effective helping and conveying respect for families is prompt response by professionals. For families who communicate an eagerness to receive services, promptness includes establishing the first face-to-face contact as soon after the referral is made as possible.

Getting Information

One of the first goals of the professional is to gather information from families that will assist in determining eligibility for services, the nature of the child's and family's needs, and the family's desire for services. How this information is obtained, however, will affect the developing relationship and role expectations between parents and professionals. Aspects of the information gathering process that should be considered include (a) where first contacts will take place, (b) the type and amount of information requested of families, (c) the format for obtaining information, and (d) the degree of control parents have in providing information.

Where the first face-to-face contact takes place may affect families' perceptions of control over the situation as well as their degree of comfort in providing information. Many parents prefer a visit to their home for this initial contact. Parents may feel more at ease in the familiar surroundings of their own home, in that, the professionals are meeting them on their own turf. Some parents have also said that professionals visiting their home can obtain a more accurate first impression of their child because the child is more at ease in this familiar setting. It should be mentioned, however, that not all parents prefer professionals to come to their home. As one parent explained, "No matter what anyone says, if a professional is coming to my house, I am going to clean up before they arrive. And because I hate cleaning house, I would much prefer to get in the car and go to someone's office." The ideal situation, therefore, may be to offer parents options of where the first meeting will take place.

In many cases, parents' early contacts with a program will include taking their child to the program site. The physical environment and the manner in which families are treated on these first visits can leave strong impressions—impressions seldom contemplated by professionals. Take a look around the lobby and waiting room of your program. What do the signs say? Is it a warm, inviting, and comfortable environment? Are parents handled impersonally by a receptionist, or does someone immediately greet the child and family and make them feel truly welcomed? Must parents wait with their children for a long time, or is their time respected by the program by promptly being attended to? Hospital clinics are renowned for crowded, uncomfortable waiting areas and for making parents and children wait a long time before seeing a doctor or other professional. Is this how parents are treated where you work? All of this may seem trivial, but it isn't. All of these things send messages to parents about who is in control of the situation and how they are expected to act.

Regardless of where the first face-to-face contact with families occurs, parents or caregivers should be adequately prepared for it. If they are not, parents are likely to assume a passive role in the interactions that take place and the professional will be in control. A brief phone call or letter prior to the first meeting can do much to improve the balance of control between parents and professionals. Parents can be told who they will be meeting, approximately how much time will be required, what types of information will be asked for, and what will be expected of them and their children. More important, parents can be encouraged to take an active role in the forthcoming visit. For example, parents may be told: "We have provided you with a brief description of our program and the services we offer. We realize, however, that you may have additional questions you want answered before making any decisions about our services. Please take a few minutes to think about and jot down any questions you would like to ask us. We will be sure to discuss these when we see you. In addition, please be thinking about any concerns or issues you would like to spend some time talking about when we meet. After all, our job is to find out what it is that you want for your child and your family and offer any information and assistance that may be helpful."

Paperwork is a necessary evil in any human service agency, and nowhere is it more plentiful than during first contacts with potential service recipients. Every program has a plethora of application forms and consent forms that must be completed and signed prior to services being rendered. One has to wonder about the necessity and nature of these forms as well as the effect they may have on families in our first interactions with them. "Was your pregnancy complicated?" "Have you ever had an abortion?" "Do you or have you ever used drugs?" "How much money do you make?" "Do you work full time?" "Is there a history of mental retardation, mental illness, or seizures in your family?" "Was your baby breast-fed or bottle-fed?" These types of questions are not all that uncommon on application forms or during initial interviews. Only the hardiest of souls would feel comfortable being queried in such a manner by a total stranger, and yet many parents of children with special needs are asked these types of questions time and time again. What information is really necessary to provide effective services? And must programs have all the information they need by the close of the first contact with families? Can some of the information be collected later, after relationships between parents and professionals have become more well-established?

At the very least, forms can be explained to parents before they are asked to complete them. They can be told why they are being asked the questions that are posed to them, how the information they provide will be used by the program or by individual professionals, and who will have access to the information they provide. Finally, an explicit statement should be made to families regarding their right not to answer questions or to withhold information they don't feel comfortable sharing with the program or professionals during these initial interactions. Thus, respect for the family's privacy is communicated and a message is given that they are the ones in control of the situation.

Giving Information

If parents are to feel comfortable providing professionals with information about themselves and their children, and if they are to be informed decision makers regarding entry into program services, they need information. They need to know who it is that they are talking to, what services the program offers, how those services might benefit their children and other family members, and the approach used in providing services. Such information can be conveyed implicitly or explicitly by all staff members who have first contacts with the family.

When first meeting a family, we are often so intent on finding out who they are and what they want that we neglect to let them know who we are. Whether parents are enrolling a child in a new child care center, taking their child to a new pediatrician, signing their child up for swimming lessons, or contemplating enrolling their son or daughter in an early intervention program, they probably want to know something about the qualifications of the people who will be providing these services. Some parents may want to know more than others, but even when little information is desired, providing some information about yourself conveys respect of the parent's position as consumer and decision maker. Extreme detail is not necessary. Information may be only a brief overview of your professional qualifications, how long you have worked with the program, and your role in providing services. Asking the parents if they have any additional questions about yourself leaves an opening for those parents who want more details.

Providing information about the program is equally important and may include the types of services offered, the scheduling of services, options and flexibility of services offered, fees for services, the number and qualifications of other staff members involved in service delivery, and the number of children and families served. In presenting such information, care should be taken to use language that is easily understood by the majority of parents, and technical jargon should be avoided if at all possible. Even then, parents are likely to forget or misinterpret some of the information presented. It may be helpful to provide families with a written description of the program and its various services, which they can later refer to. An additional benefit of providing a brochure or other written information is that parents can share the information with other family members or friends who may be involved in decision making or who are just concerned about the child's well-being. In presenting descriptions of the services offered by a specific program, care should be taken not to infer that these are the only services available to the child and family. If this happens, parents who do not feel their concerns can be addressed by that program may think there are no alternatives and ,consequently, feel frustrated or disappointed.

For parents of very young children, the network of services available in the community can be bewildering. They often don't know what is available or how to access the resources they need. Providing information about other community resources and serving as a field guide through the network beyond your own program can be an important function of an early intervention program. After all, without knowledge of the service options available to themselves and their children, parents are not in a position to make informed decisions. For some parents, information on services that are available and ideas on how to access them is all they need to take control of getting what they want.

In addition to providing factual information about services, information about your service delivery philosophy is conveyed to family members throughout these first encounters. This includes beliefs about how services to children should be provided and beliefs related to the role of the family. Statements of program philosophy or preferred intervention approaches may be put in writing or communicated in speaking to entering families, but the real messages about your beliefs will be conveyed through your actions. For example, a professional may tell a parent, "We believe that parents are children's first and most important teachers," or "Parents know more about their children than anybody else can possibly know." If, however, the professional then administers a screening test to the child and does not actively involve the parent, ask the parent questions about the child's abilities, or believe the parent when there is a discrepancy between what the parent says the child can do and what the professional observes, the initial message about the important role of parents will have been counteracted.

Providing Immediate Assistance

If families have approached your program voluntarily, it is fairly safe to assume there is something they want and are hoping you can provide. What parents hope you can provide, however, may vary considerably from one family to another. They may want to know what is "wrong" with their child, they may want to know what they can do to facilitate a specific aspect of their child's development, they may want reassurance that what they have been doing is "right," or they may want to know what the future holds in store for themselves and their child. They may also want confirmation that their child is "OK" or has potential. If the parent is encouraged to talk and the professional is a good listener, the unveiling of these desires will begin during the initial contacts with the family.

It is tempting to wait until you have more complete information on the child and family before beginning intervention of any sort. Waiting, however, can be distressing for many families. Anyone who seeks out assistance and is asked to wait, even for a short time, can feel "put off" or their anxiety may be prolonged. Offering immediate assistance or information to address concerns expressed by the family can do much to alleviate anxiety. Just as important, responding immediately to parents' concerns is a way of demonstrating that you care about the family and are a reliable resource. Thus, the relationship between parents and professionals gets off to a good start.

This is not to say that full-fledged services need to be provided immediately. In fact, the initial assistance provided to a family may be quite limited. For example, the day after a first home visit, you might mail an article or book to the family that addresses a concern they raised. You might take a few minutes during a visit to review and discuss a medical report the parents have expressed confusion about. If the parents have a specific concern about their child, such as delays in expressive language, dental care, or feeding difficulties, you might offer a few pointers or ideas they can try on their own until formal services begin. If you don't feel qualified to offer even minimal recommendations about an area of concern, you could offer to talk to someone and give the family a call back the next day or provide them with a phone number of another community resource. The bottom line is that responding quickly to parents' implicit or explicit requests for assistance lets parents know you consider their concerns and interests to be valid. It also lets parents know that you and your program can be depended on to be responsive to their needs, and that you are not locked into a standard set of services that families either fit into or don't. It lets them know that you are flexible and responsive to a range of concerns and willing to help them get what they want.

Decision Making and Program Entry

As professionals, the knowledge we have about the benefits of early intervention often leads us to assume that parents will want the services we have to offer. When such an assumption is made, however, it is likely to be conveyed to parents in one way or another, and we risk the possibility of unintentionally coercing parents into accepting services they may not really want. In other words, they may enroll in our services because we think they should and not doing so may make them look like "bad parents."

A family-centered approach to services means that parents are the ultimate decision makers in matters concerning themselves and their children, but parents will only assume this role if professionals make this role clear through their words and actions. One of the first decisions parents have to make is whether they want our services or they don't. The opportunity to make this choice must be explicitly stated by program staff and made with the further qualification that the family's decision will be accepted without judgment. Some parents may find it difficult to decide, and professionals may be called on to help them in the deliberation process. In such cases, professionals can help the family to consider the pros and cons of enrollment, the various levels of involvement with the program that they may choose (if such options are available), and the potential impacts of each decision on the child, parents, siblings, and members of the family's informal support network.

Without a doubt, it may be difficult in some situations to maintain an unbiased, nonjudgmental stance in helping families make decisions about whether or not their child will receive your services. Nevertheless, it is important to let parents know that they have a choice, to ensure that parents have the necessary information to make their decision, and to convey to parents that their decision will be respected. For parents opting not to accept services, it is important to let them know about alternative resources and that they may call again if they change their mind or if their situation changes and they would like to reconsider. Conveying an "open door" policy can make parents who are not quite ready at a given point feel comfortable in contacting the program again 6 months or a year later.

Unfortunately, there is one time when families are not in a position to make decisions about entering a program and that is when they do not qualify for services. Most programs have minimum eligibility requirements and children or families not meeting these criteria may not receive services. Nevertheless, how the issue of ineligibility is handled may have a lasting impact on a child and family. For some families, the immediate assistance you can provide during the course of determining eligibility may be sufficient to address their concerns. For families wanting more, you can provide information on or assist them in accessing other community programs and resources.

Waiting lists present another difficult situation. Obviously a policy of admitting all families who are eligible and want services is the preferred situation; but, when funding is limited and caseloads are full, this just may not be possible. Programs must then ask themselves if they can offer some type of temporary service until full services are available for a child and family. Even once-a-month group services for children and families on a waiting list may be preferred by some parents over no services at all. Enlisting the assistance of other community agencies or volunteers may make temporary or alternative services possible during a waiting period. Still another option may be to offer families the opportunity to talk to other families, either on a one-to-one basis or through an existing parent-to-parent support group. Again, parents should be informed of all alternative services and resources in the community so they can decide for themselves the preferred course of action for their family in the interim period.

Little Things That Count

For good or bad, the significance of first contacts with programs and professionals is revealed in the snapshot memories that some parents have of these experiences even years after they happen. Parents tell in vivid detail of how professionals looked at them, interacted with their children, and the words they spoke (See Resource List at the end of this chapter). For example, one mother of an 8-year-old daughter with Down syndrome frequently tells the story of her first telephone call to an early intervention program when her child was 6 weeks old. Worried and depressed, she had finally called the program and explained to the person on the other end of the line, "I had a baby born 6 weeks ago with Down syndrome." The voice replied, "Congratulations! Is it a boy or a girl?" The mother can no longer recall anything else that was said in that conversation, but she remembers those words because they were so important to her at that time. Someone had recognized that she had given birth to a baby girl and had given the expected joyful congratulations that others had neglected to offer. The voice on the other end of the line had recognized the normal, lovely part first and the problems second.

Although we don't know parents well enough at the point of first contacts to fully understand what is important to them, emphasizing the positive is usually a safe bet. This includes recognizing the parent's efforts and successes up to the time that they contacted the program and acknowledging the child's strengths and successes. Theatrics and lavish praise in conveying such recognition are not necessary or even desirable. A statement as simple as "I really admire you for how much you have learned in such a short period of time. You seem to know so much about Caitlin's medical needs," can go a long way in letting parents know that you acknowledge what they have been through and that their abilities are respected.

Recognizing the positive aspects of a child is perhaps even more important. After all, pride is a natural reaction of a parent when their child is complimented. For many parents, their child's disability and difficulties may have been repeatedly emphasized by others and pride in their child may have suffered or been squelched. Noticing a child's long eyelashes, iridescent blue irises, or delicate hands before making comments about difficulties may be a welcome relief to parents. Asking permission to hold a child, talking directly to a child, or otherwise showing your interest in the child— as a child—may also go a long way toward communicating sincere caring.

Multiple First Encounters

First encounters do not end at the point of program entry, but rather continue with each successive team member who works with the child and family. Even after the family's basic relationship with the program is well-established, their impression of and relationships with newly introduced team members will involve all of the issues we have discussed in the preceding pages. Each successive encounter with new staff members is as important as the very first in ensuring parent-professional relationships that are consistent with a family-centered approach.

Brief Encounters

In some situations, the first encounter with families may be the only encounter we have with them. An audiological assessment, an appointment with a specialist, or other type of one-shot consultation by team members or outside agencies are all examples of this type of situation. The issues addressed in this chapter still apply and may, in fact, be more important in light of the brevity of these interactions. When we have multiple contacts with a family, there are more opportunities and more time to develop a relationship, explain who we are, convey a sense of respect for the family's concerns, recognize their skills and abilities, and show that we care about their child. These are equally important when seeing a child and family for a single appointment, but the time available for accomplishing these communications is severely restricted. Therefore, even greater care must be taken to ensure that they can be fitted into our interactions. Our words and actions must be carefully chosen to accomplish our goals.

One mother told a story about a one-time interaction she had with a medical specialist more than 10 years ago. At the time she met the doctor, her child was just 18 months old. The mother, recently separated from her husband, was working full-time to support herself and the child who had multiple medical and developmental disabilities. Her self-esteem was at an all-time low and she felt guilty about the separation. Looking at the chart in front of him, the first comment from the doctor was "I see here that you are a single mother." The mother remembers that she just about burst into tears on the spot. She frantically thought through the many explanations she might give to justify the separation from her husband but, before she could offer one, the doctor continued: "I must say, I really admire you. It can't be easy taking care of this little one on your own." She never saw that doctor again, but he is still on her list of heroes. He acknowledged her successes, rather than her failures. He saw the good instead of the bad. Thus, our first encounters can have a substantial impact on parents, even if we never see the child or the family again. It may only take a few words.

In summary, our initial contacts with families set the stage for implementing a family-centered approach to service delivery. From the very beginning we can let families know that we uphold this philosophy—not by a written statement or monologue about our philosophy—but through our conversations and our actions. It is how we treat families that conveys how we feel about them and their children and what we perceive their role will be in ensuing service delivery. If we want to convey that they are the decision makers, we give them the necessary information and offer them choices. If we want to convey that we respect their opinions, we listen. If we want to convey that we are there to meet their concerns, we are responsive to their stated needs and priorities. If we want to convey that they are competent, we recognize and acknowledge their skills and abilities.

If we listen more than we speak in these initial contacts with families, we will begin to have an idea of what the family wants. We will have some notion of how their child's disability is perceived by them and the impact it has had on their daily life and future plans. Most important, we will begin to develop a picture of what is important to the family, and this will serve as a guide for future interactions with the family. Even so, our picture of what the family expects from service delivery will still be sketchy. Before jumping into recommendations and intervention plans at this point, we will need to sharpen our focus on the family's priorities. This process of clarifying child and family goals is addressed in the next three chapters.

■ REFERENCES

Oster, A. (1984). Keynote address. In *Equals in this partnership: Parents of disabled and at-risk infants and toddlers speak to professionals* (pp. 26–32). Arlington, VA: National Center for Clinical Infant Programs.

■ RESOURCE LIST

Title:	*Parents Speak Out: Then and Now* (2nd ed.)
Authors:	H.R. Turnbull and Ann P. Turnbull
Date:	1985
Publisher:	Charles E. Merrill Publishing Company
	Columbus, OH 43216

Title:	*A Difference in the Family: Living with a Disabled Child*
Author:	Helen Featherstone
Date:	1981
Publisher:	Penguin Books
	40 West 23rd Street
	New York, NY 10010

Title:	*We Have Been There: A Guidebook for Parents of People with Mental Retardation*
Authors:	Terrell Dougan, Lyn Isbell, & Patricia Yyas
Date:	1979
Publisher:	Dougan, Isbell and Vyas Associates
	1346 Roxbury Road
	Salt Lake City, UT 84108

Title:	*Exceptional Parent: The Magazine for Families and Professionals*
Ordering Info.:	Exceptional Parent
	P.O Box 3000 Dept. EP
	Denville, NJ 07834-9919
	1-800-247-8080
Cost:	$28 per year (12 issues)

■ CHAPTER 3

Understanding Family Concerns, Priorities, and Resources

If we are going to take a family-centered approach, the first order of business is to find out what families want—their expectations, their concerns, and what they hope to accomplish by involving themselves with our agency. Although this seems like a fairly straightforward task, there are times when it has been misconstrued or misunderstood. Part of the confusion may stem from the words that have been used to describe this aspect of family-centered practice. The term "family assessment" has been frequently used in the professional literature to describe the process of gathering and understanding family information. The terms "needs" and "strengths" also came into use when Part H of P.L. 99-457 (Education of the Handicapped Amendments of 1986) specified that "a statement of a family's needs and strengths" needed to be included on each child's individualized family service plan (IFSP).

There has been some concern that the use of terms such as "needs," "strengths," and "assessment" will mean that judgments or evaluations of families will be made. A quote from a parent's testimony at a Congressional hearing related to P.L. 99-457 illustrates this perspective:

> A family rated as "strong" may in fact fall apart because it is subsequently not given support. Even worse, a family rated as "weak" may be prevented from growing and coping by the perceptions of professionals. A poor rating may follow a family for years, and most likely, become self-fulfilling. To illustrate, I am not particularly interested in cleaning my house. It is not a priority with three small children who so quickly and utterly mess it up. Yet I still clean my house if any of the professionals involved in our lives are coming over. I am not willing to be judged by some, perhaps unconscious, standard.
> Jeannette Behr, Testimony

The strength of these concerns resulted in several changes in the wording of the federal regulations when P.L. 99-457 was amended and reauthorized in 1991 under P.L. 102-119. In the amendments, family "needs and strengths" were replaced with family "concerns, priorities, and resources."

Another concern, expressed by both families and professionals, relates to a family's right to privacy. A family-centered approach assumes that the better we understand families, the more effective our relationships with them will be. Research has demonstrated, however, that people's reactions to requests for self-disclosure and the amount and type of information they are willing to provide about themselves varies widely from culture to culture. For instance, Euro-Americans are willing to disclose information about a wider range of topics than are the Japanese. Ghanaians disclose readily about family matters, whereas Americans disclose more about career concerns (Seelye, 1996). Most people are more willing to self-disclose to one person than to many, and certainly least likely to disclose personal information to strangers. This cross-cultural research has implications for how we get to know families in early intervention situations, suggesting that an individualized approach be taken for each family situation. There is no one answer to the question of how professionals can present themselves as being interested in a broad range of family information without being perceived as nosy or intrusive. Yet this question is critical if we are to build a positive relationship with families. If we violate a family's sense of privacy, we may not have a second chance to repair that damage.

One mother's recollection of her family's first abortive attempt to seek services for her young child speaks to this issue. This mother described feeling extremely positive about the intervention program at the first point of contact. The people she met seemed friendly and interested, and the services that were described sounded as if they would benefit her child. It was at the second point of contact that things fell apart. The mother was asked to answer questions about her personal and family history that seemed intrusive and unrelated to any concerns she had expressed about her child. She felt she was expected to open up her life to people who were virtual strangers, not because she had identified any personal or family problems, but solely because their family was seeking help for their child. The family did not continue working with the agency as a result of that second contact.

■ OUTCOMES FOR WORKING WITH FAMILIES

The mother's experience described above reinforces the importance of making sure we are clear to ourselves and to families why we gather family information. Taking a family-centered approach, *the major purpose for gathering and understanding family information is to ensure that intervention efforts are guided by family priorities and that interventions build on family resources.* In the previous chapter, strategies were discussed for identifying family concerns and priorities when families first contact an intervention program. The process of gathering and understanding family information begins at the first point of contact and, in fact, continues throughout the intervention process. In addition, the nature and extent of information sharing will evolve, as the family–professional relationship develops. As we develop an understanding of families, they also are getting to know more about us and our agency. As families come to know and trust us, they are more likely to share personal and confidential information. They also are more likely to seek and respect our opinions. This is a circular and continuous process influenced by many factors and, as in any relationship, it takes time for trust to develop.

IDENTIFYING FAMILY CONCERNS, PRIORITIES AND RESOURCES
Outcomes for Working with Families

- To identify what families hope to accomplish through involvement with you and your agency
- To identify the immediate priorities of the family and how you might assist them with these
- To determine how families define the issues related to their child with a disability within the context of family values, structures, and accommodations to daily routines
- To identify existing family resources related to family priorities
- To establish yourself as a supportive and informed person interested in building positive, collaborative relationships with families

---

Another challenge that we face as we develop relationships with families is overcoming our professional instinct to solve problems and recommend services. This instinct is as much the result of our professional training as it is our desire as caring professionals to "help" people. A family-centered approach stresses the importance of building on and facilitating family strengths and the natural support systems available to families. If we are too quick in making recommendations about strategies for reaching family goals, we are not likely to develop an understanding of the ways that families solve problems or the resources they already have available. Also, we need to be cautious about drawing families into our professional world of services and programs in ways that isolate them from their extended family, neighborhoods, and communities.

These challenges in providing family-centered services provide a clear focus for our information-gathering activities. Our goal is to develop an ongoing understanding of where families want to channel their energies and what resources and strategies are available to the family to accomplish what they identify as being important. We are not assessing families. We are not evaluating families. We are developing an understanding of what families hope to accomplish and what, if anything, they need from us.

GUIDELINES FOR PRACTICE

Families are complex and there is so much information that can be gathered. How does one decide what is relevant and what is not? There are also many different forms, surveys, measures, and strategies described in the current literature for gathering and understanding family information (Bailey & Simeonsson, 1988; Hanson, Lynch, & Wayman, 1990; McGonigel, Kaufmann, & Johnson, 1991; Summers et al., 1990). How does one figure out which ones are practical and effective? In short, how does one go about the process of identifying family concerns, priorities, and resources in a way that builds positive relationships between professionals and families? The remainder of this chapter provides discussion, guidelines, and strategies for addressing these questions. More specifically, two aspects of the information-gathering process are described. First, we will address the *content*, or the type of family information that facilitates collaborative decision making between families and professionals. Second, we will describe the *process*, or the formats and strategies that may be used in gathering and understanding family information.

Relevant Family Information for Collaborative Decision Making

Families who become involved with early intervention programs are always asked to share information about themselves, but the type and amount of information families are asked to provide varies considerably from one program or agency to another. For example, one program may ask only that families fill out a short demographic form, whereas another program may gather a complete social history. Questions that you may want to consider as you contemplate this aspect of service delivery are: What information is absolutely necessary? What information is relevant to building a positive, collaborative relationship with families? And is this information needed immediately or can it be gathered later?

There are six broad categories of information that may be gathered from families: (a) informal support networks, (b) family values and beliefs, (c) critical events, (d) family accommodations and coping strategies, (e) family perceptions of the child's needs and strengths, and (f) family priorities. These domains of family information have been selected on the basis of their relevance in establishing collaborative relationships. It is important to keep in mind, however, that getting to know families across all these domains takes time, and gathering information of this sort needs to be done with sensitivity and with an appreciation for the family's preferences for sharing information.

Informal Support Networks

Informal supports are those people in our lives who are closest to us—relatives, friends, and neighbors—or the people we automatically turn to when we need help and support. If we think of our own lives, we can identify those we turn to. Some play an active daily role in our lives. With others, we may not be in close contact, but we know they are there when we need them or if there is a crisis. These folks are the "kith and the kin" that Emmy Werner (1984) has described as the sometimes unnoticed "protective" factors that influence the outcomes of young children "at risk." Demographic changes in our country have created the need to expand our traditional definitions of family. Perhaps the safest way to define family is to determine how each family chooses to define the term and use these individual definitions as our starting point for each family. This might provide more useful information than standard demographic details, if our interest is in determining family resources and who might be involved in intervention efforts. Understanding these support networks and how they serve as important family resources, makes us better-informed collaborators. This might be accomplished by listening to what families say, observing family interactions or, if appropriate, asking families the following types of questions:

- Who are the important people in your child's life?
- Who do you turn to for advice?
- What is happening when an event (of relevance or importance to the family) goes well?
- Who is helpful in a crisis (if crises have happened in the past)?
- What are some of the good things that have happened for your family recently?
- Who or what makes those good things happen?

Family Values and Beliefs

Our basic values and beliefs shape the roles and patterns of our lives and the decisions we make. As important as they are, values and beliefs are not always easy to articulate and sometimes operate on an unconscious level. When surrounded by others with similar values and beliefs, we sometimes forget that our view of the world is only one of many possible perspectives. For example, a belief that is predominant among the middle-class, Anglo culture is the importance of independence and autonomy. If we are of that culture, the decisions we make regarding our children are often shaped by the belief that self-sufficiency and independence are hallmarks of success. In contrast, other cultures (e.g., traditional Native American, Asian) may value cooperation and interdependence over competition and self-reliance. Consequently, families from these cultures may make child-rearing decisions based on these values. The meaning they ascribe to disabilities and to intervention may also be specific to their culture. This is not to say that all Asian families value cooperation and interdependence over self-reliance. Ethnic background is but one of many factors that shape family values. Others include, but are not limited to, socioeconomic status, religion, geographic location, and life experiences. Perhaps Margaret Mead's definition of culture as "the learned ways of a people . . .which cut across class, racial and religious lines" (Mead, 1953) best summarizes the complex nature of cultural influences.

Sometimes in our lives we encounter situations in which we are faced with difficult choices. In these situations, we may have to weigh the pros and cons of different actions and perhaps sacrifice certain beliefs to accomplish something else that is important to us. In this way, our values interweave in different ways to influence decisions we make. As a way of illustrating how family values can interconnect and shape unique decision making, let us look at two middle-class, Anglo families who look very similar, demographically. Both families are seeking to provide their child with intervention services that will facilitate the child's independence and self-sufficiency. Even so, one family has very strong beliefs about the importance of young children being raised at home until they are school age. The other family shares these beliefs to an extent, but more strongly believes in the importance of career and professional development for both parents. The type of intervention sought by these two families may be very different. The family with two parents working outside of the home may seek center-based services, with the other family possibly opting for a home-based program.

Asking a family to articulate their values and beliefs may be akin to the old saying, "Don't ask a fish about water." Cultural values and personal beliefs are so integral to our lives that we may be unaware of their influences. Even when we are aware, we might not feel comfortable sharing this personal aspect of our lives with others, especially if we do not have a close relationship with the person asking. Noticing the events and activities in which families invest time provides clues to their values and beliefs. Listening to the reasons families give for making certain decisions also provides important clues. The opportunity to do this, however, requires a trusting relationship between parent and professional—a relationship built on genuine openness and respect. If, on the other hand, families anticipate that we will not accept their decisions, they may not even discuss them with us. They may simply act, and it is left up to us to figure out why. Sometimes this is played out in broken appointments or parents not carrying out previously agreed-upon plans. At other times, parents may simply announce their decisions in a manner that makes further discussion difficult. This leaves professionals out of the decision-making process and makes further collaboration difficult.

Critical Events

There are certain events in our lives that dramatically change our patterns, roles, and/or routines. Some of these events could be categorized as "normative," or expected. For instance, the birth of a child, the death of an aging parent, retirement, or a child entering kindergarten are all examples of events that create a change in the family, but the change is one that has been anticipated. Many other people have experienced the same events and they are something that one expects to face.

Other critical events could be categorized as "non-normative", that is, they are not expected and it is not the norm to undergo such an event (Heatherington, 1984; Wikler, 1981). Examples of these include the unexpected death of a spouse, divorce, or the loss of a job. Examples particular to families whose children have disabilities might include hospitalizations and operations, diagnoses, or younger siblings surpassing the child with a disability in terms of the achievement of developmental milestones.

Critical events, whether normative or non-normative, require emotional and, sometimes, physical energy. The disruptions that accompany such events can be quite difficult, and it is often a time when families want to keep other aspects of their lives as stable as possible. It is important to be aware of critical events that a family may be experiencing and to recognize that these may be times when a family's time and energy is directed away from intervention. Initiating or suggesting changes in intervention may not be helpful at these times, unless the family perceives the change as helpful in dealing with the critical event.

Asking families in an open-ended, nonthreatening fashion about upcoming events related to their child might be appropriate in some situations. Questions such as, "I'm wondering if you have any thoughts about the upcoming evaluation/operation" provide families with a chance to say as little or as much as they want on a topic. Carefully listening to what families emphasize about an event, lets you know their hopes and concerns, and may provide you with clues about how you can play a supportive role. If a particular concern is emphasized, posing the question, "What are some ways that you can imagine getting ready for that challenge/dealing with that situation?" helps identify possible solutions to the concern. If families are initially unable to generate ideas, it is sometimes helpful to pose the question, "When you've been through similar situations in the past, what seemed to help?" It also may be that families directly ask you for your ideas on the subject.

Asking questions such as these can lead to your gaining valuable information—information about family concerns, family values and priorities, and what resources a family may already have for handling the critical event they face. Although we may have information or ideas that will assist the family in arriving at a solution to their challenges, the process of arriving at a solution seems to work best if there is a give-and-take of ideas, and this takes time and careful listening. The solutions that families generate may, in fact, be more effective than those we generate; so it is always wise to ask how a family might approach the situation before sharing our own ideas about what might work.

Family Accommodations or Coping Strategies

Each family has a unique way of dealing with or accommodating to critical events. One approach to understanding how families adapt is to consider two components: (a) family perceptions or definitions of an event and (b) family resources. The original research on this topic was conducted many years ago by Reuben Hill (1958), a family sociologist who was interested in how and why families in a community faced with a catastrophe such as a tornado responded in such different ways. Some families never recovered from the disaster. Others became stronger than ever. The differences could not be explained on the basis of resources alone (i.e., the amount of money in the bank, the number of supportive relatives, etc.). The ways that families defined the event played an important role in how they coped. Subsequent researchers (Olson et al., 1983) identified two specific perceptual coping strategies that play a role in family adaptation. These are *passive appraisal,* defined as not doing much of anything in hopes that the situation will improve on its own, and reframing, which has been explained as the process by which families attend to that aspect of an event over which they have some control. The book *Cognitive Coping, Families and Disability* edited by Ann Turnbull and her colleagues (Turnbull et al., 1993) provides research findings and insights from family members about how these kinds of coping mechanisms assist in dealing with some of the daily challenges associated with disability.

If we think about our own lives, we recognize that we use these strategies all the time. They are the ways that we keep from being overwhelmed by the demands of our lives. We often choose to focus on the aspects of a situation that seem solvable and in which we might achieve success through our efforts. The part of an event that might seem solvable to one person, however, may seem overwhelming to another. This is one way of considering why the same event might be viewed very differently by different people.

The relevance that this information has to our work with families relates again to the importance of understanding family perceptions and definitions of events and the possible resources that might be available to them for dealing with those events. If we accept the notion that passive appraisal may be a coping strategy, then it forces us to consider the issue of denial. Many of us have been trained to view denial as a negative state that should be assaulted by heavy doses of reality. Perhaps what we might label as denial is actually the family's efforts to avoid being overwhelmed by events and, thus, should be respected as their means of "buying time" for themselves.

We can often take our cues from families. We might ask ourselves, what aspect of this situation is the family talking about and attending to? This will help us know how to play a supportive role. This takes time and careful listening. Sometimes it means that families are placing higher priorities on some aspect of the situation and ignoring others that seem very important to us. We may wonder at what point we insert our opinions and ideas about what should be attended to and what should be done. As stated before, these issues require careful thought and consideration; they are the points over which we are most challenged in trying to define for ourselves what a family-centered approach means. At these points perhaps the most important consideration is determining what builds trust at a given time and what might destroy it.

We also need to recognize that coping strategies may vary among family members. A father illustrated these differences vividly in describing the difference between his and his wife's reactions to their child's diagnosis. Being an action-oriented, problem-solving type, he immediately did research on the disability and identified all of the possible resources in the community that might be of assistance. His wife wanted to move more slowly, feeling that her understanding of her child did not fit with some of the information they had received. He went on to say that when they attended meetings with professionals, they each emerged with a different picture of what had been said. He would hear facts and information; she would focus on the process of how they were treated and the qualitative aspects of how their child was described. Ultimately, their different styles were seen as a strength by the parents—as complementary approaches that enhanced the decisions they made.

This story reinforces the importance of including all family members, including siblings, grandparents, and perhaps even respected members of the community in discussions and decision making whenever possible. In reality, there is often one family "contact person" and, more often than not, this is the child's mother. This is an efficient way for families to operate and is consistent with the way that many families divide their roles and responsibilities (Rollins & Galligan, 1978). Given this reality, the question is one of how to involve family members who may be physically absent from professional contacts, but who are quite important in terms of overall family involvement. In some situations there may be a community elder, or a respected relative who has a great deal of authority with a family. Trying to identify all of those persons with power and authority in the family is important. One strategy that might be used if those persons are not physically present is to pose the question, "What does your spouse/the elder/your aunt, and so on, think about this idea/issue?" "What would he/she say about this if he/she were here now?" or (in the case of two important family members being absent) "Would your spouse and your mother see this in the same way?"

As the previous story illustrates, there will be times when individual family members may not have the same perspectives of an event or a decision. A supportive role professionals might play in those situations is to make ourselves available as a sounding board for family members. Simply listening to families when they are struggling to understand information they have received or weighing decisions that need to be made and reflecting back what they say may be the most effective way to deal with the differences in perceptions that occur in all families.

There may be times when it is possible and appropriate to involve as many relevant family members as possible in a group discussion. Determining the appropriate etiquette for how and in what order to address each person is important in these situations. For example, it might be appropriate to treat each person present as an equal participant. In that case, you might pose the same initial question to each family member about whatever issue is at hand such as, "How did things go this week with [child's name]?" or "How has it been around here since [child's name]'s hospitalization?" Personally addressing each family member acknowledges the unique and valuable perspective each has to offer. Addressing questions of this sort to siblings, when appropriate, is a strategy for recognizing the important and often unrecognized role that they play in the life of their brother or sister. In other situations, it may not be appropriate to directly address siblings who are present. Determining cultural and individual family variations in terms of how to effectively engage all of the relevant and important persons in an intervention effort is an important aspect of a family-centered approach. Developing alliances and relationships in communities takes time and careful observation, plus attention and, sometimes, direct requests for help.

Family Perceptions of Child Needs and Strengths

A basic premise of family-centered practice is that families, rather than professionals, should be the decision makers. The experiences of parenting a child with many medical and developmental needs, however, often leaves parents feeling uncertain about what is best for their child. Frequently parents come to us seeking our assistance because they are at a loss about what to do and where to go next. Often parents say, "We just want to do whatever we can to help our child."

We sometimes interpret these words as an invitation for us to develop a plan of services for the child and family that we think is best, especially when families say, "We just don't know what to do." Before immediately jumping ahead to planning further assessments or interventions, we might spend some time exploring a family's perceptions of their child's needs and strengths, the impact the child and the disability are having on the family, and, most important, what aspect(s) of the child's development is of greatest concern to the family. Taking this approach is more likely to lead to a collaborative understanding of what the next steps might be.

The greatest concern for a family may be the caregiving needs of their child. If the child is often fussy, cries for prolonged periods, does not sleep through the night, or requires complicated medical interventions, dealing with these needs may be taking up a good portion of a family's energies. Doing whatever it takes to get a good night's sleep may be a top priority for a family. A related consideration are the other childcare and domestic tasks for which families are responsible and the resources available for carrying out those tasks. Cross-cultural research in Canada with families whose young children suffered from chronic ear infections indicated that ethnic backgrounds may play a role in defining major concerns (Wuest, 1991; Wuest & Stern, 1990). In this study, the major concern for Native Canadian families was the pain and suffering their children endured—hearing their children cry was the most difficult aspect of the health problem from their perspective. In contrast, the Euro-Canadian families' greatest concern was their lack of control over the problem and that the medical profession did not have a cure. This translated into a greater tendency for Euro-Canadians to develop an adversarial relationship with health care professionals, as compared to Native Canadians. Knowledge of cultural differences of this sort, however, should always be used cautiously. Information about cultural differences can sensitize professionals who are working outside of their own communities to be alert to certain predispositions that may exist in certain communities; however, we must not assume that all families within a given culture will share the same beliefs and values. Each family must be seen as unique, and their concerns, values, and beliefs must be individually assessed.

For some families being able to engage in an activity that is an integral part of how they define quality family time may be critically important. For example, the family that believes in the importance of sitting down together each day for an evening meal may want assistance in developing strategies for making that possible. This may involve the development of feeding programs or behavior management programs for their child with disabilities, or it may involve strategies for engaging their child with disabilities in other activities while the rest of the family has dinner. A question that might be posed, if appropriate, is "What would help you most at home right now?"

What is important to one family may not be important to another family; in nearly all cases, as constantly stated in this chapter, family values determine priorities. For example, the parents of twins, one born with medical complications resulting in a hearing loss and developmental delays and the other born without problems, had a vision that their twins would enter preschool together at the neighborhood program attended by their older sibling. The positive and educational relationship between the twins was a major resource from the family's perspective. It was vitally important that intervention services did nothing to disrupt this relationship. Recommendations to this family that their daughter attend a center-based preschool for children with hearing loss were understandably met with resistance. In this situation, developing an understanding of the parents' vision for the twins would have been helpful prior to the point of recommending a specific program. Starting with parents' hopes and dreams and their existing interests and pleasures helps ensure a commitment to the intervention that follows.

In understanding a family's current perceptions, it can also be helpful to consider the changing demands and transitions associated with different phases of disability. When families first suspect that something is wrong or have just received a diagnosis, there may be certain tasks or challenges that are of immediate concern. These may include undergoing painful or difficult medical or diagnostic tests, developing relationships with a number of different professionals, and developing an understanding of the disability and what it means for the child. Families in this situation may want basic information, assistance in reconciling conflicting information or opinions, help with coordination of different professionals and agencies, or ideas for sharing information with other family members or friends. A list of questions that may be appropriate in exploring these issues is provided. Keep in mind, however, that what you ask families very much depends on what they have already told you.

- What have you been told about your child's "special needs" (or whatever term the family uses)?
- How does that fit with what you know and believe about your child?
- What do other people say about your child?
- Whose opinion makes the most sense to you?

Family concerns and questions about diagnoses are of particular relevance here. All too often it is assumed that when families have been given diagnostic information, they understand it and agree with it. Professionals may even begin discussing an intervention plan with a family, under the assumption that this the next step on everyone's mind. If, however, the family is still trying to make sense of the diagnosis, they may not be sure that intervention is even needed. Carl Dunst and his colleagues (Dunst, Trivette, & Deal, 1988) have pointed out that family–professional consensus about the nature of a presenting concern (e.g., diagnosis) is one of the three critical points for parent–professional agreement. The other two are the need for treatment and the plan for treatment.

Family Priorities

When we think of our own lives and our own priorities, we realize that we are constantly juggling and balancing work, family time and recreation, household chores, health needs, and the like. Basically, we are constantly striving to construct and sustain a daily routine that includes all of these important elements in a way that is consistent with our underlying values and beliefs. Maslow (1954) proposed that there is a hierarchy of influences that determines where families invest their energies. At the top of the hierarchy is survival and basic physiological needs (e.g., hunger, thirst). When a child or family member is faced with a life-threatening condition, this event takes precedence over everything else. Next in importance is concern with safety. According to Maslow, it is only after these basic needs have been met that families turn their attentions to the development of social and moral competence. This theoretical framework helps explain why families who are struggling with putting food on the table or locating a safe and warm place to live may have little energy or time for participating actively in child-focused services. If we do not acknowledge their situations and provide support at the basic levels, our other efforts may well be in vain.

Gallimore and his associates (Gallimore, Weisner, Kaufman, & Bernheimer, 1989; Bernheimer, Gallimore, & Weisner, 1990) have conducted an in-depth study of how families of young children with disabilities include disability issues in this ongoing balancing act. A case example from the study by Gallimore and his associates (Gallimore et al., 1989) is provided here that poignantly illustrates the ways that desperate economic circumstances impact decisions about parenting:

> A mother called the project field worker in despair because her developmentally delayed son's childcare center could no longer keep him due to his destructiveness, and she could find no other center or baby-sitter that would take him. This state of affairs put at risk the mother's effort to complete a training course that would lead to a guaranteed civil service job. The job not only meant an improved income, it also would get her off public assistance and, most importantly, provide generous medical and other employee benefits. It was not that the mother was uninterested in the cognitive development of her child; in her priorities it merely assumed a lower importance than finding a safe, inexpensive caretaking arrangement so that her job training could continue. The subsistence pressures were such she was willing to entertain temporary placement of the child in a foster home, if that was the only way she could continue her job training program. (p. 221)

The Gallimore study also reinforces the importance of attending to the differences in how events and situations are defined. For instance, a home environment defined as impoverished and deprived from one perspective might be rich in positive social experiences and interactions with extended family and neighbors from another. Or a person who might logically be considered a source of support for a family, such as a nearby grandmother with time, competence, and willingness to babysit, might also present a stress for the family in terms of other qualities, such as bossiness or having a critical attitude. According to Gallimore et al. (1989): "To oversimplify, 'social support' is not always good; and limited income or the lack of a high school diploma is not always bad" (p. 222). Before these features of a family can be evaluated, the meaning and value they have for families must be considered.

Another case example provided by Gallimore et al. (1989) illustrates how family priorities and family strategies for achieving those priorities may change over time. This mother is describing why she's considering a child care change:

> Harriet [our regular daycare woman] used to be really exercising [our daughter Kathy]—but Harriet just isn't the same anymore. She talks all the time. She doesn't leave any time to let Kathy talk back to her. . . . [e.g., She doesn't encourage her to talk] . . . . Kathy is starting to use three word sentences—

she's starting to do a lot of naming of things. When you talk to her, you need to talk to her about what she's doing. I want her to say it back to me if she can. Like, Harriet, she just keeps talking and doesn't give her a chance to say it back. . . . Harriet's a little bit on the slower side of things. She doesn't use very good English, but she's loving. We think Kathy needs to go on now and start getting something different from somebody else, but Harriet's been real-ly dependable. . . . I don't think she can teach Kathy anymore. . . . I don't want to down her, she's really a nice lady. . . very loving. (p. 223)

The family's priority—appropriate childcare—had not changed, but their definition of what is appropriate had changed as their daughter matured. This quote (p. 223) illustrates their attempt to find a new strategy for addressing their old priority. Sometimes priorities change completely, as in this example provided by another family member in the Gallimore study:

[The] laundry never got done. The house was always a mess. You must learn to change your priorities. We used to have a real clean house, we don't have it anymore. Frankly, Scott is not going to remember if the dishes were done or the laundry was folded and put away when he is 20, but he is going to remember that he can walk and talk and stuff like that. You just have to be able to look at what is important and make time for that and do the best you can with the other stuff. (p. 221)

What seems critically important is to remain receptive to each family's unique and constantly changing situation and the definitions families bring to these situations based on cultural heritage, values, and beliefs. The question of how to do this in ways that are perceived as respectful of family pri-vacy and nonjudgmental comes down to one major guideline: Let families show us the way. The information that families want to share, the ways they describe and demonstrate their interests, resources, and priorities let us know what information is relevant. This provides the starting point for getting to know each other better.

Strategies for Gathering and Understanding Family Information

This final chapter section focuses on strategies for developing an ongoing understanding of families' resources and priorities. There are various meth-ods that have traditionally been used for gathering family information, and some new ways are being described in the current literature (Bailey & Simeonsson, 1988; Hanson et al., 1990; Summers et al., 1990). The methods used may depend on the traditions of the work setting and the nature and extent to which ongoing family contact is supported or is possible.

Child/Family Histories

Many clinics and agencies use child/family or social histories as a way of gathering and understanding family information. This approach typically involves the use of a standard set of questions that is asked of each family. The questions are usually related to medical, prenatal and birth history; family background; and demographic information. The advantage of this approach is that a standard body of information is available on each child and family and can be referenced if and when needed. The disadvantage is that this approach may be perceived by some families as being intrusive and perhaps even violating their rights to privacy. As mentioned in the previous chapter on first encounters with families, the timing of asking families questions about health history (including possible drug use, abortions, and other sensitive topics) and demographic information (including income, need for public assistance, etc.) may affect whether or not families feel comfortable in providing this type of information.

Professionals who conduct child/family histories can ask themselves the following questions to ensure that histories are conducted respectfully:

- Is it necessary to ask every family every question on the child/family history form?
- If certain sensitive information is necessary, is it possible to explain to families why the information is being gathered, how it will be used, and who will have access to it?
- Can some information be collected now and some at a later point in time?

An alternative to obtaining traditional child/family histories is to ask families what information they think you should know about their child and themselves related to their expressed concern or priority. Additional information can be gathered after a trusting relationship has developed with the family and at a point when the information is relevant in terms of a family's expressed concerns or interests.

Self-Report Questionnaires

An approach that has received much attention in the literature since the passage of P.L. 99-457 is the use of self-report measures to identify family concerns, priorities, and resources. A list of some of these measures is included in Table 3–1. The primary purpose of most of these self-report questionnaires is to provide a mechanism to facilitate a professional/family discussion of family concerns, priorities, and resources for intervention planning.

Research conducted by Bailey and Blascoe (1990) is helpful in terms of understanding parent perspectives on such measures. In this study, a large number of mothers and fathers were asked to fill out the original *Family Needs Survey* (Bailey & Simeonsson, 1985) and then to answer a series of questions about the measure. Parents indicated that, for the most part, they did not feel the questionnaire was intrusive. They did feel, however, that parents should be given choices about how they shared the kind of information requested on the measure. They also felt that the wording on such questionnaires was important. For instance, they did not like the

Table 3–1. Sample Surveys and Scales for Identifying Family Concerns, Priorities, and Resources.

Family Information Preference Inventory. A. P. Turnbull & H. R. Turnbull (1986). In Turnbull, A. P. & Turnbull, H. R., *Families, professionals, and exceptionality: A special partnership.* Columbus, OH: Merrill Publishing.

> Inventory from which family chooses their current level of interest (no interest; information is of low, medium, or high priority) and the preferred format for receiving information (group meeting, individual meeting, or written materials) on 37 items (e.g., teaching child at home, advocacy and working with professionals, future planning, relaxation and family leisure, and finding and using more support).

Family Interest Survey. J. Cripe & D. Bricker (1993). In D. Bricker (Ed.), *AEPS Measurement for birth to three years* (vol. 1). Baltimore: Paul H. Brookes.

> Survey to help families identify three types of interests (child-focused, family-focused, and community-focused). For 30 items, family indicates for 30 items whether each item is a priority interest, an interest but not a current priority, or is not an interest at the time.

Family Needs Scale. C. J. Dunst. C. S. Cooper, J. C. Weeldreyer, K. D. Snyder, & J. H. Chase (1988). In C. Dunst, C. Trivette, & A. Deal, *Enabling and empowering families* (pp. 151). Cambridge, MA: Brookline Books.

> Scale in which family chooses among six descriptions (not applicable, almost never, seldom, sometimes, often, almost always) on 41 items focusing on basic resources, specialized child-care, personal and family growth, financial & medical resources, child education, meal preparation, future child-care, financial budgeting, and household support.

Family Needs Survey (Revised). D. B. Bailey & R. J. Simeonsson (1990B). Original version (1988) appears in D. Bailey & R. Simeonsson, *Family assessment in early intervention* (pp.106–109). Columbus, OH: Merrill Publishing. Revised version can be obtained by contacting the authors at the Frank Porter Graham Child Development Center, CB# 8180, University of North Carolina, Chapel Hill, NC 27599-8180.

> Survey in which family chooses from (no, not sure, yes) to the question, "Would you like to discuss this topic with a staff person from our program?" on 35 items from 6 categories: Information, Family and social support, Financial, Explaining to others, Child care, Professional support, and Community services.

Family Resource Scale. H. E. Leet, & C. J. Dunst (1988). In C. Dunst, C. Trivette, & A. Deal, *Enabling and empowering families* (p.141). Cambridge, MA: Brookline Books.

> A 31-item form focusing on growth and financial support, health and necessities, nutrition and communication, physical shelter, intrafamily support, employment, child-care, and income. Families rate each item on a 6-point scale (does not apply, not at all applicable, seldom, sometimes, usually, and almost always adequate)

Family Support Scale. C. Dunst, V. Jenkins, & C. Trivette (1988). In C. Dunst, C. Trivette, & A. Deal, *Enabling and empowering families* (pp. 157). Cambridge, MA: Brookline Books.

> Scale in which family chooses among six descriptions (not available, not at all, sometimes, generally, very, and extremely helpful) on 20 items focusing on informal and formal kinship, social organization, immediate family, and specialized and generic professional service.

repeated use of the phrase, "I need help with. . . . " As a result of this research, the *Family Needs Survey* was revised (Bailey & Simeonsson, 1990), and the statements were reworded to ask families if they were interested in talking to a staff member about the topics listed. If your program is currently using, considering using, or developing a self-report measure, it may be helpful to ask a group of culturally diverse families for feedback on the questions.

Another issue related to the use of formalized measures relates to the ways that the questions on forms define the services you provide. If we honestly feel we should provide broad-based, individualized support to families, then it is important to convey an open-ended interest family concerns, whatever these might be. A standard set of questions in and of itself creates certain boundaries or limits to how a family might respond. For example, a family that does not have adequate housing may not indicate this as a concern because it is not a choice on the form, yet it is a primary concern to the family. Thus, there are pros and cons to the use of such forms. Perhaps standard forms provide a realistic picture of what we are able to address through our agency. On the other hand, it may mean that a family may feel that their major concern is not of interest to us; therefore, they may not feel it is appropriate to mention it.

An additional issue related to written surveys is the extent to which they exclude families who simply cannot relate to written forms because of literacy levels, comfort level with filling out forms, or with written English language. Translating written documents into the native languages of those being surveyed is one strategy for reaching non-English-speaking families; however, this takes time, careful planning and resources. Included in some of the challenges associated with using translators and interpreters outlined by Lynch and Hanson (1992) is that some of the early intervention concepts are not easy to translate into other languages.

Questions you may want to consider in terms of your own use of formal self-report measures include:

■ Have you received feedback from a socioculturally diverse group of families on overall usefulness and satisfaction with a questionnaire before using it broadly?

- Are questionnaires used flexibly with family members? (e.g., are families given choices about what information is shared, whether it is shared, and how it is shared?)
- If a questionnaire is used, do you tell families how the information will be used and who will have access to it?
- Do you convey to families that you are willing to talk about a broad range of topics that affect their family, in addition to the topics covered on the questionnaires?

Informal Interviews

Another way of gathering and understanding family information is the semi-structured interview (Winton & Bailey, 1988). Using this approach, the professional has a general idea about which topics will be covered in discussions with a family. In conducting discussions with families, however, the professional uses primarily open-ended questions and follows the parent's conversational lead. Research by Jean Ann Summers and her colleagues (Summers et al., 1990) on parents' preferences about how family information is gathered suggests that the more informal the interview the better. Parents in the study stated that they preferred informal give-and-take conversations, rather than formalized questionnaires or structured interviews.

Although preferred by many families, some early interventionists feel uncomfortable about the idea of conducting informal interviews. Some professionals are concerned that an open-ended conversation with a family might lead to unanticipated issues being introduced that are beyond the interventionist's comfort and competence range. Another concern is that families will start talking about and expecting help with needs that are beyond the traditional boundaries of program services. Research has documented that, in fact, these things are likely to happen. Families do start talking about unexpected topics and concerns (Winton & Bailey, 1990) when a more informal approach is used.

This leads us to questions about the assumptions underlying a family-centered approach and how we define our roles within this framework. If we define our role as that of the expert who is expected to solve problems, then the thought of hearing about the broad array of possible family concerns would be daunting. However, if we see our role as being that of collaborator and networker—willing to assist families in generating their own solutions or accessing community resources related to their concerns—it is perhaps easier to be receptive to the "whole picture."

It is also important that we recognize and acknowledge when we feel we are "in over our heads" in trying to handle difficult issues that families may raise in our conversations with them. At these times it is important to consider turning to other resources, which can offer greater expertise and experience. Again, doing this with sensitivity is important in terms of maintaining a supportive relationship with a family. Rather than blurting out, "I need to refer you to a psychiatrist!" the first step may be to elicit from the family where they might seek other assistance. Is there anyone else they feel comfortable talking with about the issue? When they have had similar situations in the past, where have they gone for help? Questions such as these provide a starting point for joint problem solving. Acknowledging our own lack of expertise without expressing shock, horror, or making drastic recommendations is important. In cases of clear neglect or abuse, we are legally bound to contact appropriate social service agencies. If, however, that decision can be defined in terms of seeking additional support or expertise, rather than as a punitive measure, it may facilitate a continued relationship between the family and your program. The importance of working closely with other community agencies is critical at these points, if our goal is to support families when they are in crisis. It is also important to consider where we might get support for ourselves as we work in collaboration with families who are facing particularly challenging situations.

When agencies are serving families for whom English is not the primary language, it would be ideal if there were staff members available to work with these families who are familiar with the culture of these families and who are fluent in their language. When bilingual staff are not available, interpreters or translators are needed to communicate with families who do not speak English. The use of a translator, however, may not entirely resolve the issues involved in working with families who do not speak English. More detailed discussions of the considerations and cautions involved in working with translators, as well as specific strategies that may be employed when using translators are available in publications by Jeppson and Thomas (1995), Lynch and Hanson (1992), and Randall-David (1989). These readings are strongly recommended for professionals and agencies working with culturally diverse populations.

This brings us to another important question: What skills are essential for identifying family priorities and collaborative decision making with families? What are the behaviors that professionals should engage in to communicate respect, understanding, and acceptance when working with families? Throughout this chapter the importance of listening has been emphasized. Listening consists of all the verbal and nonverbal ways that we let families know we are interested, accepting, and respectful of the information they provide to us. It depends on being sensitive to the unique communication styles of individuals and families. Some families may prefer an informal, casual approach to interactions. Others may prefer a more formal approach. Some families may like to get down to the business at hand right away, while others may prefer making "small talk" first. Isaura Barrera (1994) makes the important point that the words used in any situation are a small part of the interchange. She states, "Underlying the words we speak is our 'real language'. . . a language of values, beliefs, world views, perceptions, and feelings. It is this deeper language that must be understood."

Many aspects of communication are specific to cultural heritage and background. Barrera (1994) suggests that culture and language mediators are needed to understand these deeper dimensions of communication. (See Hanson et al., 1990; Lynch & Hanson, 1992; Randall-David, 1989; Mason, Braker, & Williams-Murphy, 1995, for more information and resources on this topic.) Picking up cues from families about their style while, at the same time, they are also learning about the way you interact takes time. Perhaps the most important strategy is to move slowly and to avoid alienating a family before you have a chance to get to know one another.

Developing positive relationships with families depends on more than just listening. It also depends on effectively eliciting information from families through open-ended questioning, summarizing what has been shared, and providing information that family members request in clear and understandable language. In some situations this will mean using a translator who can effectively understand a family's native language and who can also accurately convey what the family is saying to professionals. It also means using the information families share as the basis for what happens in decision making and planning. If we listen and accept what families tell us, but then turn around and make plans for children based on other priorities, we are missing the point.

A summary of some of the tips for communicating with families described in this chapter is provided in Table 3–2.

In summary, understanding what families hope to accomplish and being responsive to their concerns and priorities is the cornerstone of a family-centered approach. Furthermore, this process is continuous and relies heavily on the development of respectful and trusting relationships between families and professionals. Creating these relationships requires an investment of time and energy on the part of professionals. It also requires effective communication skills, not the least of which is the ability to listen.

The next two chapters address the issue of child assessment. This is not to say, however, that child assessment should necessarily be the next step for all families. Our only reason for placing it next is because child assessment is often one of the first things that happens when children and families enter early intervention programs. Please keep in mind that, if we are truly family-centered, the unique concerns and priorities of each family should determine what the next step should be. Moving directly into intervention planning or service delivery may be the best way to respond to some families' priorities, with child assessment postponed until more immediate concerns have been addressed. For other families, child assessment may be exactly what is needed. The next two chapters show how flexibility and responsiveness to family priorities within the context of child assessment can make the process meaningful for all families.

TABLE 3–2. Tips for Effective Communication with Families.

Listening

Attending to what family members have to say using verbal and nonverbal listening skills

- Make eye contact in a varied and natural way when a person is talking, taking into account cultural differences that define what is "natural."
- Use natural and relaxed gestures that mirror gestures of family members.
- Show interest through your facial expressions.
- Use body language that conveys a non-critical and accepting stance toward each family member.
- Use a modulated and audible voice tone that reflects the emotional tone of the family members.
- Be comfortable with and respect silences. They often mean family members are thinking or reflecting.
- Stay on topic. Take cues from what family members have already said.
- Note words and expressions that family members use and incorporate their language into your own comments.

Reflecting Feelings

Perceiving accurately and sensitively the feelings of family members and communicating that understanding in appropriate language

- Be aware of what a family members says, as well as how it is said (e.g, body language, voice tone, glances).
- Respond to all aspects of a family member's feelings.
- Reflect feelings in a clear, concise manner.
- Reflect feelings in a manner that conveys a desire to understand and a willingness to be corrected if reflection is inaccurate, rather than conveying an attempt to interpret or diagnose.
- Do not parrot what a family member has said or overuse this technique. This may serve to alienate or inhibit communication.

Reflecting Content

Restating and summarizing the content of a family member's message or the overall content of a discussion

- Reflect the basic message conveyed by the family member without assuming more than has been said.
- Reflect the content in a clear, concise, nonjudgmental manner that allows additions, corrections, or clarifications by family members.
- When summarizing, give equal emphasis to the various items covered in the discussion.
- Intersperse this technique with other types of responses.

Effective Questioning

Developing an understanding of the family's priorities and facilitating the family's consideration of actions or options they might want to take to accomplish what they want to do

(continued)

TABLE 3–2. *(continued)*

- Begin a conversation with open-ended questions. This allows them to talk about what is important to them.
- Use only close-ended questions when precise information is needed.
- Avoid "why" questions. They tend to create an atmosphere of defensiveness.
- Keep questions simple and ask them one at a time.
- Make sure you have a clear understanding of a problem or situation before seeking solutions to it.
- Ask questions in a way that conveys interest and curiosity about the relationships between the people, events, and values related to what is happening, rather than attempting to analyze or diagnose.
- Ask about times or situations when things were working well and explore what contributed to that positive state of affairs.

REFERENCES

Anderson, M., & Goldburg, M. (1991). *Cultural competence screening and assessment.* Chapel Hill, NC: National Early Childhood Technical Assistance System (NEC*TAS).

Bailey, D. B., & Blascoe, P. (1990). Parents' perspective on a written survey of family needs. *Journal of Early Intervention, 14*(3), 196–203.

Bailey, D. B., & Simeonsson, R. J. (1985). *Family Needs Scale.* Chapel Hill, NC: Frank Porter Graham Child Development Center, The University of North Carolina.

Bailey, D. & Simeonsson, R. J. (1988). *Family assessment in early intervention.* Columbus, OH: Merrill Publishing.

Bailey, D. B., & Simeonsson, R. J. (1990). *Family Needs Survey* (rev.). Chapel Hill, NC: Frank Porter Graham Child Development Center, The University of North Carolina.

Bernheimer, L. P., Gallimore, R., & Weisner, T. S. (1990). Ecocultural theory as a context for the individualized family service plan. *Journal of Early Intervention, 14*(3), 219–233.

Braun, L., & Swap, S. (1987). *Building home-school partnerships with America's changing families.* Boston, MA: Wheelock College.

Barrera, I. (1994, June/July). Thoughts on the assessment of young children whose sociocultural background is unfamiliar to the assessor. *Zero to Three,* 9–13.

Education of the Handicapped Act Amendments of 1986, Pub. L. No. 99-457. (October 8, 1986.) Title 20, U.S.C. §1400 et seq. *U.S. Statutes at Large, 100,* 1145–1177.

Gallimore, R., Weisner, T. S., Kaufman, S. Z., & Bernheimer, L .P. (1989). The social construction of ecocultural niches: Family accommodation of developmentally delayed children. *American Journal on Mental Retardation, 94*(3), 216–230.

Hanson, M., Lynch, E., & Wayman, K. (1990). Honoring the cultural diversity of families when gathering data. *Topics in Early Childhood Special Education, 10*(1), 112–131.

Heatherington, M. (1984). Stress and coping in families. In D. Doyle, D. Gold, & S. Markowitz (Eds.), *Children in families with stress* (pp. 7–33). San Francisco: Jossey-Bass.

Hill, R. (1958). Social stresses on the family. *Social Casework, 39,* 139–150.

Jeppson, E., & Thomas, J. (1995). *Essential allies: Families as advisors.* Bethesda, MD: Institute for Family-Centered Care.

Lynch, E., & Hanson, M. (1992). *Developing cross-cultural competence: A guide for working with young children and their families.* Baltimore: Paul H. Brookes.

Maslow, A. (1954). *Motivation and personality.* New York: Harper & Row.

Mason, J., Braker, K., & Williams-Murphy, T. (1995). *An introduction to cultural competence principles and elements: An annotated bibliography.* Portland, OR: Portland State University, Research and Training Center on Family Support and Children's Mental Health.

McGonigel, M., Kaufmann, R., & Johnson, B. (Eds.). (1991). *Guidelines and recommended practices for the individualized family service plan* (2nd ed.). Bethesda, MD: Association for the Care of Children's Health.

Mead, M. (Ed.). (1953). *Cultural patterns and technical change.* Paris: UNESCO.

Olson, D., McCubbin, H., Barnes, H., Larsen, H., Muxen, M., & Wilson, M. (1983). *Families: What makes them work.* Beverly Hills, CA: Sage Publications.

Randall-David, E. (1989). *Strategies for working with culturally diverse communities and clients.* Bethesda, MD: Association for the Care of Children's Health.

Rollins, B., & Galligan, R. (1978). The developing child and marital satisfaction of parents. In R. Lerner & G. Spanier (Eds.), *Child influences on marital and family interaction* (pp. 71–102). New York: Academic Press.

Seelye, H. (Ed.). (1996). *Experiential activities for intercultural learning* (Vol. 1). Yarmouth, ME: Intercultural Press.

Summers, J.A., Dell'Oliver, C., Turnbull, A.P., Benson, H.A., Santelli, E., Campbell, M., & Siegal-Causey, E. (1990). Examining the individualized family service plan process: What are family and practitioner preferences? *Topics in Early Childhood Special Education, 10*(1) , 78–99.

Turnbull, A., Patterson, J., Behr, S., Murhy, D., Marquis, J., & Blue-Banning, M. (1993). *Cognitive coping, families and disability.* Baltimore: Paul H. Brookes.

Werner, E. (1984). *Child care: Kith, kin and hired hands.* Baltimore: University Park Press.

Wikler, L. (1981). Chronic stresses of families of mentally retarded children. *Family Relations, 30,* 281–288.

Winton, P. J., & Bailey, D. B. (1988). The family-focused interview: A collaborative mechanism for family assessment and goal-setting. *Journal of the Division of Early Childhood, 12*(3), 195–207.

Winton, P. J., & Bailey, D. B. (1990). Early intervention training related to family interviewing. *Topics in Early Childhood Special Education, 10*(1), 50–62.

Wuest, J. (1991). Harmonizing: A North American Indian approach to management of middle ear disease with transcultural nursing implications. *Journal of Transcultural Nursing, 3*(1), 5–14.

Wuest, J., & Stern, P. (1990). Childhood otitis media: The family's endless quest for relief. *Issues in Comprehensive Pediatric Nursing, 13,* 25–39.

■ CHAPTER 4
Rethinking Child Assessment

The assessment of children through developmental checklists and standardized or criterion-referenced tests is standard practice for most early intervention programs. In fact, federal law mandates a process of evaluation and assessment for children entering the early intervention system. Federal regulations governing Part H of the Individuals with Disability Education Act (IDEA) stipulate that an "evaluation" must take place within 45 days of the initial referral and must be conducted to determine the child's initial and continuing eligibility, which includes identifying the child's level of functioning across a variety of developmental domains. The regulations further stipulate that such evaluations must be comprehensive, nondiscriminatory, multidisciplinary, and conducted by qualified personnel. In addition, the regulations specify the need for "assessment" activities, which are defined as the ongoing procedures used throughout the child's eligibility to identify: (a) the child's unique needs, (b) the family's strengths and needs related to the development of the child, and (c) the nature and extent of the early intervention services needed by the child and the child's family. State laws must comply with these federal regulations and usually provide additional details about how child evaluations and assessments are to be conducted (Meisels & Provence, 1988). In response to these regulations, child evaluation is often one of the first items on the agenda for families interested in receiving early intervention services.

Despite the good intentions of state and federal regulations governing child evaluation and assessment, their interpretation and implementation can result in practices that conflict with a family-centered approach. For example, children and families may be denied immediate access to services because there is a long waiting list for child evaluations. In some of these situations, services may be available, but the agency responsible for conducting evaluations has a backlog. If families are permitted to enter the services immediately, the 45-day timeline for evaluation would not be met, and so enrollment is postponed. There may also be situations in which parents are not interested in having their child participate in a comprehensive, multidisciplinary evaluation. The information or services the parents want may be quite specific but, to get what they want, their children have to go through a complete evaluation. Finally, there are numerous "war stories" told by parents about their experiences in having their children evaluated. Child evaluations can, indeed, be very stressful for families. Ken Yockey (1979) poignantly describes his family's experiences when their daughter, Debbie, was 4 years old and received her first psychological evaluation. This father's story is titled "Playing Blocks with Psychologists," and excerpts from his story are presented below.

> It was made very clear to us that we must remain quiet, speak only when spoken to, and under no circumstances were we to encourage our daughter in any way while the tests were being conducted. It was something like going to watch my son play in a Little League baseball game, and being told I wasn't allowed to cheer, except this was much, much worse.
>
> For Barb and me, these tests for Debbie couldn't have been any more important than if they had been college entrance exams. I remember thinking to myself at one point, "For God's sake Deb, the blue post, put the damned thing on the blue post." I knew she could do it. I had seen her do it a thousand times. I could almost feel Barb thinking the same thing. But we said nothing . . . . Debbie, on the other hand, simply did not understand or appreciate the seriousness of the situation at all. Nobody had explained to her that this was a test, and that her parents' egos and mental health might hang in the balance.
>
> When the psychologists report arrived, we met once again with our pediatrician . . . . it confirmed what we suspected all along . . . . mental retardation . . . . The report also said that, in the opinion of the psychologist, my wife Barbara was having a difficult time "accepting" Debbie's mental retardation, and that she was being "overly protective." It's odd, but it wasn't until that moment Barb and I realized that we were being tested, too. (pp. 26–29)

In this chapter, traditional notions of child evaluation and assessment are challenged as we view the process from a family-centered perspective. According to federal regulations (Part H), evaluation is defined as the procedures used to determine a child's initial and continuing eligibility for services. Assessment is defined as the procedures used to determine a child's specific strengths and needs and to identify the type of services needed by the child and family. In keeping with current thinking that evaluation and assessment should be part of a continuous process, we use the term "assessment" hereafter to refer to that process. For, in fact, we perceive it to be unfortunate that there is often an unnecessary separation of activities related to child evaluation and child assessment in service delivery to infants, toddlers, and preschoolers with special needs. We begin this chapter with a discussion of the purposes of child assessment from this alternative perspective. This is followed by discussions of the structure of assessment, the content of assessment, and the methods used in assessing young children.

■ THE PURPOSE OF ASSESSMENT

Although many of the traditional reasons for child assessment are valid within a family-centered approach, there is a shift in focus that calls for a modification of previously accepted policies and practices. As in the past, many of the purposes of child assessment center on the gathering of information about the child. The difference, however, lies in who the information is being gathered for. From a family-centered perspective, the purpose of child assessment is to gather information that addresses the concerns and priorities of the family, rather than primarily obtaining information that professionals feel they need to design appropriate services for a child. Although professionals must meet certain obligations set forth by agency policies or state laws, care should be taken not to sacrifice the priorities of the family to comply with such regulations. When regulations are unavoidable, it is best to be up front with families about why certain procedures must be followed and request their cooperation.

CHILD ASSESSMENT
Outcomes for Working With Families

- To determine and document the child's eligibility for early intervention services
- To provide families with the information they want about their child
- To underscore the child's accomplishments and abilities as well as the parents' contributions to these achievements
- To ensure that parents are informed decision makers in matters that affect them and their child
- To obtain information about the child that contributes to the development of an appropriate and effective plan of action

---

Most families want information about their child. They may want to know if their child is showing delays in his or her development, the reason for their child's delays or differences, what they can do to facilitate their child's development, or where they can find the services or resources they want to help their child. Supplying parents with the information *they* want should be the primary focus of the assessment process. This can only happen if we know what their concerns and priorities for their children are *prior* to conducting assessments. This is the first order of business.

The unique characteristics of each child and family give rise to wide variations in parents' desires for information. It is, therefore, unrealistic to think that a standard set of procedures for conducting assessments will adequately address the concerns of all families. Rather, assessments must be custom-tailored to be responsive to the unique priorities of each family (Johnson, McGonigel, & Kaufmann, 1991; Kjerland & Kovach, 1990). This requires flexibility on the part of agencies and the individual professionals within agencies who perform assessment services. Obviously, the degree of flexibility that agencies have may be limited by the availability of funds, the number of professionals on staff, the disciplines represented on the staff, as well as by the number of families they are expected to serve. Nevertheless, even with severe shortages of resources, adaptations can be made by the program and by individual professionals to meet the unique information needs of each family.

Another purpose of child assessment is to provide families with information about their children that they may not have otherwise been aware of or have thought to have been concerned about. Suppose, for example, a family's primary concern is that their 18-month-old child is not talking. During the assessment process, it is noted that the child, although attempting to walk, is unsteady and appears to have increased muscle tone in his or her legs. The professionals should provide this information to the family, even though motor development was not an expressed concern or priority at the outset. The manner in which this additional and unexpected information is provided to the family, however, is critical. The purpose of telling the parents is not to *convince* them that they need to be concerned about the child's walking, that they need to have further assessments conducted, or that intervention in this area should be a priority. Instead, the purpose is to provide them with the same information that the professionals have and, thereby, allow them to make an informed decision as to whether or not this aspect of their child's development should be considered a priority.

Above all, child assessment should contribute to the development of an appropriate intervention plan. Although this assessment purpose is not unique to a family-centered approach, what is meant by "appropriate" is different from traditional notions. As discussed in Chapter 6, Intervention Planning, a family-centered approach dictates that the goals included on the intervention plan should be based on the family's priorities. Similarly, the strategies for accomplishing these goals should take into consideration the routines, values, and competing priorities of all family members. And finally, it is the family, rather than the professional, who is ultimately responsible for deciding the content of the plan. The extent to which the assessment process provides parents with information that helps them make these decisions will determine the degree to which the intervention plan is appropriate.

THE STRUCTURE OF ASSESSMENT

A wide variety of formats are used for conducting child assessments. Formats vary from state to state as a function of the bureaucratic systems that are in place and how those systems have defined the roles and responsibilities for each agency. Variations in state laws governing early intervention services can also affect how assessments are conducted. Even within states, formats for conducting assessments are likely to vary from community to community and from one program to another as a function of resources that are available.

In some cases, a multidisciplinary assessment may consist of only two or three professionals from different disciplinary backgrounds. In other situations, child assessment may be conducted by a team of six to eight professionals. Assessments may be conducted by the same program that will be providing services to the child and family, or they may be provided by an agency whose sole function is to conduct child assessments. Assessments may be conducted in the family's own home, in a classroom setting, or in a clinic that is specifically designed to assess young children. The length of time allotted to child assessment may also vary, ranging anywhere from 1–2 hours to a tightly scheduled, full 8 A.M. to 5 P.M. day of assessment activities. In addition, all assessments may be conducted on the same day and in the same location, with all team members observing and sharing information, or they may be spaced out over time and take place in a variety of locations, with little ongoing communication among the various professionals. What formats, if any, are most conducive to a family-centered approach? In attempting to answer this question we must consider the effects that each format may have on families and their children.

As mentioned above, the primary purpose of child assessment should be to provide parents with the information they want about their child. Thus, one condition that should be met by any assessment format is that it provides parents and professionals with a true picture of the child's abilities. If this condition is not met, we cannot possibly provide the family with accurate information. In an article appearing in *Exceptional Parent* magazine, Elizabeth Moon speaks for herself and many other parents as she describes the frustration she experiences when her child performs poorly in testing situations. Her article is entitled "Test Child/Real Child."

> The child being evaluated can't jump over an eraser on the floor and clings to his mother's hand. The real child, at home, hops down a line of six laundry baskets, slowly but gleefully.
>
> The child being evaluated can barely totter up a few stairs holding an adult's hand, putting both feet on each tread. The real child climbs stairs well, if slowly, by himself, one foot per tread, sometimes skipping a tread.
>
> It seems obvious that an evaluation which doesn't find the "real child" can't form a basis for diagnosis or treatment. Whether a child "should" or "shouldn't" be that different during evaluation is beside the point; the real child is **both** children, but the one we want to encourage is the lively, competent, adventurous one at home. We can't do that if we don't know what his real abilities are.
>
> Elizabeth Moon
> *Exceptional Parent*, June 1992 (p. 16–17)

What are the assessment formats that allow the "real" child to emerge and, thus, enable us to provide parents with accurate information? One has to question formats that involve long hours in an unfamiliar environment, wherein the young child is confronted with multiple strangers and is being asked to perform numerous tasks in highly structured activities. Although it may be argued that the standardization population was tested under unfamiliar conditions as well, the chances are that they were not subjected to a battery of tests over the course of a single day. And no argument related to the accuracy of test results will counteract the stress experienced by parents as they watch their child fail item after item—especially when they know their child is capable of performing these skills under more favorable conditions. Is it any wonder that parents tell so many "war stories" about child assessment, or that some parents don't agree with professionals' conclusions that are based upon assessment results?

Recognizing that traditional models of multidisciplinary assessment may not be conducive to getting the best performance from infants, toddlers, and preschoolers, several alternative formats have emerged in the field of early intervention. Play-based and arena assessment techniques are becoming increasingly popular for use with very young children (Foley, 1990; Linder, 1993; Wolery & Dyk, 1984). These models and others have sought to provide a more naturalistic context for conducting child assessment by limiting the number of professionals who interact with the child, providing increased opportunities for parent involvement, and observing the child while he or she is engaged in social interactions or toy play.

When evaluating the efficacy of assessment formats, another issue to consider is whether the assessment process can be individualized to meet the unique information needs of each family. From a family-centered perspective, the ideal situation would be to have a variety of assessment models from which each family could choose. Given the limited resources available in most communities, however, such an ideal situation is unlikely to exist. Instead, professionals will probably have to be flexible and offer choices within a single model of assessment to individualize the process for children and their families.

Suppose, for example, that a parent is concerned their 20-month-old child is not walking independently. Their expressed priority is to find out why the child is delayed in walking and, more important to them, what they can do to help their child learn to walk. In addition to providing the family with information and suggestions related to their child's motor development, the program may also need to determine eligibility for services because this is a new referral. Should this family be required to go through a full-scale, multidisciplinary evaluation (e.g. psychological, speech-language, nutrition, social-emotional, medical, educational, and physical therapy assessments) to get the information they want about their child's walking? At this point, all the family might really want is for their child to be evaluated by a physical therapist, and yet the program must comply with federal and state regulations by documenting the child's current level of functioning across a number of developmental domains. It may also be true that the child's disability extends beyond the obvious delay in his or her motor development, and more extensive assessment may reveal these related difficulties.

If we respect the parent's role as decision maker and honor our commitment to individualized services, we would offer the full-scale evaluation but allow the family to select what they thought would best meet their priorities. If they chose only a physical therapy evaluation, an alternative method of determining eligibility requirements might be needed. One alternative could be to administer a standardized, multiple-domain test such as the *Batelle Developmental Inventory* (Newborg, Stock, Wnek, Guidubaldi, & Svinicki, 1984) in addition to the physical therapy evaluation. Descriptions and comparisons of the various multiple-domain tests available are provided by McLean & McCormick (1993). Use of a multiple-domain test would at least provide normative information on the child's levels of functioning across a variety of developmental areas and, thus, satisfy administrative requirements. Another alternative would be to use a nonstandardized developmental checklist such as the *Brigance* (Brigance, 1978) or the *Hawaii Early Learning Profile* (Furuno et al., 1979) and identify the proportion of delay between the child's chronological age and developmental age across areas. Whether or not these alternatives are in line with state regulations would need to be carefully considered. An arena assessment or other variation of transdisciplinary assessment might be another option. For example, the physical therapist and the parent could work together in assessing the child's motor functioning while other members of the assessment team observe and screen for delays in other areas of development.

THE CONTENT OF ASSESSMENT

An emphasis on developmental levels or age equivalents and the use of standardized or criterion-referenced tests frequently results in assessments focusing on what is "wrong" with a child. In other words, these tests only provide us with information about the degree to which an individual child's performance diverges from that of the typically developing child. Without a doubt, this type of information is important in our work with young children. We need it to determine eligibility for service provision, and many parents want this type of information to increase their own understanding about their child. If, however, the content of assessment stops there, it is understandable that the assessment experience may not be a pleasant one for some families. After all, how many parents *really* want to hear how their child doesn't measure up to other children of the same age? When parents do ask for this type of information it may be because they believe it is important to be as fully aware as possible about their child, but chances are they also want to hear something positive.

A mother of a 4-year-old child with severe and multiple disabilities once explained the negative impacts that testing can have on a family. The family had received services from a home-based early intervention program since shortly after the child was born, and the child's fourth annual assessment was scheduled for the following week. "I just dread it," the mother said. "I absolutely dread it. Every year, for about 2 weeks before Ryan's assessment, I get so depressed. I just hate going through the assessment only to hear, once again, about how far behind he is. I know he's behind and I know he'll never catch up. They know it too. What's the point of it?" She sighed and then continued, "When I'm at home with him, I can just enjoy him for who he is. I know he has problems, but I don't need to be reminded of how far behind he is year after year."

This same mother enjoyed the relationships she had with the professionals who came to her home, and she often came up with creative ideas for encouraging her son's development. She just hated assessments. In fact, in the same conversation just described, the mother had remarked that she only participated in the assessments because she didn't want to be perceived as a "difficult parent" or have the professionals think she was "denying" her son's disabilities. Furthermore, the professionals who conducted the assessments were the same professionals who provided services to her son, and she didn't want to give them a hard time because she liked them very much.

Now, it wasn't that the staff was insensitive to this mother's feelings. They may not have been aware of the degree to which this mother dreaded Ryan's annual assessment, but they did know she didn't look forward to it. They tried to make the assessments as positive as possible by emphasizing what the child could do rather than what he couldn't do, and they lavished compliments on the mother about how she interacted with her son and her creativity in working with him. Obviously, this was not enough.

Emphasizing the child's and family's strengths is a good start toward making assessments family-centered, but further adjustment appears warranted for at least some families. Among the problems in using standardized tests and developmental checklists are that they are static measures. By static, it is meant that they provide us with a snapshot of the child's level of skill development at the time of testing, but provide little information about the child's potential and movement toward future skill acquisition. Nor do they provide us with information about how to facilitate the child's learning.

Development is a term that denotes movement, change, or growth—it is active. And yet, our assessment of development through tests and checklists provides a static, single-frame snapshot of this active concept. Parents are often far more interested in where their children are going and how they can help them get there than they are in how their child tests at a particular time. Acceptance of the child's level of functioning at the time of testing is passive, but hope for the child's future development encourages parents to be positive and to take action. Can child assessments be conducted in such a way as to incorporate a more active view of development?

One way this can be accomplished is to include an assessment of the child's ability to learn new skills and the teaching strategies that best facilitate such learning. The individual practitioner can incorporate this strategy into even the most traditional, test-oriented assessment processes. For example, when you are administering a test and the child fails an item, take a few minutes to try to figure out how the child might best learn the skills or concepts that are required for successful performance of the test item in question. Ask the parent what they think is going on and how he or she would approach teaching the skill. Try out these ideas as well as a few strategies that you might have in mind. By exploring teaching strategies, the parent goes away from the testing situation with ideas about what they might do at home rather than just seeing what the child cannot do. In some cases, the parent may even leave the situation with their child having performed a skill that he or she had never done before.

The idea of assessing learning potential and discovering effective intervention strategies may be further expanded in organizations that are open to innovation and supportive of a family-centered approach. Take, for example, the situation involving the mother of the 4-year-old with severe and multiple disabilities described earlier. Perhaps this mother was correct in questioning what the point was of repeated testing when her child's scores changed very little from year to year. The time devoted by the professional team, as well as the time spent by the child and his mother, probably could have been put to more productive use. A quick update of developmental levels could have been achieved through a checklist or multiple-domain test, and the remaining time spent investigating the child's capacity for learning and identifying strategies to accomplish the priorities this mother had in mind for her child. Some may argue that such activities should not be considered assessment. If, however, the purpose of child assessment is to provide families with information and to guide intervention planning, it seems to qualify.

Another problem in relying on standardized tests and developmental checklists is that they are typically context-free. They provide us with an age level of skill performance with little or no consideration of the child's behavior in his or her natural environment. These tools may be appropriate for determining eligibility for services, gaining normative information, and establishing diagnoses, but their value in terms of providing information that will contribute to the development of intervention strategies is questionable. For some children, their value in determining diagnoses and developmental levels may even be questionable. This is especially true for children with severe or multiple disabilities (McLean & McCormick, 1993) and for children of diverse cultural heritage (e.g., Mattes & Omark, 1984). In addition, for children with communication difficulties, their familiarity with the examiner may play a role. For example, the work of Fuchs, Fuchs, Power, and Dailey (1985) has revealed that, although children without disabilities perform equally well with familiar and unfamiliar examiners, children with communication difficulties perform more poorly when the examiner is someone whom they are not familiar with.

Increasing awareness of the need for more functional assessments has resulted in the development of a number of alternative assessment methods. For example, play-based assessment (Linder, 1993) and arena assessment (Foley, 1990; Wolery & Dyk, 1984) rely heavily on professional observation of children in more naturalistic play situations—although still in environments that are unfamiliar to the child being tested. Others (Vincent, Davis, Brown, Teicher, & Weynand, 1983; Vincent et al., 1986) have developed questionnaires and interviews for obtaining information from parents about how their children function in everyday routines. To go one step further, some professionals are offering families the opportunity to evaluate their own children using developmental scales or checklists. (See Chapter 5 for more detail on the role of families in assessment.) There is, however, no magic to be found in the use of any of these alternative methods. The point being made here is that the integrity of our interventions may be seriously jeopardized if the content of our assessments does not consider child behavior within the context of daily routines. As pointed out by McLean and McCormick (1993), "interventionists must be able to move beyond the documentation of the presence or absence of a specific skill or concept to an analysis of the use or quality of the skill or concept" (p. 49). McWilliam (1992) further reminds us that "the use of context-free assessment has often led to the practice of context-free, nonfunctional objectives such as 'will stack four blocks' or 'will make a circle with a crayon.'"

METHODS OF ASSESSMENT

By and large, current methods of assessing infants, toddlers, and preschoolers are not in line with the principles of family-centered practices. Enablement and empowerment are difficult to achieve when, for the most part, our methods remain professionally directed. The use of professional jargon, reliance on nonfunctional, standardized tests, and the division of child development along professional discipline boundaries all contribute to distancing parents in the assessment process. Words of encouragement for parents to "join the team" and become active participants in the assessment process cannot override the messages sent by our methods. All too often the message is clear: "We are the experts, we know what to do, so let us get our job done." If we want to change this message, we must begin to change our methods.

First, let us consider the settings in which child assessments take place. Assessments are typically conducted on professional turf. This may be in a professional's office, a therapy room, classroom, or a testing room specifically designed for assessment—complete with one-way mirrors, intercoms, and headsets for listening to what takes place. Although these settings may be familiar and comfortable for the professionals, they are probably not familiar to many parents and their children. It is difficult, at best, for families to feel in control of the assessment process or to assume an active role when they are on professional turf. As Elizabeth Moon (1992) points out, the setting in which assessment takes place may also affect the child's behavior and, therefore, the validity of test results.

Recognizing the effect of setting, some early intervention programs have elected to provide parents with the option of conducting assessments in the family's home or the child's regular preschool setting. These programs typically combine naturalistic observations of the child in familiar routines with more traditional methods of assessment. If home assessments are not possible, another option may be to bring "the family's home" into the professional setting. In today's technological world, this is easily accomplished through lightweight, hand-held camcorders. The purchase of a camcorder would be a relatively minor expenditure for most programs. Some families may even have their own video equipment. A professional or the parents themselves could videotape the child in daily routines related to the family's areas of concern. The videotapes could be brought to the assessment or sent ahead of time for viewing by the professionals responsible for conducting the assessment.

Still another option is to make the professional setting more familiar and comfortable for the child and family. Clinic-style waiting areas may be replaced with a more home-like environment, and therapeutic testing areas may be abandoned in favor of rooms that resemble kitchen areas, living rooms, or playrooms. Families may also be asked if they would like to bring the child's favorite toys, familiar objects (baby blanket, pacifier) or snacks with them to lend some familiarity to the setting and to encourage more natural interactions. Above all, our assessment settings and methods should not circumvent children's accessibility to their parents or disrupt familiar patterns of parent–child interaction. Separation of young children from their parents for the purpose of assessment should rarely, if ever, occur.

A second consideration is the common practice of massed assessments. Parents and children are frequently subjected to long assessment days in which a number of different assessments are conducted by an equal number of examiners representing a variety of professional disciplines. This is probably more true for initial evaluations than for subsequent assessments, but it may occur at any time. Behind this practice is the belief that a more thorough understanding of the child's abilities can be achieved when a number of discipline perspectives are included in the assessment. With a more comprehensive picture of the child, a more complete intervention program can be developed. Although such intentions are laudable, they may fail to consider the potential negative impacts of the method on the child and family. We might also ask ourselves if this is really what families want and, if they do, can the same outcome be achieved in ways that are less stressful?

Play-based assessment and arena assessment have been mentioned in previous sections of this chapter as alternative methods of assessing young children. Both methods address the present concern, in that, they limit the number of professionals who interact directly with the child. In doing so, they also shorten the time required for completing the assessment process, while still allowing for input from a variety of professionals. The innovative structure of these methods alone, however, is not sufficient to ensure that a family-centered approach is being used. The content of the assessment must also be taken into consideration. If the content of the assessment is not individualized and guided by family priorities, the method will not be family-centered.

The key to achieving family-centered assessment is understanding the concerns, priorities, hopes, and beliefs that parents have about their children. No amount of professional expertise or innovation in assessment methodology will override the need for this information. Once obtained, this information should be used to direct all assessment activities. In fact, it may be wise to have a written statement, using the parents' own words, of what they hope will be accomplished as a result of the assessment. Prior to the assessment, this statement or list of questions, concerns, and priorities could be shared with all professionals who are slated to participate in the child's assessment. Decisions about the format, content, or testing instruments selected for the assessment could be made by professionals and families together, taking into consideration what would best meet the family's identified priorities. Similarly, the number of professionals and the discipline backgrounds represented in the assessment process could be decided on using the parents' list. Perhaps we could even evaluate the quality of our assessments by determining the degree to which the parents' questions, concerns, and priorities were addressed at the conclusion of assessment activities.

In conclusion, child assessment is one of the oldest and most institutionalized practices in early intervention. It also involves more professional disciplines than any other aspect of services in our field. As a result, it may be the most resistant to change. At the same time, child assessment continues to be the first order of business for many children and families entering early intervention services. The experiences that families have in the initial assessment of their children is likely to influence what they perceive their roles to be in subsequent early intervention services. If we want families to feel in control of planning for themselves and their children, those messages should be given at the outset. This will only be accomplished if our assessment of children reflects the same family-centered approach as the rest of our services.

Dramatic changes in how child assessment is conducted are unlikely to occur in many programs—at least not for some time to come. Change may come more easily for some programs, either as a function of progressive administrators, or because of a smaller and more cohesive staff. Even if wide-scale changes are not possible, there are smaller changes that individuals or programs can make to bring child assessment more in line with a family-centered approach. The next chapter provides the interested reader with some specific ideas for incorporating family-centered principles in traditional assessment settings.

REFERENCES

Brigance, A. (1978). *Brigance Diagnostic Inventory of Early Development*. Woburn, MA: Curriculum Associates.

Foley, G. M. (1990). Portrait of the arena evaluation: Assessment in the transdisciplinary approach. In E. D. Gibbs & D. M. Teti (Eds.), *Interdisciplinary assessment of infants: A guide for early intervention professionals* (pp. 271–286). Baltimore: Paul H. Brookes.

Fuchs, D., Fuchs, L., Power, M., & Dailey, A. (1985). Bias in the assessment of handicapped children. *American Educational Research Journal, 22*, 185–197.

Furuno, S., O'Reilly, K. A., Hosaka, C. M., Inatsuka, T. T., Allman, T. L., & Zeisloft, B. (1979). *The Hawaii Early Learning Profile*. Palo Alto, CA: VORT Corporation.

Individuals with Disabilities Education Act Amendments of 1991, Pub. L. No. 102-119. (October, 7, 1991.) Title 20, U.S.C. §1400 et seq. *U.S. Statutes at Large, 105*, 587–608.

Johnson, B., McGonigel, M., & Kaufmann, R. (1991). *Guidelines and recommended practices for the individualized family service plan*. Washington, DC: National Early Childhood Technical Assistance System (NEC*TAS) and Association for the Care of Children's Health.

Kjerland, L., & Kovach, J. (1990). Family-staff collaboration for tailored infant assessment: A guide for early intervention professionals. In E. D. Gibbs & D. M. Teti (Eds.), *Interdisciplinary assessment of young developmentally disabled children* (pp. 164–182). Baltimore: Paul H. Brookes.

Linder, T.W. (1993). *Transdisciplinary play-based assessment: A functional approach to working with young children* (rev. ed.). Baltimore: Paul H. Brookes.

Mattes, L. J., & Omark, D. R. (1984). *Speech and language assessment for the bilingual handicapped*. San Diego: College-Hill Press.

McLean, M., & McCormick, K. (1993). Assessment and evaluation in early intervention. In W. Brown, S. K. Thurman, & L. F. Pearl (Eds.), *Family-centered early intervention with infants and toddlers: Innovative cross-disciplinary approaches* (pp. 43–80). Baltimore: Paul H. Brookes.

McWilliam, R. A. (1992). *Family-centered intervention planning: A routines-based approach to early intervention.* Tucson, AZ: Communication Skill Builders/Psychological Associates.

Meisels, S. J., & Provence, S. (1988). *Screening and assessment: Guidelines for identifying young disabled and developmentally vulnerable infants and their families.* Washington, DC: Zero to Three/National Center for Clinical Infant Programs.

Moon, E. (1992) Test child/real child. *Exceptional Parent Magazine, 22*(4), 16–17.

Newborg, J., Stock, J. R., Wnek, L., Guidubaldi, N. J., & Svinicki, J. (1984). *The Batelle Developmental Inventory.* Allen, TX: Developmental Learning Materials.

Vincent, L., Davis, J., Brown, P., Broome, K., Funkhouser, K., Miller, J., & Grunewald, L. (1986).*The parent inventory of child development in nonschool environments.* Madison: University of Wisconsin, Department of Rehabilitation Psychology and Special Education.

Vincent, L., Davis, J., Brown, P., Teicher, J., & Weynand, P. (1983). *Daily routine recording form.* Madison: University of Wisconsin, Department of Rehabilitation Psychology and Special Education.

Wolery, M., & Dyk, L. (1984). Arena assessment: Description and preliminary social validity data. *Journal of the Association for the Severely Handicapped, 9,* 231–235.

Yockey, K. (1979) Playing blocks with psychologists. In T. Dougan, L. Isbell, & P. Vyas, *We have been there: A guidebook for parents of people with mental retardation* (pp. 24–40). Salt Lake City: Dougan, Isbell, & Vyas Associates.

■ CHAPTER 5

Applying Family-Centered Principles To Child Assessment

Whereas the previous chapter focused on assumptions and philosophical issues related to child assessment procedures, this chapter provides specific guidelines and strategies for conducting child assessments in a family-friendly way. We recognize that within early intervention there is a long history of evaluating young children and, over the years, certain standard procedures have been developed. Our intent in this chapter is to provide ideas and strategies for all professionals who conduct child assessments, including those who may feel constrained by demands or regulations that are imposed upon them by the agency or system within which they work. Strategies related to two major components of child assessment are provided: (a) planning and conducting assessments and (b) mutual sharing of assessment information.

PLANNING AND CONDUCTING ASSESSMENTS

We can all think about times when we were included in planning for an activity such as a social event or a professional function. Most of us would agree that our commitment and interest in the activity was heightened by our own participation in the planning process. Thus, our own experiences might prompt us to include the family more directly in the planning of their child's assessment. In addition, we might consider the consensus issue raised in Chapter 3 and recognize that the likelihood of achieving consensus on the "nature of the presenting concern," "the need for treatment," and "the next steps to take" may be improved if we begin based on the family's ideas about what areas of child functioning are assessed and the manner in which these assessments are conducted.

In trying to gain an idea of the family's concerns and priorities about assessment activities, the following questions might be useful: "What is your biggest concern about your child?" "What kinds of information would be most useful to you at this point?" and "How might we help you get this information?" Using questions such as these to acknowledge family members as the "directors" of the upcoming process may ensure that the family's primary questions and concerns have been solicited and addressed.

Previous Assessment Information

If a child has been assessed previously, professionals may want to get more information about what took place during those prior assessments to more effectively plan the upcoming one. To gather more information, the professional may want to ask questions such as:

- What kinds of assessment activities were performed with your child in the past?
- Which types of activities seemed to work best?
- What part did you play in the assessment process?
- What information from the assessment was useful to you?

In asking about the family's previous experiences with assessment, the professional may gain a good deal of information about both the child and family. In particular, listening to the family's reactions to recent assessment experiences may help professionals know more about what additional information the family wants. A perfect example is the mother who, when asked about a previous assessment, said, "Well, I'll tell you one thing that I don't want and that's for someone to tell me again how far behind my son is. What I really need to know is what I can do to help him." This mother was clearly not asking for developmental levels, but was seeking practical activities and ideas for working with her son every day.

Listening to the kinds of questions that families ask can also provide clues about what the family hopes to gain from the assessment. For example, the parent who asks, "Do you think my son is retarded?" is expressing the need for a very different type of information from the parent who says, "I know my child is not developing normally, but what can I do to help her reach her potential."

The "Nuts and Bolts" of Assessment

Where and when will the actual assessment take place? Who will be involved in the assessment activities? What roles might family members play in these activities? These are all questions that can be decided jointly between family members and professionals. There are various strategies that may be used in such joint planning. For example, Linda Kjerland of Project Dakota has created a short checklist that parents might be invited to use (see Table 5–1). Conversations with families could take place with the discussions structured around questions similar to those on the Project Dakota checklist.

Preassessment planning may take place as part of the general information gathering with families or may be part of a discussion or meeting that primarily focuses on specific aspects of the upcoming assessment. When a separate preassessment planning meeting or discussion is held, parents may be encouraged beforehand to think about what issues they

TABLE 5–1. Project Dakota checklist for preassessment planning.

1. What questions or concerns do others have (e.g., babysitter, clinic, preschool?)

2. Are there other places where we should observe your child?
   Place:
   Contact Person:
   What to Observe:

3. How does your child do around other children?

4. Where would you like the assessment to take place?

5. What time of day? (The best time is when your child is alert and when working parents can be present.)

6. Are there others who should be there in addition to parents and staff?

7. What are your child's favorite toys or activities that help him become focused, motivated, and comfortable?

8. Which roles would you find comfortable during assessment?
   ___ a. sit beside your child
   ___ b. help with activities to explore her abilities?
   ___ c. offer comfort and support to your child?
   ___ d. exchange ideas with the facilitator?
   ___ e. carry out activities to explore your child's abilities?
   ___ f. prefer facilitator to handle and carry out activities with your child?
   ___ g. other

Note. Preassessment planning form. Copyright by Dakota, Inc., 1380 Corporate Center Curve, Suite 305, Eagan, MN 55121. Reprinted with permission.

want to address within assessment, to talk about their concerns with others they feel are important to the process, and to notice the kinds of activities or actions that may improve their child's performance. The following sections outline more specific questions and topics that might be addressed in those preassessment conversations with families.

Where and When

Ideally the assessment should occur at a time and place that allows maximum participation by the child's caregivers and within a context that promotes typical interaction with the child. Through questions such as "What times of day are best for your child?" "When is she or he feeling best?" "How could we see what is typical of your child?" and "Are these times that would be convenient for conducting an assessment?" the professional may both acknowledge the family's familiarity with their child and gain understanding of the contexts and settings that may facilitate the child's

best and typical performances. The professional may gain a more representative sample of the child's behavior by asking the family to indicate all
possible locations for assessment (e.g., home, daycare, grandparents'
house) and by working to vary any one context to include a variety of
interactions with people and objects. Asking family members, "What are
things your child enjoys doing?" "What toys does he or she play with?"
"What are places that are fun for your child?" and "Are those places possible locations where an assessment might take place?" are useful in determining the location(s) for child assessment.

These questions presume that professionals have the flexibility within their job settings to honor family preferences. If this flexibility is not
possible, there may be choices that parents can make within the constraints present in the work setting. Perhaps you can offer different locations where an assessment can be conducted within a center-based program. Perhaps you can use "flex" schedules wherein professionals work
some early evening or Saturday hours to provide more options for parents
who work outside the home. If it is not possible to offer choices of times
and locations for assessment, there may be other choices within the
assessment process that families can make.

Who to Include in Assessment

In determining who will be present for the assessment, the professional
may want to use questions as a means to help the family identify their preferences. Here are some questions that might be used:

- Who do you feel knows your child well?
- Who might be able to contribute to our understanding of your child?
- Who might gain from this experience?
- Who would you like to be present for the assessment?
- Who would you like to be a part of helping your child in the future?

Through this questioning process, parents may be encouraged to consider those who are or could be important in shaping their child's development and to consider involving those persons from the beginning.
Involving the important people in the child's life in the assessment process
may not only help the family with future plans for the child, but can also
serve to eliminate the need to interpret assessment results to others.

As indicated by legislative mandates, assessment interactions and
activities need to be sensitive to sociocultural factors and must take place
in the family's native language. As indicated by Barrera (1994), the core of
any assessment is communication, the transfer or extraction of information and meaning between two or more persons. Therefore, for professionals who are not bilingual or who are not members of the family's cultural group, an interpreter or cultural mediator may be necessary (Moore
& Beatty, 1995). A cultural mediator may help identify and develop optimal

social, cognitive, and linguistic contexts to maximize the transfer of information (Barrera, 1994; Tikunoff, 1987). As suggested by Moore and Beatty (1995), interpreters or cultural mediators may take many roles within the assessment process, such as referral source for the community, liaison with parents, communication link between staff and parents, parental advocate, "cultural gauge" for what may or may not be relevant for the family, source of information from parents, interpreter during assessments and meetings, and translator of written materials (e.g., tests, reports, checklists). In these situations, family preferences for the type of role played by the interpreter or cultural mediator is important and their membership on the assessment team is essential. For those interested in gaining more information about working with interpreters or cultural mediators within the assessment process, helpful resources include Anderson and Goldberg (1991), Barrera (1994), Lynch and Hanson (1992), and Moore and Beatty (1995).

Roles Family Members Might Play

Traditionally, family involvement in child assessment has consisted of asking them to provide background information about the child, such as medical and developmental histories. More recently, some families are being asked to provide detailed accounts of their child's day-to-day activities, to describe their child's characteristics and behaviors, to relate the types of strategies that have been tried with the child, or to relate what has worked or not worked. Many professionals have recognized that asking parents broad questions such as "How would you describe your child?" or "What kinds of activities does your child like?" can provide valuable information not available through typical assessment tools. As areas of concern are identified (e.g., communication or motor delays), the use of specific questions such as, "How does your child let you know that he or she is hungry/mad/happy?" "When your child has difficulties, what have you tried that seems to help?" and "How does your child respond to help?" can also provide useful information.

Some professionals have found it useful to ask the family to describe daily routines as a way of gaining understanding of who is involved in the child's life, how the activities take place, and the ways that family members have adapted to the child's disability. By asking family members to describe their child and their child's behaviors, the professional both acknowledges the contributions of the family in the assessment process and benefits from the detailed information that can be provided. In addition, this information can help professionals understand the ways in which the family's sociocultural background and beliefs may influence the child's and family's day-to-day activities and what they believe to be important.

Increasingly, families are being encouraged to observe and participate in assessment activities. An example is the current use of arena assessment in which family members, the child, and two or more professionals observe and assess the child. Questions such as, "Can you show us how you get your child to . . ." or "Could you feed your child and show us the things you have tried that seem to work with your child?" may encourage the parent to take a more participatory role in assessment. Additionally, a family member may be asked to administer certain test items (e.g., "Please try to get your child to stack these blocks") and thus may actually perform part of the assessment. More information on the use of arena assessments and variations in the arena model are available in articles or books by Foley (1990), Linder (1993), and Wolery and Dyk (1984).

In situations in which the family observes from another room (e.g., using a one-way mirror), it may be helpful for a professional to watch with the family and describe the activities, the reasons for performing them, and answer any questions the family may have. If parents must observe alone, it may be helpful to provide paper and pens for them to write down their questions.

An additional way that family members may take part in assessment is through performing observations of their child in other environments (e.g., home, playground, preschool). More formal observation checklists can be used to identify the presence or absence of certain behaviors, or informal methods can be devised wherein family members identify a behavior and simply note its occurrence. Examples might include charting specific behaviors such as the number, type, and mode of expressed intentions or the occurrence of question asking (Crais & Roberts, 1991). In determining observation activities with families, professionals need to be particularly careful not to overburden families with additional tasks. Thus, joint decision making is especially important in planning observations that parents are expected to perform on their own time.

In attempting to gain information, professionals can also ask parents to interpret their child's actions and reactions. In this role, family members have the opportunity to use their past experiences with the child to provide information about what they believe their child is doing, saying, feeling, or thinking. A prime example of the need to have family members as interpreters, is in the assessment of early developing communication skills. In attempting to determine a child's intention for doing or saying something (e.g., change in body posture, saying "no" to favorite food), caregivers are often the best source of information. Another situation in which the family may serve as the child's "interpreter" is when the professionals and family are from different cultural or ethnic groups. Asking family members to interpret their child's behaviors in the context of their own sociocultural background may be helpful in sorting out which behaviors are "expected" and those that may indicate concerns.

Family members can also be asked to validate activities throughout the assessment process. In knowing how and in what ways their children can function best, caregivers can often assist professionals in choosing appropriate activities and contexts and, thereby, improve the overall accuracy of the assessment process. Caregivers can also be asked to validate the results gained from the assessment and to determine whether the results reflect the child's typical behavior. To gather validation information from family members, the professional may use questions such as:

- How did you feel about the assessment today?
- Did you feel that the tests/activities used were helpful in understanding your child?
- Do you think the results reflect your child's typical performance?
- Did we achieve the objectives you indicated were important to you today?
- What other skills or behaviors does your child do that we were not able to see today?
- How could we gain more accurate information about your child?

In this way, not only can families help validate and interpret the results gained from the assessment, but they can also feel certain that their own reactions to and concerns about the accuracy of the findings will influence the reporting and use of the assessment results.

Finally, caregivers can be asked to evaluate their children by posing questions such as: "Do you think your child can do . . .?" "What would happen if you were to . . .?" or by completing developmental checklists or administering specific tests. The types of evaluation activities that families are now being asked to perform are diverse and include: (a) performing screening measures (Bricker, Squires, & Mounts, 1995; Dopheide & Dallinger, 1976); (b) documenting sensory behaviors (Dunn & Oetter, 1991); (c) completing parent report questionnaires (Dale, 1991; Fenson et al., 1993; Rescorla, 1989); and actually administering some tests, such as developmental assessments (Bloch & Seitz, 1989; Bricker, 1993; Brinckerhoff & Vincent, 1987), disability inventories (Haley, Coster, Ludlow, Haltiwanger, & Andrellos, 1992), and tests of articulation (Andrews & Andrews, 1990).

Specific tools and activities that can be used to facilitate family participation in assessment activities are listed in the resource section at the end of this chapter and are more fully described in Crais (1993, 1995). Of primary importance in discussing family involvement in assessment activities, however, is the recognition that not all families will want or choose to participate in assessments, much less to do so in an active manner. Parents who have been involved in early intervention for some time may be "burned out" from the activities created for them by professionals. Other families may view professionals as the "experts" and may see their own skills as inadequate for evaluating their child. In these instances, it is useful to examine why it is that family members may be reluctant to participate actively in assessment.

As for any of us when provided choices, families will react differently depending on the way information and choices are presented. By indicating through words and actions that the contributions family members make are valued, and by being responsive to the family's preferences for assessment activities, professionals may facilitate their participation. Some families may be willing to perform assessment activities that can fit within their day-to-day activities or ones that seem critical to their idea of what should be assessed. Additionally, family members may suggest other ways that they can participate in assessing the child.

We should also keep in mind that some families may not have the energy or time to devote to assessment activities. We must balance our encouragement of family participation with a clear message that they are free to make the choice. Recognizing and supporting the family's preferences for the type and level of participation in assessment is critical to building a positive relationship. In discussing choices with families and supporting those choices, professionals again confirm the power of families to make their own decisions for their child and themselves.

Variations Across Work Settings

For those professionals in job settings with limited access to families before assessment or in agencies with limited personnel, these ideas may seem almost impossible. In the event that families are not seen before the assessment and there is no face-to-face opportunity to identify their concerns (e.g., school or residential setting), perhaps it is possible to use some type of preassessment form that can be sent to families ahead of time. A telephone conversation with the family can also serve as a way of gathering some of this information. Perhaps the office personnel could send out the form with a cover letter, or teachers/staff could send a note and preassessment form home with the child. Following up such correspondence with a phone call can also be helpful in clarifying the family's concerns and preferences.

If evaluating a child as part of a multidisciplinary or interdisciplinary team process, there may be enough time before the assessment takes place that someone could discuss assessment options with the family. Some clinic-based programs have personnel who either visit the home or meet with the family at the center sometime before assessment to discuss the family's priorities and concerns. Perhaps this person could include questions specific to the family's preferences for assessment. If an interpreter or cultural mediator will be involved, program staff could provide this person with options and information relative to the assessment. A final option is to include a discussion about assessment preferences at the beginning of the assessment session. Although this alternative may limit the options available to the professional and the family during the assessment itself (e.g., types of assessment activities, roles of family members), combining it with some of the previous strategies may enhance the outcome.

Some professionals may feel unable to include parents when state or agency guidelines mandate that particular tests or types of tests be administered. When standardized tests are required, professionals may ask how they can engage families more fully in assessment and still maintain the rigorous test conditions necessary to achieve accurate results. Perhaps, in addition to the standardized test, family members could be asked to complete developmental checklists or behavioral checklists? After all, many professionals supplement test scores with nonstandardized measures to provide more information about the child's behaviors within natural contexts. Is it possible for family members to take part in assessing their child with these nonstandardized measures? In addition, professionals have used variations from the "standards" for years when assessing children with disabilities. Perhaps we should consider the changes necessary to offer families more active roles in assessment as just another "variation."

An example of the kinds of variations made recently by one professional during her scheduled home-based assessments may stimulate ideas for others. In attempting to provide more family-centered services, this professional reviewed her current practices and then began to slowly modify her assessment activities. She started by sending a preassessment form to families and calling them to discuss the upcoming assessment. Rather than beginning with a standardized developmental screening (e.g., bringing toys and playing with the child herself), she began by spending more time talking with the parents and observing the child and parents together. By orienting her questions to the parents' concerns and priorities, asking them to complete a few developmental checklists, and to play with the child themselves, she was able to get a better picture of both the child's developmental level and the family's concerns about the child.

Another example of changes made to gain parents' participation is an innovative school-based preschool program which initiated "home-visit week" during the first week of school. During this week, rather than hold class, the teachers of the program visited each child's home to meet the family and to discuss the family's immediate concerns and priorities for the child. During the visit, the family was asked to help perform various assessment activities with the child and to make decisions about the child for the upcoming school year. In this way, not only did the family members become active participants in their child's assessment, but the teachers also noted enhanced participation by the families throughout the year. These are just a few of the many possible variations for gaining active participation by families.

Family–Professional Disagreement

As mentioned previously, families and professionals will not always agree on what is most important for assessment or how assessment should occur.

Take, for example, a mother whose primary concern was that her son was a messy eater. The professionals working with this mother and her son were far more concerned about the limited variety of foods in the child's diet than she was about the mess the child made at the table. In this situation, the assessment could focus on examining *how* the child ate and/or *what* he ate and why. If the professionals focused primarily on the issue of *what* he ate and ignored the mother's concern, there may be a mismatch in expectations for the assessment and the subsequent plans for intervention. If the professionals ignored their own reservations and focused the assessment primarily on the mother's concern, how might this impact the growth and development of the child?

We are not advocating that professionals ignore their own professional knowledge, skills, or opinions in situations like that just described. We are, instead, suggesting that there are often multiple ways to address a family's preferences, and it may be helpful to consider the value of pursuing different routes at different times. There may be alternative ways of approaching this type of situation that recognize both professional and family perspectives and also promote positive feelings and outcomes. One available option is to take a "wait and see" approach. Through this choice, we might suspend our professional opinions for a time and support the family's immediate preferences for assessment. Depending on the outcomes achieved, we could then decide whether to express our concerns or priorities. In addition, as we develop a relationship with the family, they are more likely to be interested in our views. As trusting relationships develop, families often ask for professionals' opinions about their children.

Another alternative is for professionals to express to the family their own concerns, thoughts, and feelings about an issue at hand. This is particularly important when a professional feels an area for assessment is critical to the child's health or progress and the family has not mentioned or expressed concern about it. If ideas can be expressed in a way that does not overpower the family, they may be more willing to consider such an area as important for assessment and may be more open to the results. For some families, talking about these issues may be difficult or uncomfortable, and the professional needs to recognize and respect individual variations between and within families. When facing a mismatch between the family's and professional's views, it is often helpful for the professional to try to understand the family's perspective. This may increase the professional's appreciation for the family's position and may possibly pave the way toward the elimination of the conflict or, at least, soften its impact.

Summary

Collaboratively planning and conducting child assessment can have many benefits for both families and professionals. This type of assessment process can not only be more satisfying to families and professionals, it can also provide a more accurate and representative picture of the child and family. When considering planning and conducting assessments, remember two old adages. First, the amount of time spent planning an activity directly relates to the success of the activity. Second, for all parties to feel central to an activity, they must be active participants in the planning. Thus, increased time spent in collaboratively planning and conducting child assessments may afford benefits impossible to calculate for both families and professionals.

MUTUAL SHARING OF ASSESSMENT INFORMATION

When families relate their memories of previous assessment experiences, what kinds of impressions stand out in their minds? Are their thoughts full of empathetic professionals who were expert listeners and careful sharers of information, or do they recall professionals who disappointed and disheartened them? Quite often the latter set of perceptions are those that come to mind, and it is the negative or insensitive words or behaviors that are remembered (Olson, 1988). As professionals, we know that families have not always been satisfied with the way assessment information has been shared. We also know that the way information is shared with families can affect how the information is perceived, the resulting relationship between the family and the professional(s), and the follow-through on plans made after assessment.

The reactions of families to assessment information can be highly variable, often depending on their past experiences, their own resources, their knowledge of the diagnosis, their view of the child, their feelings about the validity of the results, and the extent to which they have participated in the actual assessment process. For some families, the results may be negative, but they confirm the family's suspicions and thus are welcome in helping them settle on a diagnosis or a direction for planning. For other families, a "positive" outcome, such as finding out that their child does not have a hearing loss, may be viewed as unsettling because of the lack of a diagnosis and the need to continue searching for what is causing the child's difficulties.

Time delays in presenting assessment results can also cause negative feelings on the part of parents. The time spent waiting between an assessment and being told the results can be a difficult and anxious time for families. Although some families may have a rough idea of what the assessment outcome will be, they may not know the specific results or the immediate or long-term implications for their child. Other families may have fewer indications of the outcome and may be surprised by the results.

In a survey of parents following the diagnosis of their child's hearing impairment, Martin, George, O'Neal, and Daly (1987) reported a number of ideas that parents felt would improve their interactions with professionals. Some parents in the study advocated that the professional could (a) demonstrate positive counseling characteristics, (b) include the entire family in ongoing services, (c) make group and individual counseling available if desired by parents, (d) provide more information (e.g., services, remediation techniques, realistic expectations, printed materials), and (e) provide opportunities to meet other parents of children with disabilities.

As professionals, we too have strong feelings about interacting with families about assessment results. In a recent survey (Olson, 1988), a group of professionals noted that they particularly disliked (a) relaying painful information, (b) responding to parents' grief and anger, and (c) being viewed as unknowledgeable. One difficulty for many early intervention professionals is the limited training they received in working with families when, at the same time, we are expected to work more closely with families (Bailey, Simeonsson, Yoder, & Huntington, 1990; Crais & Leonard, 1990). Given the dissatisfactions reported by both parents and professionals, consideration must be given to determine how to share assessment information in a way that is useful to families, that will guide families and professionals in decision making, and that is understood and valued by family members. In determining how best to share information with families who are from sociocultural backgrounds that differ from that of the professionals involved, interpreters or cultural mediators can again be helpful. By gaining insight into a family's preferences for how information is best shared, understood, and valued, professionals can tailor the interactions to meet the immediate needs of the family.

There are multiple ways that information about assessment may be shared including (a) ongoing discussions throughout the assessment process (b) a post-assessment meeting held immediately or a short time after the assessment, and (c) telephone follow-ups and/or written reports. As reported by several researchers and clinicians (Brinckerhoff & Vincent, 1987; Dunst, Trivette, & Deal, 1988; Luterman, 1991), the more families participate in the assessment process, the more active and satisfied they are with the outcomes. Thus, in our attempts to alter the assessment process to include more collaboration with families, we must also examine new models for sharing information.

One strategy that is being used more often by professionals is discussing the family's and professional's observations and findings throughout the course of the assessment. In this way, discussion of the "findings" of each assessment activity may be tied directly to the behaviors just seen and, therefore, may be clearer and more useful to the family. Moreover, when the family and professional are engaged in discussion about immediate behaviors and activities, they can generate ideas and strategies together for how the child's behaviors or development may be facilitated. In addition, the discussion of assessment findings throughout testing, may help limit the amount of information that is traditionally discussed at the end of the assessment process.

To facilitate an examination of the "sharing" process, the remainder of this chapter focuses on issues surrounding the sharing of assessment information and provides ideas and suggestions for how this process may be more positive for both families and professionals. The information is divided into the following components:

- Beginning the discussion
- Providing a diagnosis
- Long-term implications
- Differences in individual style
- Little things that count
- Closing the discussion
- Assessment reports
- Follow-up contacts
- Variations across work settings

Beginning the Discussion

One strategy for beginning the discussion of assessment findings is to ask the family what issues/concerns they wish to discuss first and then following their lead in topic organization. If information can be provided in response to requests or questions posed by family members, the information is more likely to be of use and to be remembered. Another starting point may be asking family members to discuss their own assessment findings or to comment generally on the assessment process as observed. Families who have performed observations or assessments at home or on-site, can be asked to provide their own impressions of their child's abilities, particularly focusing on the child's areas of strength. Families, however, will vary in their ability to describe their assessment findings or their perceptions of their child. In some cases, the professional may want to provide more direction to the family by asking questions such as, "From what you observed and know about your child, what things is your child able to do well?" "What kinds of things are difficult for your child?" and "What skills do you think your child most needs to learn next?" In addition to gaining the family's perspectives, parents' responses to these questions can serve as a means of validating the results of assessments conducted by professionals.

Following or during a family's discussion of their child's abilities, professionals can provide information based on their own assessments and observations. Kjerland and Kovach (1990) suggest that someone write down on a wall chart the contributions made by all participants, noting with initials who contributed which comments. With this type of visual record, it is easy to see when the professional is contributing more than the family, and when it may be better to allow the family more time to talk.

At some point, the professional and family may find it useful to look over the list of observations and more directly identify what they think are the "strengths" and "needs" of the child. In this process, it is helpful to first gain the family's perceptions of their child's strengths and needs and then the professional can add to the list any items that they felt were left off. Whether a new list of strengths and needs is written or particular items are starred on the original list of observations, this visual representation helps the participants have a clear record of the items identified.

The next step in the discussion is to determine whether any additions, revisions, or clarifications of the family's concerns about their child have occurred as a result of the assessment. Useful questions might include, "From what you know of your child and what you saw today, what are your main concerns?" "Are your current concerns the same as those you expressed to us at an earlier time?" "What does this information mean to you?" and "Are there additional areas that you feel need further assessment?" In some cases, the professional may want to ask more directed questions such as those recommended by Kjerland and Kovach: "What are the things that are most important?" "What stands out about your child now?" or "What comes to mind when you see these strengths and needs?"

Providing a Diagnosis

Some families may view the assessment process as a way to understand what is "wrong" with their child, to give a name to the difficulty if possible, and to determine what is next for their child. We, as professionals, may also be drawn to a diagnosis due to issues within the early intervention system that often force us to determine a diagnosis in order to provide further services. Some families, for personal or cultural reasons, may not be receptive to the idea of having their child "diagnosed" or labeled. A recent trend in early intervention has been to defer the use of diagnostic labels and to view assessment as an ongoing process. Extending the time for professionals and families to observe the child and gather information promotes more accurate findings and also keeps the focus on setting immediate goals that are based on the current behaviors of the child. Even when diagnoses are not provided, however, most of us share with families some type of assessment information about the child's strengths and difficulties, the need for further observation or testing, and/or the child's need for intervention. Thus, although a specific diagnosis or label may not be provided, the family is typically left with the notion that their child is "not okay" and may need special help.

If a diagnosis is decided on and shared, some parents may have difficulty accepting the accuracy of the diagnosis, particularly when it comes as a surprise or when it is especially painful (e.g., autism, mental retardation, profound hearing loss, cerebral palsy). Even when a broad term such as "developmental delay" is used, families may still indicate doubt or confusion about what it means for their child. Is there a way that we can deliver "bad news" without being perceived as the "bad guys" by parents? Can we reduce the discomfort we feel in sharing diagnoses with families?

When parents display verbal or nonverbal signs of doubt or disagreement about a diagnosis, professionals often feel compelled to "convince" the parents that they are right and may continue to provide information in the hopes that the parents will eventually agree with them. One mother tells the story of being told during the initial evaluation that her young son was autistic. When she expressed her doubt and questioned the diagnosis, one of the professionals held up a tambourine behind the child's head and banged it loudly. After receiving no response from the young boy, the professional said, "Now, do you think that's normal?" Years later, the mother remembers the event quite painfully and describes her frustration at not being given the time to discuss her reservations, her anger in having this diagnosis so painfully and forcefully thrust upon her, and her doubts about the overall results and methods.

One strategy that may help in dealing with uncertainty or disagreement regarding a diagnosis or the results of assessment, is to ask family members about their feelings and reactions to the information. This focus on the family's uncertainty may prompt a frank discussion of their reservations or concerns. The use of active listening strategies are also useful at this time. If the diagnosis is a tentative one, it is useful to explain the professionals' uncertainty to the family and point out that further observation and assessment will be needed to confirm or reject the diagnosis. Other methods of handling these types of situations include: (a) reviewing the presence or absence of behaviors that led to the diagnosis; (b) providing a list of possible diagnoses (e.g., hearing loss, cognitive deficits, autism) and indicating why you or the family think each may or may not be likely; (c) offering further testing if you think it may be beneficial; (d) offering to help parents seek out additional resources if they want more information about the diagnosis or a second opinion; or (e) in situations where parents were not initially present during testing (e.g. hearing testing), suggesting that the parents be present during retesting. And, as previously suggested, the opportunity to actively participate in the assessment of their child often allows the family to contribute in concrete ways to the assessment discussion and facilitates the match-up of family and professional views (Brinckerhoff & Vincent, 1987). Finally, if the observations, opinions, and perceptions of family members are solicited throughout the discussion of assessment results, there may be less likelihood of disagreement at the point of diagnosis or in later planning.

Discussion of Long-Term Implications

How do professionals decide whether to discuss any long-term implications of a child's disabilities? Are prognostic statements necessary to the future development of the child and family? And, if it seems imperative to discuss these issues, can those with a negative impact be handled in a way that is less burdensome to families? Furthermore, how do professionals decide when and in what ways to discuss these issues?

In thinking about these questions, it is often helpful to look first at families' perceptions of receiving this type of information. Scores of parents have related their stories of the dreadful predictions or pronouncements professionals have made in the past about their children. One mother of a 2-year-old related that following the child's stroke at 1 year of age, the neurologist told her that her daughter would never walk or talk. The devastation that this prognosis had on the family was quite powerful and both parents went through a period of true hopelessness. Fortunately, through the persistent efforts of the child and her family, she began to make progress and now she both walks and talks. Thus, some families, although burdened initially, may be resilient to these "prophecies" and indeed may be challenged to overcome the odds and prove the professionals wrong. Other families may be demoralized and slowed down by the perceived long-term implications and may, in fact, make important and costly decisions based on limited information.

The need to provide a "reality check," as we professionals have often called this strategy of forcing families to "face the facts," seems rooted in the belief that families need to see things as we do and to move on quickly to the "next stage." As suggested in Chapter 3, families need time to digest critical information, and holding onto hope in the face of predictions of negative outcomes may represent an adaptive coping response on the part of families. In addition, we are also beginning to recognize the benefit of allowing families to "move" at their own pace and to determine for themselves what and how much they need to know, and especially when they want to know it.

One strategy that seems consistent with a family-centered approach is to let the family lead us as to whether, when, and how much they wish to discuss their child's future. In this way, only the amount of information that the family wants and may be ready to receive is shared with them. Many families, given time, will ask for professional advice and opinions on what may happen in their child's future. As they look toward and plan for the future, they may recognize a need to enlist the services of professionals. When they do, the professional should be as clear as possible and let the family's questions guide how much information is desired.

Some families may ask from the outset, "What will happen to our son in the future?" or "Will my child ever be able to walk/talk/feed himself?" In response to the first question—a request for a general prediction—it is often helpful to ask families for more specifics before giving an answer. Questions such as "How far ahead are you thinking about—next month, next year or beyond that?" or "Is there anything in particular about the future that concerns you?" may help the family identify what it is they really want to know. Although providing alternatives such as, "Do you mean will she/he go to school, will she or he use sign language, will she or he ever catch up to other children?" may be useful to some families, but for others it may open up thoughts about the future that they are not ready to consider. In addition, providing examples may serve to focus on areas that are of no concern to the family while ignoring areas of primary interest. If professionals ask the family to clarify their concerns first, they will be much more able to offer the type of response desired by the family.

As for questions about the child's future in a specific skill area, the professional may not have an answer. Certainly a "best guess" can be provided, but the professional can also suggest to the family that more time and information are needed to provide a definite or more complete answer. If there are any positive comments to be made about the child's progress in this area, it is useful at this point to share that information. For example, following the assessment of a young boy with a severe physical disability, the mother asked whether her son would ever walk. The professional answered honestly that she did not know, but that the youngster was certainly learning how to stand and the physical therapist had been very positive about the importance of this skill for future walking.

A final strategy for handling family's questions about the future is to ask them to be first in sharing their thoughts and feelings. What do they see as possible outcomes for their child? In this way the professional may be able to get an idea of the time frame, behavior or skill area, and depth of information the family may have in mind. Information on what they know about the disability or diagnosis and their own perceptions of the impact on their child may also be gained. Throughout these types of discussions, it is also helpful to recognize and attend to misperceptions, particularly those that may have a negative effect on the family or child (e.g., believing that every child has to learn to crawl before being able to walk).

In summary, there are times when professionals feel it is necessary to discuss the future with family members. And many parents are, in fact, concerned about the future and will actively seek out predictions from professionals. Professionals should not avoid talking with parents about such issues, but they should follow the family's lead whenever possible. The future is a very sensitive topic and must be handled both delicately and honestly. If we listen carefully to parents and empathize with their situations we will probably be off to a good start.

Differences in Individual Communication Styles

When parents are asked about how they would like assessment information to be shared with them, the interpersonal skills of professionals are nearly always mentioned. In regard to counseling skills, a number of parents in the Martin et al. (1987) survey noted that professionals need to (a) be supportive listeners, (b) be capable of helping the parents work with their emotions, (c) offer realistic hope for the future, (d) be willing to spend time with them, and (e) provide more resource information.

In seeking to achieve a better match in communication styles between professionals and families, it is often helpful to use the words families use and highlight the issues they express. This is particularly important for families who are from different sociocultural backgrounds from the professionals involved. Using familiar terms rather than the jargon we are prone to exchange with other professionals can help in "normalizing" our interactions with families. It is also helpful to keep in mind that spoken information is not easily remembered, especially when a number of details are provided or unfamiliar terms are used. In fact, much of the literature on postassessment conferences suggests that parents are typically able to recall only about half of the information they are given. Is it necessary that we provide all the assessment information at one time, or is it possible to share some portions at a later time?

As many parents and professionals have noted, family members may also not "take in" important information during a discussion of the assessment results due to the messages going on in their heads (e.g., "This is awful, what will we do now?" or even "I'm glad we finally know why he's been acting this way"). Professionals who encourage parents to participate in conversations about assessment results may be in a better position to judge what parts of the offered information parents are receiving. Questions such as, "Is this new or unexpected information for you?" "Is this information useful in understanding your child?" "How do you think this will impact your daily life with your child?" and finally, "What further information do you need?" may prompt families to share their feelings. Providing parents with a written summary of the information they have been given and the discussions that took place is also helpful for families.

Little Things that Count

When presenting disturbing information to families, avoid trying to "cheer up" the family by suggesting that the problem could be much worse (e.g., "At least the retardation is not severe.") or by reframing the situation (e.g., "Look at this as an opportunity to . . ."). This kind of response may only invalidate the parents' feelings and give them the sense that you think they should not feel badly. Allowing the family to use their own strategies for coping will send the message that you are listening to and are supportive of them. Some parents and professionals have also noted that the child's presence during the discussion of the assessment results increases the likelihood that the child is positively acknowledged, and the child's presence may, in fact, reduce the stigma of the diagnosis (Cunningham & Davis, 1985). Cunningham and Davis also noted that with the child present, parents may perceive the professional's interactions with the child during the conference as positive.

In considering whether to include the child in conferences, choices can be discussed with the family and the wishes of the family enacted. The presence of siblings and other relatives can also be explored with the family. It is useful in thinking about assessment sharing discussions, to remember that family members differ widely in how they may wish the discussion to take place. The more we can request and honor their preferences, the more likely the discussion will be beneficial to the family.

Closing the Discussion

In closing the discussion, it is often helpful for someone to "sum up" the major points or issues covered. The use of this strategy can serve as a means to review the discussion and to gain consensus regarding: (a) what was important, (b) what, if any, next steps will be taken, and (c) who will be responsible for taking them. Although professionals often do the summing up, family members may be asked if they would like to do it. If parents are assured that the purpose of the summarizing is only for clarification and they feel comfortable with the professionals involved, they may appreciate this opportunity. Asking parents to take the lead, however, should be done with the clear message that it is voluntary and not expected. If a professional does the summing up, useful questions to stimulate closing comments from family members may include:

■ From today's discussion, what are the issues that you feel are the most important?
■ From what you have heard and seen, how do you interpret this information?
■ What aspects of today's discussion do you feel are important to share with others?
■ Where would you like to go from here?

Depending on the family's preferences and the professional's constraints, further discussions or activities can then be planned.

Toward the close of the discussion it is helpful to ask families what would be most helpful to them in terms of "next steps." Are they interested in more information, referral to other agencies, meeting other parents of children with similar disabilities, parent support groups or individuals, or just time to adjust to the new information? At this point, some families will know exactly what they want and will express it openly, whereas others may be overwhelmed by the whole experience. To help families who seem less sure of what they think the next steps should be, professionals can suggest ideas or options from which families may choose.

Another useful strategy is to review with the family the objectives they identified for the assessment and discuss the extent to which they felt each objective had been accomplished. If preassessment planning forms (see Table 5–2) or information gathering forms (as described in Chapter 3) such as the *Family Needs Survey* (Bailey & Simeonsson, 1990) have been used, professionals can refer to these and ask the family whether their

TABLE 5–2. Birth to five assessment tools for facilitating family participation in assessment.

Ages and Stages Questionnaires (ASQ): A Parent-Completed Child-Monitoring System. **(1995). D. Bricker, J. Squires, & L. Mounts, Baltimore: Paul H. Brookes.**

Set of 11 developmental questionnaires periodically sent to parents of children at-risk between 4 and 48 months. Areas screened include: Gross and fine motor, communication, personal-social, and problem-solving. Also has Spanish version. Article describing the results of work with the precursor to this tool: Bricker, D. & Squires, J. (1989). The effectiveness of parental screening of at-risk infants: The infant monitoring questionnaires. *Topics in Early Childhood Special Education, 9,* 67–85.

Assessment, Evaluation, and Programming System: AEPS Measurement for Birth to Three Years **(Vol. 1). (1993). D. Bricker (Ed.). Baltimore: Paul H. Brookes.**

Criterion-referenced assessment, evaluation and family participation components. Areas included: fine & gross motor, adaptive, cognitive, social-communication, and social. Also includes a *Family Report Measure* for parents to assess their child and a *Family Interest Survey* to gain information on child, family, and community interests. Volume 2 includes curricular materials.

Assessing Linguistic Behavior (ALB). **(1987). L. Olswang, C. Stoel-Gammon, T. Coggins, & R. Carpenter, Seattle: University of Washington Press.**

Birth to two observational and administered scales: Cognitive antecedents, play, communicative intention, language production, and comprehension. Video available of children at different levels of development for first four segments.

Carolina Curriculum for Infants and Toddlers with Special Needs **(Second Edition). (1991). N. Johnson-Martin, K. Jens, & S. Attermeier, and B. Hacker, Baltimore: Paul H. Brookes.**

Criterion-referenced assessment of birth to 24-month-old children with special needs. Areas included: Tactile integration, fine motor, auditory localization, object permanence, functional use of objects, control of physical environment, gestural imitation and communication, feeding, vocal imitation and communication, responses to communication from others, gross motor (prone, supine, upright).

Child Development Inventories. **(1992). H. Ireland, Minneapolis: Behavior Science Systems.**

Parent completed instrument used to identify a child's skills across fine motor, gross motor, social, expressive language, language comprehension, general development, self-help, letters, and numbers. Age range covered is 15 months to 6 years. Other associated tools include a parent interview format and screening tools for: infant development (0–15 months), ages 1–3 and 3–6, and kindergarten readiness.

(continued)

TABLE 5–2. *(continued)*

___

Communication and Symbolic Behavior Scales **(First Edition). (1993). A. Wetherby, & B. Prizant, Chicago: Riverside.**

Developed for 9–24-month-old preverbal to verbal children. Observation, interaction, and parent interview. Measures communicative functions and means, reciprocity, social-affective signaling, verbal symbolic and nonverbal symbolic behavior. Includes eight communication temptations; unstructured, directed, and combinatorial play; and comprehension items. Also includes *Caregiver Perception Rating* form for caregivers to complete after the assessment to gain their perceptions of the child's behavior and performance during the assessment.

Family Administered Neonatal Activities. **(1989). I. Cardone, & L. Gilkerson, Zero to Three, 10(1), 23–28. Washington, DC: Bulletin of the National Center for Clinical Infant Programs.**

Uses Brazelton's (1984) *Neonatal Behavioral Assessment Scale* (2nd ed.). (I and II). Clinics in Developmental Medicine, No. 88, Philadelphia: J. B. Lippincott to involve parents in observing and interpreting their newborn's actions and reactions. Focus is on confirming parent's perceptions of the newborn through observations.

Infant-Toddler Language Scale. **(1990). L. Rossetti, East Moline, IL: LinguiSystems.**

Developed for birth to 3-year-olds. Includes parent questionnaire & test protocol to gather observed, elicited, and parent report information. Areas assessed include: Play, interaction-attachment, gesture, pragmatics, language comprehension and expression. Parent questionnaire includes questions regarding concerns, interaction and communication development, and a vocabulary checklist for comprehension and production.

Language Development Survey. **(1989). L. Rescorla, The language development survey: A screening tool for delayed language in toddlers.** *Journal of Speech and Hearing Disorders, 54,* **587–599.**

Vocabulary checklist used as a screening tool to identify children with language delays at two-years of age. Includes 14 semantic categories. The survey is printed and described in the referenced article.

MacArthur Communicative Development Inventories. **(1993). L. Fenson, P. Dale, S. Reznick, D. Thal, E. Bates, J. Hartung, S. Pethick, & J. Reilly, San Diego: Singular Publishing Group.**

Parent report instruments used to determine child's comprehension & production vocabularies. For children 8–16 months (words, gestures, imitation), and for children 16–30 months (production vocabulary, word combinations). Article describing the use and results of the instruments: P. Dale (1991). The validity of a parent report measure of vocabulary and syntax at 24 months. *Journal of Speech and Hearing Research, 34,* 565–571.

(continued)

___

TABLE 5–2. *(continued)*

Parent/Professional Preschool Performance Profile (5Ps) **(1987). Variety Pre-Schooler's Workshop, 47 Humphrey Dr., Syosset, NY 11791.**

> Behavioral scales from 6 to 60 months designed for home-school collaboration. Areas included: social, motor, cognitive, self-help, language, and classroom adjustment. Parents and teachers complete the assessment based on their own observations of the child's performance, respectively at home and school. Then the parents and teachers meet to discuss ways to facilitate desired behaviors seen at home or school in the other setting. Available in English and Spanish.

J. Platt, & T. Coggins (1990). Comprehension of social-action games in prelinguistic children: Levels of participation and effect of adult structure. *Journal of Speech and Hearing Disorders, 55,* **315–326.**

> Provides a developmental hierarchy of social-game participation of children 9 to 15 months of age. Includes typical social routines (e.g., peek-a-boo) and describes the behaviors expected of children at different levels.

System to Plan Early Childhood Services (SPECS). **(1990). S. Bagnato, & J. Neisworth, Circle Pines, MN: American Guidance Service.**

> Judgment-based assessment by professionals and family members of children age 2–6 years across: communication, sensorimotor, physical, self-regulation, cognition, and self/social. Focuses on team assessment and program planning through consensus building.

identified objectives have or have not been met. If some objectives were not met, are they still important to the family? And, if so, can we help them access the appropriate resource? Barbara Hanft (1991) suggests using this type of pre- and postassessment format to help the family identify continuing areas of concern and the need for support or information. It is also helpful to "leave the door open" for families to contact professionals involved in the assessment at a later time if they have additional questions or concerns. Providing the family with the telephone number of a contact person, and the best times and days to reach that person, can effectively send the message that someone will be available.

Once again, think of your own experiences in consultative discussions with professionals (e.g., doctor, car mechanic) and try to remember what aspects of the discussion were positive. Were you asked what your major concerns were? Were you allowed adequate time to provide the information you felt was important? Did you feel listened to and believed? Did you get the information you needed? Did you understand and value the outcomes? Thus, as professionals we might ask ourselves how the families we serve might respond to these same questions following an assessment of their child by our program.

Assessment Reports

One method of follow-up for most agencies is the preparation of a written report, even if it is only a screening summary outlining the child's performance. Most agencies also send out a copy of the report to the child's family and, with family approval, to the referral source or to other professionals or agencies who will be serving the child and family. Written reports serve two major functions. First, they serve as a method for sharing detailed information with other professionals, and second they provide families with assessment information. How can we be assured that assessment reports are in line with family-centered principles?

In recent years, many professionals have begun to change their written reports to make them more understandable and useful for family members and other lay persons who may benefit from the report. Just as verbal discussions about assessment information with families is better handled without the use of jargon, so too is the writing of reports. In recognizing that parents are the ultimate consumers of assessment results, the information shared should be concise and aimed toward facilitating the family's use of the information for further decision making. The report should clearly address the main concerns expressed by the family and, whenever possible, use words that are familiar to the family in describing the child.

For health insurance agencies and other third-party payers, certain terms and diagnoses may need to be used for families to receive their benefits or reimbursement. Some families may feel offended by these expressions and terminology. If the professional is in doubt about the family's reactions to what will be written, it may be worthwhile to check out the family's perceptions and preferences about terms and diagnoses before completing the report. When specific terms are necessary, it is important that the terms are discussed with the family and their purpose explained. Interpreters or cultural mediators can be helpful in providing explanations to family members as well as informing the professionals preparing the report about terms or content that may be new or not "in keeping" with the family's beliefs and values.

All reports should acknowledge the participation and contributions made by everyone present. One helpful strategy for indicating joint participation is to interweave throughout the report the information provided by both professionals and families. Including observational information and everyday examples of behaviors along with test scores, will help the report more fully represent both the family's and professional's views of the child. Some professionals and agencies are offering parents the option of reviewing and commenting on a draft of the report before it is printed in final form. The initial drafts of reports can either be sent home to the family or can be reviewed in a later home- or center-based discussion with the family. Kjerland and Kovach (1990) suggest that families should have a chance to review and edit the report before the creation of the individualized family service plan (IFSP). In recognizing the family's right to approve what is said and concluded within reports, we are again acknowledging the family's decision-making power and perhaps bolstering their confidence and competence in making decisions about their child.

Follow-Up Contacts

Personal telephone calls or visits are another means of providing services to families after an assessment. Professionals may want to ask parents if they would like to be contacted at a later date to discuss the assessment process and to talk about further needs and concerns. Parents have reported the helpfulness of receiving a follow-up call from professionals and the relationship building qualities it may engender. We can all think of our own experiences when a service provider (e.g., medical facility, newspaper carrier, carpet cleaner) took the time to call and ask how satisfied we were with the service and whether we had encountered any problems. Follow-up phone calls, visits, or written correspondence are also important for responding to requests that families may have made during the assessment. This may include a phone number or address, a journal article, a chapter from a book, a catalog, or anything else related to the family's priorities or interests. This type of responsiveness on the part of professionals communicates to families that you care and are dependable.

Variations Across Work Settings

The type of agency in which we work, the size of our caseloads, our billing policies, and numerous other characteristics of our jobs will place constraints on how assessment information can be shared with families and the degree to which follow-up contacts are possible. For those professionals who typically see a child and family on only one occasion, discussion of assessment findings usually takes place during or immediately after assessment activities have been completed. Thus little time may be available for deliberation and planning. For some, the discussion may be delayed a short time to allow for the professional(s) who evaluated the child to compile the results and recommendations. When assessment activities have taken place in the home, the professional and family may have more unstructured time for a discussion of findings and next steps. In school-based programs, a meeting is typically held several days or more after assessment activities have been completed and usually involves multiple professionals. And for many programs, the assessment report is sent home to the family without further contact with the professionals who performed the assessment.

Regardless of the timing or location for sharing assessment results, professionals can still focus on the importance to the child and family of the information shared, the collaborative way in which it is shared, and the preferences of families for what and how information is shared. Unless families have participated in the assessment or are otherwise prepared for the assessment sharing discussion, the professional will typically be in control and it may be hard for some families to take an active part. Time spent in helping families prepare for these discussions can be invaluable, whether it is in increasing their own observations/assessments of their child, reviewing options for the discussion, or in helping them draw together their own thoughts and impressions of their child. Time spent in preparing reports that are readable and useful to family members and that represent the family's views of the child is also important. These efforts to meet families "in the middle" may go a long way in developing positive relationships surrounding assessment.

In summary, it is clear that assessment activities are extremely important to both families and professionals in setting the tone and the expectations for all subsequent interactions. When families and professionals are partners in assessment, they work together to achieve commonly agreed upon goals and outcomes, they develop relationships built on trust and respect, and they seek to strengthen the child's and family's feelings of confidence. As families and professionals work together to determine the assessment parameters, activities, and results, they are shaping the future for what will happen for the child and family. When professionals serve as collaborators and facilitate decision making by families, we set the stage for the continued exchange of ideas and information. In applying family-centered principles from the time of our our first contacts with families, through the identification of family concerns, priorities, and resources, and in conducting child assessments, we will hopefully have established a mutual relationship on which further interactions may be grounded. In the next chapter, we explore the possibilities for goal setting and intervention planning that may be built on the collaborative relationship we have so carefully established.

REFERENCES

Anderson, M., & Goldberg, P. (1991). *Cultural competence in screening and assessment: Implications for services to young children with special needs ages birth through five.* Chapel Hill, NC: National Early Childhood Technical Assistance System (NEC*TAS).

Andrews, J., & Andrews, M. (1990). *Family based treatment in communicative disorders.* Sandwich, IL: Janelle Publications.

Bagnato, S., & Neisworth, J. (1990). *System to plan early childhood services.* Circle Pines, MN: American Guidance Service.

Bailey, D., & Simeonsson, R. (1990). *Family Needs Survey* (rev.). Chapel Hill, NC: Frank Porter Graham Child Development Center, The University of North Carolina.

Bailey, D., Simeonsson, R., Yoder, D., & Huntington, G. (1990). Preparing professionals to serve infants and toddlers with handicaps and their families: An integrative analysis across eight disciplines. *Exceptional Children, 57*(1), 26–35.

Barrera, I. (1994, June/July). Thoughts on the assessment of young children whose sociocultural background is unfamiliar to the assessor. *Zero to Three,* 9–13.

Bloch, J. (1987). *Parent/Professional Preschool Performance Profile*. Syosset, NY: Variety Preschooler's Workshop.

Bloch, J., & Seitz, M. (1989, July). Parents as assessors of children: A collaborative approach to helping. *Social Work in Education*, 226–244.

Bricker, D. (1993). *Assessment, Evaluation, and Programming System: AEPS Measurement for Birth to Three Years* (Vol. 1). Baltimore: Paul H. Brookes.

Bricker, D., Squires, J., & Mounts, L. (1995). *Ages and Stages Questionnaires (ASQ): A Parent-Completed Child-Monitoring System*. Baltimore: Paul H. Brookes.

Brinckerhoff, J., & Vincent, L. (1987). Increasing parental decision making at the Individualized Educational Program meeting. *Journal of the Division of Early Childhood*, *11*, 46–58.

Crais, E. (1993). Families and professionals as collaborators in assessment. *Topics in Language Disorders*, *14*(1), 29–40.

Crais, E. (1995). Expanding the repertoire of tools and techniques for assessing the communication skills of infants and toddlers. *American Journal of Speech-Language Pathology*, *4*(3), 47–59.

Crais, E., & Leonard, R. (1990). P.L. 99-457: Are speech-language pathologists prepared for the challenge? *Asha*, *32*(4), 57–61.

Crais, E., & Roberts, J. (1991). Decision making in assessment and early intervention planning. *Language, Speech, Hearing Services in Schools*, *22*(2), 19–30.

Cunningham, C., & Davis, H. (1985). Early parent counseling. In M. Craft, D. Bicknell, & S. Hollins (Eds.), *Mental handicap: A multidisciplinary approach* (pp. 162–176). London: Bailliere-Tindall.

Dale, P. (1991). The validity of a parent report measure of vocabulary and syntax at 24 months. *Journal of Speech and Hearing Research*, *34*, 565–571.

Dopheide, W., & Dallinger, J. (1976). Preschool articulation screening by parents. *Language, Speech, Hearing Services in Schools*, *7*, 124–127.

Dunn, W., & Oetter, P. (1991). Application of assessment principles. In W. Dunn (Ed.), *Pediatric occupational therapy: Facilitating effective service provision* (pp. 75–123). Thorofare, NJ: Slack.

Dunst, C., Trivette, C., & Deal, A. (1988). *Enabling and empowering families*. Cambridge, MA: Brookline Books.

Fenson, L., Dale, P., Reznick, S., Thal, D., Bates, E., Hartung, J., Pethick, S., & Reilly, J. (1993). *MacArthur Communicative Development Inventories*. San Diego: Singular Publishing Group.

Foley, G. (1990). Portrait of the arena evaluation. In E. Gibbs & D. Teti (Eds.), *Interdisciplinary assessment of infants: A guide for early intervention professionals* (pp. 271–286). Baltimore: Paul H. Brookes.

Haley, S. M., Coster, W. J., Ludlow, L. H., Haltiwanger, J. T., & Andrellos, P. J. (1992). *Pediatric Evaluation of Disability Inventory: Development, Standardization, and Administration Manual, Version 1.0*. Boston, MA: New England Medical Center.

Hanft, B. (1991). *Identification of family resources, concerns and priorities within the IFSP process*. Baltimore: Maryland Infants and Toddlers Program.

Ireton, H. (1992). *Child Development Inventories*. Minneapolis: Behavior Science Systems.

Kjerland, L., & Kovach, J. (1990). Family-staff collaboration for tailored infant assessment. In E. Gibbs & D. Teti (Eds.), *Interdisciplinary assessment of infants: A guide for early intervention professionals* (pp. 287–298). Baltimore: Paul H. Brookes.

Linder, T. (1993). *Transdisciplinary play-based assessment-Revised.* Baltimore: Paul H. Brookes.

Luterman, D. (1991). *Counseling the communicatively disordered and their families* (2nd ed.). Austin, TX: PRO-ED.

Lynch, W., & Hanson, M. (Eds.). (1992). *Developing cross-cultural competence: A guide to working with young children and their families.* Baltimore: Paul H. Brookes.

Martin, N., George, K., O'Neal, J., & Daly, J. (1987). Audiologists' and parents' attitudes regarding counseling of families of hearing-impaired children. *Asha, 29*(2), 27–33.

McLean, M., & Crais, E. (1996). Procedural considerations in assessing infants and toddlers. In M. McLean, D. Bailey, & M. Wolery (Eds.), *Assessing infants and toddlers with special needs* (pp. 46–68). Columbus, OH: Merrill.

Moore, S., & Beatty, J. (1995). *Developing cultural competence in early childhood assessment.* Boulder: University of Colorado at Boulder.

Murphy, A. (1990). Communicating assessment findings to parents. In E. Gibbs & D. Teti (Eds.), *Interdisciplinary assessment of infants: A guide for early intervention professionals* (pp. 299–307). Baltimore: Paul H. Brookes.

Olson, J. (1988). *Delivering sensitive information to families of handicapped infants and young children.* Moscow, ID: Outreach to Infants in Rural Settings, Special Education Department, University of Idaho.

Rescorla, L. (1989). The language development survey: A screening tool for delayed language in toddlers. *Journal of Speech and Hearing Disorders, 54*, 587–599.

Sheehan, R. (1988). Involvement of parents in early childhood assessment. In R. Sheehan & T. Wachs (Eds.), *Assessment of young developmentally disabled children* (pp. 75–90). New York: Plenum Press.

Tikunoff, W. (1987). Mediation of instruction to obtain equality of effectiveness. In S. Fradd & J. Tikunoff (Eds.), *Bilingual education and bilingual special education* (pp. 99–132). Boston: College-Hill Press.

Winton, P. (1988). Effective communication between parents and professionals. In D. Bailey & R. Simeonsson (Eds.), *Family assessment in early intervention* (pp. 207–228). Columbus, OH: Merrill Publishing.

Wolery, M. & Dyk, L. (1984). Arena assessment: Description and preliminary social validity data. *Journal of Severely Handicapped, 9*, 231–235.

RESOURCES

1. Suggestions for additional ways to take a family-centered approach throughout the assessment process can be found in articles by Crais (1993, 1995); McLean and Crais (1996); Kjerland and Kovach (1990); and Sheehan (1988).

2. Excellent resources for reading about other approaches to sharing assessment information include Murphy, 1990; Olson, 1988; and Winton, 1988.

3. Inservice materials through which continuing education credits can be obtained include:

Developmental Screening and Family-Centered Care. (1994). Gainesville, FL: Institute for Child Health Policy, University of Florida.

> This curriculum was intended for individuals or groups to promote skills in conducting developmental screening and testing, and effectively collaborating with families. Includes a self-study curriculum, pre- and post-tests, and exercises at the end of each section.

Increasing Family Participation in Assessment of Children Birth To Five. (1994). Crais, E. Chicago, IL: Riverside Publishing.

> The focus of the materials is on providing background information relevant to working more collaboratively with families (e.g., enhancing communcation skills, service coordination, sociocultural awareness) and practical strategies and tools for increasing family participation in assessment. These materials include a manual, audiotapes, and a post-test.

4. Other information about alternatives to child assessment can be found in *Transdisciplinary Play-Based Assessment*, Linder (1993); and an entire volume of *Topics in Early Childhood Special Education* (1990) edited by J. Neisworth & R. Fewell and entitled, "Judgment-Based Assessment."

5. An excellent and inexpensive videotape for demonstrating child-centered and family-centered assessment is *First Years Together: Involving Parents in Infant Assessment*. (1989). Raleigh, NC: Project Enlightment.

■ CHAPTER 6

Family-Centered Intervention Planning

When we talk about intervention planning, one of the first thoughts that comes to mind is the completion of forms. By law, for each child served we must have a written document on file that documents the child's current levels of development and outlines the goals and objectives of service provision, the types of services offered, and intervention strategies that will be implemented to accomplish stated goals and objectives. For infants (birth to 3 years) this document is the individualized family service plan (IFSP), while for preschoolers (ages 3 to 5 years) it may be an IFSP or an individualized education plan (IEP). Although much attention has been given to the format and content of IFSP and IEP forms, such written products are perhaps the least important aspect of the intervention planning process. As pointed out by McGonigel and Johnson (1991), "Far more important are the interaction, collaboration, and partnerships between families and professionals that are necessary to develop and implement the IFSP [IEP]." (p. 1). Thus, the *process* by which the intervention plan is developed is of primary importance and this process begins with our first contact with families. Although federal and state laws may differentiate between IFSPs and IEPs, in this chapter we will use the term IFSP to refer to intervention plans for both infants and preschoolers. If a family-centered approach is followed, there should be little difference in intervention planning between the two age groups and the term IFSP best reflects this approach.

The primary purpose of the IFSP process is to develop a blueprint for action. This involves clarifying and prioritizing the family's goals, identifying resources and strategies for making goals into realities, and assigning responsibility and time lines for implementing the plan. The process, as well as the written document, thus serves as a means for coordinating the efforts of all involved toward meeting the family's priorities and communicating the decisions that have been reached. Above all else, the IFSP should be guided by the values and decisions of the family rather than those of the professionals providing services. After all, it is the family that will ultimately be affected by the outcome of the interventions. It is they who will be left to live with the results.

■ SETTING THE STAGE FOR FAMILY PARTICIPATION

The need for an IFSP or any other type of written intervention plan is a concept that arises from the realm of human service professionals. As a result of our training and experience, the writing of goals, objectives, and service agreements are a natural part of our work. For many parents of young children with disabilities, however, the concept may be quite foreign and perhaps even intimidating. Thus, we are faced with a dilemma—we want parents to direct the development of the IFSP, and yet we are the ones who are actually more familiar and comfortable with its format, content, use, and importance.

If we want parents to take an active role in the development of the IFSP, we must take the time to familiarize them with the rationale for its existence and the process by which it will be developed. We must also provide them with all of the information they need to make decisions. Above all, we should do our best to make the process and the final product family-friendly by using language, concepts, and formats that are familiar to families. The more we can take the IFSP out of the professional realm and make it fit into the realm of the family, the more likely parents will feel confident in assuming a leadership role and perceive the final product as useful.

To begin with, parents should be informed of the IFSP well in advance of any meetings related to its development and, certainly, before even the most preliminary drafts of forms are completed. For families who are new to your program, the IFSP can be introduced early, along with explanations of the program's philosophy and services, and more detailed information can be given as the process of identifying parents' concerns, priorities, and resources continues. Families who are already receiving services should be notified of upcoming reviews and revisions of their IFSP far enough in advance to allow them to think about it and prepare themselves for participation.

For some parents, written information about IFSPs and guidelines for family participation may be helpful. An example of such a guidebook is *Into Our Lives* (see Resource Section). For other parents, however, such guidebooks may be inappropriate or unhelpful. Regardless of the methods used to prepare families for participation in the development of the IFSP, the point made here is that parents should be as aware of the process and the time lines of IFSP development as the professionals who are working with them. Only with full knowledge of the process and the importance of their input, can parents make informed decisions as to what they would like included on the IFSP and their level of participation in its development.

■ INDIVIDUALIZING TEAM COMPOSITION AND PROCESS

The concept of teamwork in the development of intervention plans is well ingrained in most of us as a function of our professional training.

Consequently, our approach to intervention planning typically involves a meeting or series of meetings in which the professionals working with a child and family get together to coordinate their findings and ideas related to intervention planning. The importance of involving families in the process is also well-known by most professionals; therefore, parents are typically invited to participate in some if not all of the group meetings concerning goal setting and intervention planning. Unfortunately, professional time is often at a premium. Caseloads are high and schedules are tight, resulting in the need to limit the amount of time devoted to intervention planning for any given child and family. The amount of time that parents have available to attend meetings may also be limited. To accomplish all that must be done in the time available, drafts of goals and intervention strategies may be developed by professionals prior to a group meeting and then subjected to the approval of parents at the meeting. Although this gets the job done and some parents may be satisfied with the resultant product, the extent to which families are actively involved in the process and the degree to which intervention plans truly reflect parents' priorities must be questioned.

A family-centered approach to intervention planning requires rethinking our traditional notions of teamwork in the process of arriving at goals and intervention strategies. First, group meetings may not be the method of choice for developing a plan of action, or these meetings may have to be supplemented or preceded by more extensive discussions with parents. Second, the preferred method for developing intervention plans may vary from one family to another. We may need to individualize the process for each family served. Third, family-directed intervention plans will probably require that more time be spent with the family by at least one professional to ensure a complete understanding of what the parents want for themselves and their children and to identify any preferences they may have for intervention strategies.

A full team meeting may not be an ideal setting for parents to sort through their thoughts about priorities, goals, and strategies for intervention. The time pressures of such meetings, and the bombardment of new and perhaps confusing information from a number of professionals, may not be conducive to parents making decisions that will affect their child's development, their own daily lives, and perhaps their family's future. This is not to say that parents don't need the information available from all members of the team, for indeed they do. The question we must ask ourselves and families is when and how to present such information in a manner that helps parents effectively use it in making decisions that are truly their own. If we are willing and able to be flexible, we can ask parents how they prefer to proceed with the process of developing an intervention plan. Even then, we should probably present alternatives from which they can choose.

One option is to conduct all intervention planning, from identifying goals through the development of specific strategies for accomplishing those goals, with all members of the team present. At the other extreme, all intervention planning may be done in the family's home with a single professional. In the latter case, information from other professionals may be gathered in a variety of ways. For example, the professional working with the family may serve as a conduit of information from other team members, or the family may converse with other team members on a one-to-one basis as information is needed for decision making. Parents may also be offered the option of working with a single professional for some aspects of the intervention planning process (e.g., goal identification), but meet with the entire team for other aspects (e.g., developing intervention options). Still another option that may be offered is to have a selected sub-group of professionals (two or three team members) work with the family to develop the IFSP.

In addition to the professionals working within your own program, there may be other people who play a significant role in the lives of children and families and who should be included in the process of developing an intervention plan. These people may be professionals from other programs or agencies or they may be members of the family's informal support network, such as a babysitter, grandparents, an older sibling, or the boyfriend or girlfriend of a single parent. Although parents should decide whether or not these people will be included and how they will participate in intervention planning, they may not request that they be included unless we introduce the possibility first. For example, if you know from previous conversations that there are close bonds between the child's parents and grandparents, you might say to the parents: "You've mentioned your own parents quite often during our conversations and, from what you have said, they seem quite attached to Rebecca and that you count on them for support. Do you think you'd like to include them in our discussions of what Rebecca needs and how to go about meeting her needs?"

In the sections that follow, methods of encouraging active family participation in the intervention planning process are described, from the prioritization and clarification of goals through the development of interventions strategies to the actual writing of the IFSP document. These methods are described without regard for the setting in which the process takes place or the number of professionals who may be involved. It is hoped, however, that the methods presented below can be easily adapted for use in the variety of settings in which intervention planning takes place.

■ CLARIFYING AND PRIORITIZING FAMILY GOALS

The first step in ensuring that the IFSP addresses family priorities is to have a sound understanding of what those priorities are and to communicate them to all involved in developing the intervention plan. Although we have already discussed the identification of child and family goals at some length in previous chapters, the present discussion focuses on the further specification of goals and the development of a plan of action. The more precise families can be about their priorities, the better position we will be in to lend our expertise in helping them to accomplish their goals.

Reviewing Parent-Identified Goals

Through the course of our conversations with parents, a number of child and family priorities may be discussed. Some of them will be precise and talked about in great detail; others may be mentioned in passing or perhaps only alluded to. Furthermore, parents' concerns and priorities may change over time, as they acquire new information about their child or as a function of changing family situations unrelated to their child with special needs. Although such changes are likely to continue, the development of an intervention plan helps the family take stock of where they are at a given time, and identify the direction they would like to take. It is a time for pinpointing a few specific changes they want to make to enhance the development of their child and the quality of life of all family members.

Some parents may be capable of identifying very specific goals on their own, but for many it is helpful to have someone talk them through the process. To begin, you can summarize for the family what you have heard them talk about in previous conversations and ask if they would like any of these things addressed by the IFSP. For example, you might say something like, "Over our past few times together, you have mentioned a number of things that you are concerned about or would like to see happen for your child and your family. As we want to put together an intervention plan that you find truly helpful, perhaps the best place to start is to go over the things we have already discussed and let you tell us what you think is most important. If all of the professionals working with you know what your priorities are, we can work together to come up with ways to deal with those things that are most important to you."

With an introduction like this, you can proceed to outline the various issues that the parents have raised. It may be helpful to keep an ongoing list of these topics as the conversation ensues, so that you can refer back to it when the time comes for prioritizing. As each topic is discussed, ask the parent(s) if this is still a concern or goal and list only those that they verify. Be careful not to restrict the listing of potential goals to those things that can be addressed by the services offered by your own program. After all, what is important to the family has nothing to do with whether or not you are in a position to provide help. The goals they establish for their child and themselves should be independent of the boundaries of your services. After you have exhausted the topics the parents have raised in previous conversations, be sure to ask them if they have any further concerns or thoughts about what they would like to accomplish and add these to the growing list. At this point, you will probably have a somewhat lengthy list of goals to choose from. Don't be concerned if many of them are still vague or broadly stated, the time for clarification will come later.

Include Areas of Relative Strength

Before moving on to prioritizing goals, you might want to check out a few areas that the parents have neglected to mention. For example, one area that is frequently overlooked are child strengths. Parents and professionals, alike, have a tendency to concentrate on things that a child can't do well and work on remediating those deficits. Even when a child's areas of relative strengths are recognized and applauded in conversations with the parents, skills in these areas are rarely identified for inclusion on an intervention plan. The long-term, negative effects of focusing on a child's deficits is pointed out by a mother whose daughter, Marti, has mental retardation:

> They're always trying to "fix" Marti—as if they can't accept the fact that she's handicapped. They spend all their time working on things she can't do without giving her a chance to enjoy the things she can. It fosters a bad self-image. Everyone buys into it. Instead of seeing a wonderful little girl who loves to play and make friends and be with people, they see a poor little girl who can't walk. (Simons, 1985, p. 48)

The frequency with which child strengths are seemingly overlooked and undervalued by professionals prompted Robin Simons (1985), author of *After the Tears*, to include the following in her advice to parents of children with disabilities:

> Your child also needs time to enjoy his successes before moving onto the next challenge. Too often professionals see children's development as stepping stones, rushing them from one task to the next. Ask them to slow down. Your child deserves every bit of enjoyment and gratification he can milk from each success. A little extra bit of resting on his laurels will do more to bolster self-esteem than it will to delay future gains. (pp. 61–62)

It seems a shame that child strengths are not emphasized more, considering that skills in these areas may be called upon to compensate for deficits in other areas of development. In addition, working on skills in children's areas of strength allows families to see the successful results of their parenting efforts and take pride in their child's accomplishments. So, it may be wise to take a few minutes to investigate parents' interests in identifying goals in these areas.

Let us suppose, for example, that you are working with a child who is severely physically disabled and nonvocal as a consequence of cerebral palsy. Even so, the child seems intrigued by other children, as she smiles and laughs at the antics of her big brother at home and her friends at preschool. The parents have also mentioned in passing that she loves books and they read to her every night at bedtime for an hour or more. In this case, the goals for the child will, in all likelihood, include the development of motor skills and expressive speech—perhaps through augmentative communication methods. If the parents do not mention the child's areas of strength, you might open the topic yourself by saying something like, "Although we already have quite a long list of things you would like to see your child learn to do, I'm still left wondering about a few things you've mentioned before. In our conversations, you have told me that she seems to really enjoy being around other children and loves reading books with you. It sounded as though these were things you thought were important to her and important to you, too. Is there anything you'd like to see happen to expand her interest, her abilities, or her enjoyment in these areas?"

Addressing Family-Level Issues

So far, we have only talked about identifying child-level goals. What about family-level goals? To what extent should those aspects of family life that are not directly related to the child be addressed in the development of intervention plans? If you will recall from Chapter 1, one of the basic principles of a family-centered approach is that the family, rather than just the child, is viewed as the unit of intervention. Therefore, any goals or interventions related to enhancing the functioning of the family as a whole or the well-being of individual family members are appropriate for including on the IFSP.

More than a decade of research (e.g., Bailey & Simeonsson, 1984; Bailey et al., 1986; Barber, Turnbull, Behr, & Kerns, 1988; Dunst, Trivette, Hamby, & Pollack, 1990) has shown us that family-level issues directly or indirectly affect the development of the child and vice versa. And for more than a decade, parents' stories (e.g., Dougan, Isbell, & Vyas, 1979; Featherstone, 1980; Simons, 1985; Turnbull & Turnbull, 1985) have told us of the far-reaching effects of a child's disability on the family. Emotional distress, isolation, financial problems, marital stress, physical exhaustion, strained relationships with relatives and friends, transportation difficulties, sibling reactions, and restrictions on parents' personal growth and development are just a few of the many effects of disability that have been reported by families. Taking a family-centered approach, any of these would be appropriate to include on an IFSP. But how do we determine which, if any to include on a given family's intervention plan? The answer, of course, is to ask the family.

One might think that families would be eager to receive such broad-based assistance, but this doesn't always seem to be the case. In fact, a recent survey of 539 families in North Carolina (McWilliam et al., 1995) showed that, for the majority of parents polled, their priorities for intervention were child-level goals. Some of the families in the study also stated that they wanted the focus to remain on the child, whereas others appreciated the concern that professionals expressed about aspects of family life that were not directly related to the child.

In discussing the results of their survey and interviews with families, McWilliam et al. (1995) make several points that have implications for addressing family-level issues. First, if being family-centered means responding to family priorities, and family priorities are related to child-level interventions, then providing child-level interventions in such cases would be consistent with a family-centered approach. They caution, however, that this would only be true if it were made clear to families that addressing family-level issues is also an option. Second, they suggest that,

> addressing family-level concerns might be a developmental process: the more professionals attend to families' priorities the more likely they are to develop close relationships with families. With such a relationship, a family is more likely to see the early interventionist as a potential resource for addressing family-level needs. (pp. 56–57)

Based on this evidence and the experiences of thousands of interventionists, we can probably expect that the majority of goals parents want included on the IFSP will be related to child outcomes. Furthermore, this is more likely to be true for families first entering our programs than for families who have been involved in our programs for a prolonged period. Our first objective, then, is to ensure that families are aware that family-level issues may also be addressed by the IFSP. Strategies for conveying this information have already been discussed in previous chapters of this book (Chapter 2, First Encounters with Families, and Chapter 3, Understanding Family Concerns, Priorities, and Resources). Nevertheless, invitations to include family-level goals should be re-issued during the development of the IFSP.

For example, suppose that during your initial conversations with a family they mentioned that the hospital or doctor bills were piling up, that they didn't like to take their baby out for a walk because the neighborhood was dangerous, or they were frustrated by the fact that the child's grandparents didn't seem to understand the severity of the child's disability. During your listing of concerns and priorities you might say, "I seem to remember you mentioning during one of our visits that you were uncomfortable about taking the baby out for a walk because you felt your neighborhood wasn't safe. Is that something that still bothers you?" If the parent(s) say that it still is a concern and that they wish they could find or afford housing in a better neighborhood, you could follow up with, "I don't know if I can help you with that directly, but would you like for us to work together and look into the possibility of finding a safer place to live—some place where you feel more comfortable taking the baby out for walks?" If they say yes, then you can add it to your ongoing list of priorities. The same type of questioning could be used for any family-level issue that parents have mentioned in the past. Even if parents say that they are not interested in your assistance, at the very least you have let them know that you are prepared to address such concerns should they ever want your assistance.

As a final note on this topic, professionals should keep in mind that some parents may be very sensitive about including family-level issues on the IFSP. They may not want the fact that they are having financial struggles, marital problems, or in-law troubles put in writing for all to see. These issues may be viewed by families as very personal and private matters. If you have been privileged by a family to be told of such concerns, but the family prefers that these concerns not be shared with others or included on the written IFSP, what do you do? In short, just because a family priority is not on the IFSP, doesn't mean that you can't provide assistance. Also keep in mind that, by federal law (Part H of the Individuals with Disabilities Education Act Amendments of 1991, P.L. 102–119), the inclusion of any information related to family strengths and needs on the IFSP is completely voluntary on the part of families. In fact, it may be a good idea when discussing family-level issues to let parents know that they have the option of including or not including family-level priorities on the IFSP. And, in some cases, talking with parents about how a family-level priority might be worded on the IFSP could make them feel more comfortable with allowing it to be included.

Reviewing Professional-Identified Goals

Other areas that might warrant investigation are the concerns that professionals have about the child that have not been mentioned by the parents as possible goals for intervention. It may be that the parents have overlooked these goals, but it may also be that they are unaware of or disagree with the opinions of the professionals. We owe it to parents to inform them of concerns we have based upon our professional knowledge and expertise. At the same time, this information should be presented in such a way that parents are given permission to disagree with us without denigrating their integrity as parents.

For example, suppose that during an assessment a physical therapist is concerned that a child with cerebral palsy is not getting adequate support from an umbrella stroller that the parents employ for transporting the child and for other seating needs. The physical therapist has suggested to the parents that more traditional adaptive seating equipment, such as a wheelchair or travelchair, is needed. You know that the physical therapist discussed this concern with the parents at the close of the assessment, but the parents have not mentioned it since then. To open up the issue for discussion, you might say, "One thing you haven't talked about since your child's assessment is the physical therapist's suggestion that you substitute a travelchair or wheelchair for the umbrella stroller you are using now. The physical therapist obviously thought this was important, but I was wondering how *you* felt about it. Is it something you want to look into any further?"

Suppose the parents indicate that they are not interested. They may or may not offer an explanation for their lack of interest. The first thing to do is to support their decision by saying "That's fine." or "I think I can understand how you might feel that way." Before closing the subject, however, you might want to inquire whether they felt the physical therapist offered an adequate explanation of his or her concern and whether they would like to talk any further about this issue with the physical therapist. The aim here is to ensure that the parents have received and understood an explanation about the concerns related to positioning—that they are making an informed decision. You might also ask whether they are satisfied with the seating and transportation methods they are currently using for their child, or if they would like to investigate alternative methods other than a wheelchair or travelchair. No doubt it can be difficult for us to accept a parent's decision when it goes against what we have been taught to be good practice. Nevertheless, it is the parent's decision to make. Besides, what will be gained if we push the issue to the point of conflict? Chances are they will not comply with our recommendations regardless of what we say. But if we support their decision, they can return to us for assistance without losing face.

Prioritizing Identified Goals

Once all of the issues are laid out on the table, it is time to ask the family to select and further clarify those goals that will be addressed by the intervention plan. You might begin the process with, "We have talked about a lot of things that you want for your child and your family. Although all of them seem worthwhile, it would help us to know where you want to start. Are any of these things more important to you than others?" Any number of areas for change may be identified, including both child and family goals. The purpose of prioritizing is not necessarily to reduce the number of goals, but rather to insure that those things which are most highly valued by the family are addressed by the intervention plan. Again, the parents' priorities may not necessarily coincide with the opinions held by the professionals involved in the planning process.

There will be times when parents will identify goals for their children that seem unrealistic to professionals. For example, when parents of young children with disabilities are asked what they would like to see their children learn, "walking" and "talking" are often high on their list of priorities. How does one handle the situation in which a parent identifies these goals for a child whom the professionals think may never walk or talk, or for whom walking or talking is a long way down the road? One way to handle this situation is to first validate the parent's concern and desire by saying, "Wouldn't it be great if [child's name] could learn to walk/talk." or "I can see where walking/talking would be important to you."

The next step is to discover the parent's concerns or priorities that underlie their desire for their child to walk or talk. To do this, you might say something like, "I'll bet life would really be different if [child's name] woke up tomorrow and was walking/talking. I wonder what that would be like? How would things change?" Providing you have been sincere in the asking, the parent may then disclose some concerns or priorities that *can* be addressed. For example, suppose a family had initially said they wanted their child to be able to talk. At this point, they might say something like, "Maybe all of the crying and screaming would stop if [child's name] could tell me what he wanted. As it is, I have to go around for 20 minutes or more trying to figure out what he wants." Now that is a concern that a professional can help the parent address—even if the child never learns to talk. Other reasons the parent may offer for wanting the child to talk may, likewise, be addressed in a variety of ways. Finding out *why* a parent selects the priorities they do is an important step in intervention planning and is described further in the next section.

Establishing Functional Significance

In addition to prioritizing goals for intervention, a further clarification of selected goals is important. This may be done concurrently with or following the establishment of priorities, but it should be done before identifying strategies for intervention. The more specific the goal, the more likely it is that professionals will understand the true intent of the family in identifying it as a priority, and the more likely that the parents' true desires will be addressed.

Remember that goals are outcomes—what is hoped will be accomplished as a result of intervention. This seems so obvious and hardly worth mentioning, and yet all too often goals and intervention methods are confused in our planning for children and families. For example, "Sara will receive speech and language services two times a week" and "Mr. and Mrs. Phillips [parents] will attend a parent advocacy workshop" are not goals but methods—a means of achieving something else. In the case of speech and language services, the actual goal may be "Sara will learn to say and use the names of favorite toys to request these items from caregivers." In the case of the advocacy workshop, the goal may be "Mr. and Mrs. Phillips will be aware of their legal rights and the rights of their child related to an inclusive placement in a public school program." The major point being made here is that goals that are appropriately stated as outcomes leave open the possibility of any number of alternative strategies for achieving them. If, however, intervention methods are misconstrued as goals, there are no alternatives.

A well-stated goal has a context. It will tell us something about the circumstances in which we hope to see the desired changes occur. Parents can identify these circumstances for us if we take the time to pose a few simple questions. For example, suppose a parent wants their child to play more with other children. We might ask them, "Do you have any specific children, times, or places in mind?" "Can you tell me more about the types of situations where you would like to see your child playing with the other kids?" or "What kind of playing did you have in mind—who would it be with and what might it look like?" Some parents may not have a clear idea of what this play might look like, but they will know that playing with other children is something they want their child to be able to do. In such cases, the professional working with the family might make several suggestions for the parents to choose from or discuss the various possibilities to help the parent(s) figure out what they want.

Without specification of contexts for goals, we are usually left with rather vague and nonfunctional goals such as "James will display understanding of object permanence," "Julie will use labels for familiar objects and people in her environment," or "Ben will be able to crawl independently." Although these might be developmentally appropriate goals for these children, the goals tell us nothing of the functional outcome of accomplishing these skills. What are the consequences of the children mastering these developmental milestones? How will it affect them and the other people in their lives? Will James be able to find his pacifier in his crib when he drops it or engage in a game of peek-a-boo with his mother? Will Julie be able to tell her parents what she wants and, as a result, have fewer crying jags? Or will Julie's father feel fulfilled when his daughter calls him "Da da" for the first time? Perhaps Ben's mother will be able to cook the family meal with less stress because Ben can get his own toys or go to her when he wants attention. Moving away from the use of developmental checklists as a means of identifying goals for children and targeting skills within the context of the child's and family's daily routines provides us with a clearer picture of the hoped for outcomes of intervention. The resultant functional goals are also more familiar to families, in that, they refer to those things they encounter on a daily basis.

The determination of family priorities through the assessment of home routines has become increasingly popular, and a number of strategies and instruments incorporating this approach are now available (Brinckerhoff & Vincent, 1986; Lynch, 1988; McWilliam, 1992; Vincent, Davis, Brown, Teicher, & Weyland, 1983). These strategies typically involve the listing of family routines, parents' assessment of how their children function within routines, and the degree to which family members are satisfied with what goes on within each routine. Based on such information, outcomes for intervention are identified.

What about those skills that are specifically related to a child's participation in the classroom? Can the family participate in identifying these goals as well? To do so, the parents must first be knowledgeable about what the classroom routines are and how their child participates in each routine. This may be done through ongoing communication with the parents or through parent conferences. The drawback of this type of exchange, however, is that the child's performance in the classroom is filtered through the eyes of the professional. Consequently, the parents cannot draw their own conclusions. One way to solve this problem is to have parents observe their children in the classroom. If this is not possible, a videotape showing the child in the various routines of the classroom may serve the same purpose. No matter how a parent gains this knowledge, they will be in a better position to participate in identifying what skills would benefit the child most and to discuss any concerns they might have.

One useful method for parent participation in identifying child goals for classroom environments has been described by McWilliam (1992). Using this method, professionals and parents describe and discuss the child's functioning within his or her daily routines at home and in the classroom. Based on this information sharing, decisions are made about child goals and appropriate strategies are developed for accomplishing these goals. The final written product is a routines matrix in which classroom routines are listed and specific goals and intervention strategies are identified for each routine. The benefits of the family-centered, routines-based approach developed by McWilliam (1992) is described by Kathy Grabowski, the director of a center that adopted this strategy for developing IFSPs:

> The rewards have been tremendous. A new level of trust and communication exists between staff and families . . . While we had always been warm and positive with families, we did little to build on their feelings of competence as advocates and parents of their child. Though we had some inevitable professional suspicion that parents would not be consistently accurate in their descriptions of their children's needs, no parents have proven this to be true in our experience. Most parents were quickly and easily able to tell us what they wanted for their child. We broadened families' perspectives by explaining how a child's needs at home are related to the classroom. In return, our own outlooks were broadened, and subsequently families and staff place more value on the need for shared goals. (McWilliam, 1992, p. 160)

■ IDENTIFYING OPTIONS FOR INTERVENTION

Once goals have been established, it is tempting to offer solutions or advice as quickly as possible. Through our professional training and experience, most of us have acquired a variety of proven methods for promoting children's skill development in our areas of expertise, and we want to share this knowledge to help parents and children. After all, isn't that why they come to us for services? Most parents are, indeed, interested in benefiting from our professional expertise. Nevertheless, recommendations made too hastily can subvert the use of knowledge that parents have to offer, the resources and supports that families may already have in place, and our own understanding of factors that may limit the impact of intervention strategies we may suggest.

Prior to offering your own ideas, take some time to find out what the parents have been doing to accomplish the goal being addressed. Ask them, "Is this something you have been working on already?" and, if so, "Perhaps you could tell me a little more about what you have been doing and how you think it has been working." If they have not yet addressed the goal on their own, or if they have and don't feel that their efforts have been effective, you could ask them, "Do you have any other ideas about what might work or what you might need in order to accomplish your goal?" If parents feel that their efforts have been at least somewhat successful, you could ask them if they were satisfied with the rate of progress they had achieved or if they can think of anything that might help make their present efforts even more effective. By asking such questions, professionals will glean a picture of the resources already available and being used by the family, potential barriers to intervention, as well as parents' levels of skill and knowledge.

The degree to which professionals offer suggestions for intervention strategies will, in part, be determined by how satisfied the parents are with what they are presently doing and the resources already available to the family. But even when things are going reasonably well, professionals may have ideas to share with the family. As one of the family's sources of support, we have a certain obligation to provide them with information about alternative strategies and resources that may suit their needs. The key is to provide such information in a manner that allows the family to freely choose the options that they think are best rather than feeling in conflict with us if they do not accept the methods we offer. To do this, perhaps we need to first acknowledge in our own minds that best practices depicted in textbooks and professional journals are not necessarily what will be best for every family. To convey this to families, we need to restrain our enthusiasm for any one method of intervention, lest it impinge upon the family's ability to choose freely among the other options available. This does not mean that we cannot discuss with parents the pros and cons of the various options available. Indeed we should, but we should try to do so as objectively as possible and tell parents that what really matters is what will work for them. They know best what is practical and what is consistent with their values of child rearing and family life.

In an ideal world, early intervention programs would offer a complete menu of services to choose from and flexibility within each service, such that a truly individualized program of services could be designed to meet the goals established for each child and family. Unfortunately, such an ideal world does not exist in communities across our nation. By and large, most early intervention programs adhere to a single model of service pro-vision (e.g., home-based, classroom-based, or clinic-based services) and alternative service methods may or may not be available through other agencies in the community. Professionals are, therefore, often locked into a single model of service delivery in which they must try to meet the many and varied goals of the children and families they serve. Fortunately, even under such restrictive circumstances, flexibility and creativity on the part of administrators and individual professionals can yield the adaptations necessary to accomplish most goals.

Let us say, for example, that we are working in a classroom-based program. In identifying goals for intervention planning, the mother of a 3-year-old girl with severe cerebral palsy conveys that she is exasperated by her daughter's incessant crying and attention-seeking while trying to make dinner and also attend to the needs of an 18-month-old sibling.

> I dread leaving work at 5 o'clock knowing what lies ahead of me for the next two hours," says the mother. "I pick up the kids from their child care centers on the way home and it's 5:45 by the time we walk in the front door," she continues. "We're all starved and I have to start getting dinner ready right away. My husband doesn't get home until 6:30 or 7:00, so I'm on my own with the kids. Shannon [3-year old] is cranky and wants me to hold her, read to her, or help her play with toys. She whines or cries if I don't attend to her every few minutes. I don't blame her though . . . I mean, she can't really do anything for herself. If I don't entertain her, she can only sit there doing noth-ing. So, she cries and I perform."

Little wonder this mother would like to see some changes in this aspect of home life, but what can we offer as a classroom-based program?

As stated earlier, the best place to start is to ask the mother what she has been doing, how it has worked, and what she thinks it would take to make this aspect of the evening schedule less hectic for her. Joint problem solving between the mother and professional(s) can yield a number of options from which to choose. Some of the options may involve changes that can be worked on directly by the classroom staff. For example, per-haps the mother has come to the conclusion that Shannon would be less demanding if she weren't reliant on adults for playing with toys. If she had some way to handle toys by herself, she wouldn't feel so helpless and might be content for longer periods of time. One strategy for assisting Shannon might be to introduce her to adapted toys with switches that she can operate even with her limited movements. Shannon could be taught to use these switch-operated toys in the classroom and generalization to the home environment could be accomplished through home visits, notes from the teacher sent home in Shannon's bag, phone calls, or videotapes of Shannon using the switches and toys at school.

Other options to meet this family-identified need may have little or nothing to do with what takes place in the classroom on a daily basis.

Suppose, for example, the mother doesn't think that adapted toys would make significant changes in Shannon's behavior at this time of day, or perhaps she likes the idea but feels it would take a lot of time and wants more immediate relief. The mother says that what would be really helpful would be to have someone who would help entertain the children while she prepares dinner, or to have only one of her children to contend with at this time of day. Exploring the resources available to the family might open up a number of options. There may be a relative or friend who could pick up one or both of the children at the end of the day and take them home. The mother could go straight home and have dinner started before the children arrived home. A teenager in the neighborhood may also be available to babysit one or both children in the home for an hour or so while dinner was being prepared. Although these strategies may have nothing to do with the classroom services offered by the program, they are potential means to meet one of the family's priorities and, thus, are worthy of the time we devote to discussing them with the family.

■ THE WRITTEN PLAN

As stated at the beginning of this chapter, the process of intervention planning culminates with the development of a written document. Although much has been written about the format used for the written IFSP and a number of model formats have been developed from which to choose (e.g., Bennett, Lingerfelt, & Nelson, 1990; Dunst & Deal, 1994; Deal, Dunst, & Trivette, 1989; McGonigel, Kaufmann, & Johnson, 1991), it is important to keep in mind that the format, alone, has little to do with whether or not an intervention plan is family-centered. Rather, it is the *process* leading to the written plan that will determine the degree to which it is family-centered. If the process is family-centered, and if the content of the plan represents the outcome of that process, an appropriate IFSP should result, regardless of the format used. In fact, there is no one best format for writing IFSPs. What works well for one program, region, or type of clientele may not work well under different circumstances. The following guidelines are offered to assist programs in choosing or developing an IFSP format and to help individual professionals and teams transfer the information and decisions made during the IFSP process to the written page.

Plans Should be Useful and Used

The best criterion for judging a written intervention plan is that it is perceived as useful by families and professionals and that it is used. The most sophisticated, comprehensive, and well-worded IFSP is of little value if, shortly after it is signed, it is placed in a file cabinet, desk drawer, or dining room credenza, never to be referred to again. If an IFSP does not function to guide and coordinate activities for both the family and the professionals involved with the family, it is of little use other than to satisfy bureaucratic regulations related to service delivery. Some of the characteristics of intervention plans that are useful and used are provided in Table 6–1. We have already discussed many of these in the preceding sections. The rest will be discussed in the remaining sections of this chapter.

When you think about it, an IFSP is actually a fancy "To Do" list that is written for more than one person to work from. The listing of services, intervention strategies, activities, and person(s) responsible is an agreement as to who will do what to meet the goals that have been established. For the goals to be accomplished, each person responsible for implementing the IFSP must understand what they are supposed to do, keep in mind and fulfill their responsibilities on the "To Do" list, and let others know of their progress in doing their part.

As we all know, a "To Do" list is of little help if it is not easily accessible. The booming business of daily, weekly, and monthly planning books, as well as the latest computerized versions of these, are testimony to the need for frequent referral to our "To Do" lists if the items on them are to be remembered and done. The criteria for accessible and useful IFSPs was once described by the mother of a young child with disabilities as being able to pass the "Piggy Magnet" test. On a home visit, a professional who was just beginning to work with the family asked the mother if she could see the child's intervention plan. The mother said she only vaguely remem-

---

TABLE 6–1. Characteristics of intervention plans that are useful and used.

♦ Parents understand and agree with the content

♦ Parents have a sense of ownership of the plan that is developed by them

♦ The plan includes goals that are important to the family

♦ Activities for accomplishing goals are enjoyable for the child and the family

♦ Activities are embedded within daily routines

♦ There is a high likelihood of accomplishing goals within a relatively short period of time

♦ Resources are available and accessible for implementing activities (e.g., time, money, emotional support, energy, space, materials)

♦ The intervention plan is amenable to frequent changes and updating

♦ The plan is reviewed frequently and planning is a continuous process

♦ The written plan passes the "piggy magnet test"

bered receiving the document, but she knew where it would be if she had a copy of it. She walked over to the hall closet and from the top shelf she retrieved a large laundry basket that was nearly full of papers. "These are all of the important papers that I've gotten from the program," she announced. "If I've got it, it will be in here somewhere." When asked about the usefulness of the IFSP, the mother replied, "It doesn't pass the piggy magnet test." The professional asked what she meant and the mother explained: "The number of pieces of paper that come into this house every week is incredible. I have piles of papers on every counter top we own and it's hard to keep track of it all. If there's anything I need to remember or use—a grocery list, doctor's appointment, bill, or a coupon for salad dressing—I hang it on the refrigerator. See that piggy magnet over there?" she asked, pointing to the refrigerator. The entire front of the refrigerator was covered in pieces of paper held in place by a massive collection of magnets in the shape of fruits, animals, and advertising logos. Among the collection was a rather grotesque 3-inch pig, shaped out of dough and wearing a straw hat. "That's the biggest and strongest magnet I own," she said. "If something can't be held up by that pig, it's as good as gone."

Use the Parents' Own Words

In writing an IFSP, we should ask ourselves who we are writing it for. Are we writing it for the administrative auditors of our permanent files? Are we writing it for the other professionals on the team? Are we writing it for professionals in other community agencies? Or are we writing it for the family? Obviously, all of these people are potential readers and users of the IFSPs we write, but who is it really designed for? The answer to this question will influence how it is written. If we want families to have a sense of ownership of the IFSP—that it indeed represents the plan they have decided upon in previous meetings and conversations—we should use their words on the form rather than our own professional jargon. By doing so, any lack of understanding of the plan's contents will be on the part of the professionals rather than on the part of the family. If professionals have to ask parents to explain the meaning of items on the IFSP, the roles of authority are reversed. The parents are in charge of the plan.

Goals Supersede Services in Importance

Care should be taken not to translate the parents' goals into our own system of organization. That is, we shouldn't revamp the parents' goals to fit professional categories such as gross motor skills, fine motor skills, cognitive skills, self-help skills, and so on. Nor should we change parents' goals to reflect the division of services among the various professional disciplines represented on the team (e.g., physical therapy goals, speech-language goals). Instead, a status of primacy should be given to family-identified goals, wherein the goal is set first and a listing of what each person on the team will do to contribute to the achievement of that goal follows. For example, suppose a family says that it is important to them that their child with physical disabilities and cognitive delays gets more enjoyment out of being in the company of other children. More specifically, they would like to see their child be able to play with toys in the company of another child and participate more actively in structured group activities such as singing, storytime, or art activities. This end may ultimately be achieved through the combined efforts of the parents and several professionals on the team, and through activities implemented in the various settings the child is in throughout the day or week. Even if everyone involved has different items on their "To Do" list in working toward enhancing the child's ability to play with other children, they should be grouped together to show a coordinated effort toward this common goal. Doing so also provides written documentation of the joint planning involved in the development of the plan and joint responsibility for its implementation. An example of how objectives and activities related to the family's priority that their child get more enjoyment out of being in the company of other children can be grouped together to show a coordinated plan is provided in Table 6–2.

The routines matrix for use in classroom programs developed by McWilliam (1992) is another way of displaying the coordination of activities across disciplines and settings in addressing families' priorities for their children. An example of a completed routines matrix is shown in Figure 6–1. In addition to coordinating activities toward a common goal, the routines matrix is refrigerator-friendly, that is, it will pass the piggy magnet test. Routines matrixes may also be used in home-based programs (e.g., Bennett et al., 1990). The basic format of the matrix would be the same, but home routines (e.g., nap time, meals, car travel, bath time) would be listed across the top of the form.

Include Ongoing, Successful Activities

Many of us cheat just a little when we develop our own personal "To Do" lists by including one or two tasks that we have already done or know we will do even if it is not on the list. Why? Because it is exhilarating to cross the item off the list and, thereby, prove to ourselves that we have been successful or made progress. We like to get credit for what we have done. No matter how bizarre such behavior may seem, many of us do it—and probably a good many more than will actually admit to it. Maybe this phenomenon should be taken into consideration in the writing of the IFSP.

We have already talked about including goals in areas of child and family strengths, but perhaps we should expand this notion to including activities that families are already doing and want to continue doing for themselves and their children. If we don't, the IFSP will just add more

TABLE 6–2. Example of grouping objectives, activities, and services on the IFSP to reflect a coordinated effort toward a common family priority.

Family Priority: **Erin will actively participate in group activities with other children (toy play, singing, art activities)**

Objectives	Person(s) Responsible
Erin will learn the hand movements accompanying 3 songs that the children sing in morning circle	Teacher Parents
Erin's parents will be given videos of morning circle and the words to Erin's favorite songs	Teacher
Erin will learn to use a switch to activate popular battery-operated toys (e.g., Ferris wheel, race cars)	Teacher Physical Therapist
Paint brushes and other art equipment will be adapted (built-up handles) to make them easier for Erin to use	Physical Therapist
Erin will learn the names/sounds of familiar animals (e.g., dogs, pigs, cats) found in her favorite storybooks at home and school	Speech-Language Pathologist Teacher Parents
Erin will point to pictures in familiar storybooks upon request ("Show me —"; "Where's the —")	Teacher Speech-Language Pathologist Parents
Erin will learn to say "no" rather than slapping at other children who take away her toys or in other ways annoy her	Teacher Parents
Erin will attend community-based programs for children (e.g., library, arts center, YMCA pool)	Parents

things to do on top of the things that they are already doing. For example, if a family believes strongly that reading to children is important, and if the parents faithfully read a bedtime story to their child every night, why shouldn't this be on the IFSP? They will probably continue to do so regardless of its being written on the intervention plan, but why shouldn't it be included? Doing so allows us all to acknowledge the parents' existing efforts and successes in doing something they think is important. Doing so may also help professionals on the team understand more fully what par-

Figure 6–1. Sample intervention matrix. (From *Family-Centered Early Intervention Planning* by R. A. McWilliam, 1992, p. 96. Tucson, AZ: Communication Skill Builders. Reprinted with permission.)

Child: _____ Martin _____ ID: _____ From: _____ 4/1/92 _____ to _____ 6/30/92 _____

*T = Teacher; **F** = Family; **SC** = Service Coordinator   SE   SLP   PT   OT

Priority #	*Person Responsible	Objective	Arrival	Free Play	Meals	Structured Activity	Circle	Music	Art	Outdoors	Transitions	Nap	Personal Hygiene	Home	
1		Use two-word combinations (signs OK)	X		X	X	X				X			X	6
2		Play beside one other child		X		X			X	X					4
3		Follow one-step direction				X		X	X		X				4
4		Play with large-movement toys (riding toys, playground equipment, etc.)		X						X					2
5		Look at person talking to him	X			X								X	3
6		Imitate play with toys		X		X									2
7		Indicate diaper is wet/dirty											X		1-12
8		Use spoon with little spilling			X								1		1
			2	3	2	5	1	1	2	2	2		1		≥23

ents are already doing for their children and families. As a result, perhaps they will be more cautious in suggesting that families add more activities to already full schedules, or at least more understanding if parents hesitate to accept recommendations for new services or activities.

Coordinate with Other Programs and Informal Supports

Just as the efforts of team members and parents need to be coordinated within our own programs, so too should the efforts of professionals and agencies outside our program be coordinated with ours. The concerns and priorities of families should be the common ground—the touchstone—for all services regardless of which agency is providing them. After all, the hopes and aspirations that parents have for their children and families are not dependent upon whose building they are in. They remain the same no matter who is providing services. Ideally, all agencies and professionals involved with a family and child would be included in the development of a single intervention plan that addresses all of the family's priorities. In reality, however, there may be a number of barriers to interagency coordination, not the least of which may be the difficulties inherent in scheduling time to plan together and the territoriality or turf issues that so often exist between community agencies.

Even amidst the worst of relationships between community agencies, there are things that we can do on our own to ensure that the IFSP takes into consideration the services provided by others. At the very least, we can list the other agencies involved with the family on the intervention plan and describe the services provided. If some of these other services are related to goals we are also addressing, we can list their services and intervention strategies along with our own under the appropriate goal. If their services are aimed at meeting a family goal that our own services are not addressing, we can still list the goal and identify the external agency as responsible. Finally, with the parents' permission, we may forward a copy of the written plan we have developed to the other agencies that are involved. Although doing these things may not result in truly coordinated service delivery, acknowledging the services provided by other agencies on the IFSP may provide parents and ourselves with a more complete picture of child and family goals and how resources are being combined to achieve them.

Plans Should Be Flexible

In the next chapter we discuss in more detail the issues of families' changing priorities over time, therefore only a brief mention of this issue is offered here. Suffice it to say that family priorities, concerns, and resources do change. Changes may occur as a result of unexpected crises, the acquisition of additional information, or merely as an unexplainable change of perspective on the part of parents. Whatever the reason, family priorities are very likely to change and sometimes change quite often. If the IFSP is to be useful and used, it will need to be able to accommodate the changing priorities of families. If goals, objectives, and intervention strategies cannot be added, deleted, or otherwise altered on the IFSP form, the plan will soon be outdated and serve no purpose other than bureaucratic paperwork.

Given the changing priorities of families, one has to wonder just how complex the IFSP should be. How much time should be spent outlining intervention strategies that may not be needed in another month or two? Just how far in the future should we plan and at what level of detail? Can any of us really develop a plan of action for our children or ourselves for an entire year?. . . . for 6 months?. . . . 6 weeks? Perhaps all of the family's priorities should be listed on the IFSP, but detailed planning of intervention strategies should be reserved for those goals that will be addressed immediately or in the very near future. With frequent review of the plan, progress can be assessed, family priorities can be checked and changed when necessary, and detailed intervention strategies can be developed for newly added priorities. Deal, Dunst, and Trivette (1994) have suggested a fairly uncomplicated format for IFSPs that allows professionals to keep a running account of family-identified needs and actions that have been taken to meet these needs. The status of each family priority is reviewed frequently, and items are added or deleted on an ongoing basis to reflect the family's accomplishments and changing needs. Deal et al. (1994) have also developed a simple rating system for evaluating the achievement of family priorities. Their rating system is:

1 = No longer a need, goal, or project
2 = Situation unchanged; still a need or project
3 = Implementation begun; still a need, goal, or project
4 = Outcome partially attained or accomplished
5 = Outcome accomplished or attained, but not to the family's satisfaction
6 = Outcome mostly accomplished or attained to the family's satisfaction
7 = Outcome completely accomplished or attained to the family's satisfaction. (p. 70)

In short, IFSPs need not be as complicated as we once thought they should be. They do need to meet certain legal requirements, but within these requirements there is a lot of latitude. We are accustomed to thinking of intervention plans as static, once-a-year forms that need to be completed and filed to retain our funding and our ability to provide services to a child. If we can cast away these old notions and see the development and the writing of the IFSP as an ongoing process rather than as a static, once-a-year event, it may be a relief to all involved. In other words, perhaps we should view the writing of intervention plans as more like writing on a chalkboard than carving in a stone tablet.

■ OVERCOMING ADMINISTRATIVE BARRIERS

As unfortunate as it may be, the fact remains that state and local administrative agencies still place a heavy emphasis on the written intervention
plan. The reason for this is quite clear: The written IFSP or IEP is a permanent product that is readily accessible and easily scrutinized to assess
compliance with state and agency regulations. State auditors can just pull
files and determine if appropriate procedures are being followed. It is a
matter of accountability. It would be far more difficult and expensive to
observe the process of developing the intervention plan. Even if it was
possible, it would be exceptional for a state to have in place a measurement system that determined compliance with regulations in this fashion.
(See Chapter 8 for a description of innovative monitoring systems in Alaska
and Kansas.)

All too often, the regulations governing the written intervention plan
are unsupportive or even counterproductive to the family-centered
process described in this chapter. For example, using the family's own
words in writing child goals may result in written plans that may be
viewed by unenlightened supervisors or state auditors as being "unprofes-
sional" and, therefore, unacceptable for entry into the child's permanent
file. Some agencies have extremely strict rules about how goals and objectives must be worded and the type of performance criteria that must be
used. We have heard of more than one school system that requires specific, measurable objectives and criteria for accomplishment such as "Child
will exhibit correct performance on 7 out of 8 trials."

Does this mean that professionals working in settings where such regulations exist and are enforced cannot be family-centered in their intervention planning? Of course it doesn't, but it does mean that there will be
challenges to overcome. Some professionals may take a straightforward
approach and challenge the system. This may be done piecemeal, by making incremental changes in how IEP or IFSP documents are written and
defending these changes to supervisors or auditors. Others may choose to
take a more direct approach by gathering support and advocating for
changes in the regulations or interpretations of the regulations. Support
may come from parents, colleagues, and supervisors or program directors.

Many professionals, however, are not inclined to be so bold. Rather
than directly confronting regulations, they may choose to work around
them. They may explain to parents the necessity of writing traditional
intervention plans and continue to write IEPs or IFSPs in strict accordance with regulations. Even so, they may follow a family-centered
process in understanding family priorities and developing strategies for
intervention. In addition to the official intervention plan that is placed in
the child's permanent file, they may also choose to have an "unofficial"
plan that more closely reflects a family-centered approach. In remembering the criteria of passing the "piggy magnet test," this unofficial document

need not require a great deal of extra time or effort. It can simply be a short list of goals or priorities that reminds parents and professionals what everyone is working toward and has agreed to do. This list can be updated and changed more frequently than the official intervention plan and will, in all likelihood, be more useful to all involved than the official document. As mentioned earlier, a routines matrix may also serve as a useful, working plan for action.

The most important thing to remember from this chapter is that it is the *process* of developing the intervention plan rather than the final *written product* that will determine whether or not a family-centered approach has been taken. Furthermore, the intervention planning process must be *flexible* enough to accommodate the unique characteristics and preferences of each family we serve. Finally, intervention planning is an *ongoing process* that involves the continuous exchange of information between professionals and families and the frequent updating of plans in response to the changing concerns, priorities, and resources of the family. This continuous exchange of information will be addressed further in the next chapter on day-to-day service delivery—the heart of family-centered practices.

■ REFERENCES

Bailey, D. B., & Simeonsson, R. J. (1984). Critical issues underlying research and intervention with families of young handicapped children. *Journal of the Division for Early Childhood, 9*, 27–37.

Bailey, D. B., Simeonsson, R. J., Winton, P. J., Huntington, G. S., Comfort, M., Isbell, P., O'Donnell, K., & Helm, J. (1986). Family-focused intervention: A functional model for planning, implementing, and evaluating individualized family services in early intervention. *Journal of the Division for Early Childhood, 10*, 156–171.

Barber, P. A., Turnbull, A. P., Behr, S. K., & Kerns, G. M. (1988). A family systems perspective on early childhood special education. In S.L. Odom & M.B. Karnes (Eds.), *Early intervention for infants and children with handicaps* (pp. 179–198). Baltimore: Paul H. Brookes.

Bennett, T., Lingerfelt, B. V., & Nelson, D. E. (1990). *Developing individualized family support plans: A training manual.* Cambridge, MA: Brookline Books.

Brinckerhoff, J. L., & Vincent, L. J. (1986). Increasing parental decision-making at the individualized education program meeting. *Journal of the Division for Early Childhood, 11*, 46–58.

Deal, A. G., Dunst, C. J., & Trivette, C. M. (1994). A flexible and functional approach to developing Individualized Family Support Plans. In C. J. Dunst, C. M. Trivette, & A. G. Deal (Eds.), *Supporting and strengthening families: Volume 1, Methods, strategies, and practices* (pp. 62–72). Cambridge, MA: Brookline Books.

Dougan, T., Isbell, L., & Vyas, P. (1979). *We have been there: A guidebook for parents of people with mental retardation.* Salt Lake City: Dougan, Isbell, and Vyas Associates.

Dunst, C. J., & Deal, A. G. (1994). A family-centered approach to developing individualized family support plans. In C. J. Dunst, C. M. Trivette, & A. G. Deal (Eds.), *Supporting and strengthening families: Volume 1, Methods, strategies, and practices* (pp. 73–88). Cambridge, MA: Brookline Books.

Dunst, C. J., Trivette, C. M., Hamby, D. M., & Pollack, B. (1990). Family systems correlates of the behavior of young children with handicaps. *Journal of Early Intervention, 14,* 204–218.

Featherstone, H. (1980). *A difference in the family: Living with a disabled child.* New York: Penguin Books.

Individuals with Disabilities Education Act Amendments of 1991, Pub. L. No. 102-119. (October 7, 1991.) Title 20, U.S.C. §1400 et seq. *U.S. Statutes at Large, 105,* 587–608.

Lynch, E. (1988). Ecological interview form for infants and preschoolers. In M. J. Hanson & J. P. Shonkoff (Eds.), *Early intervention: Implementing child and family services for infants and toddlers who are at-risk or disabled* (pp. 679–699). Cambridge, UK: Cambridge University Press.

McGonigel, M. J., & Johnson, B. H. (1991). Chapter 1: An overview. In M. J. McGonigel, R. K. Kaufmann, & B. H. Johnson (Eds.), *Guidelines and recommended practices for the individualized family service plan.* (2nd ed.) (pp. 1–5). Bethesda, MD: Association for the Care of Children's Health.

McGonigel, M. J., Kaufmann, R. K., & Johnson, B. H. (1991). *Guidelines and recommended practices for the individualized family service plan* (2nd ed.). Bethesda, MD: Association for the Care of Children's Health.

McWilliam, R. A. (1992). *Family-centered intervention planning: A routines-based approach to early intervention.* Tucson, AZ: Communication Skill Builders/Psychological Associates.

McWilliam, R. A., Lang, L., Vandivere, P., Angell, R., Collins, L., & Underdown, G. (1995). Satisfaction and struggles: Family perceptions of early intervention services. *Journal of Early Intervention, 19*(1), 43–60.

Simons, R. (1985). *After the tears: Parents talk about raising a child with a disability.* San Diego: Harcourt Brace Jovanovich.

Turnbull, H. R., & Turnbull, A. P. (1985). *Parents speak out: Then and now,* (2nd ed.). Columbus, OH: Charles E. Merrill.

Vincent, L. J., Davis, J., Brown, P., Teicher, J., & Weyland, P. (1983). *Parent inventory of child development in nonschool environments.* Unpublished manuscript. University of Wisconsin, Department of Rehabilitation, Psychology, and Special Education, Madison.

■ RESOURCES

Materials For Parents

Title:	*After the Tears: Parents Talk About Raising a Child with a Disability*
Author:	Robin Simons
Date:	1985
Ordering Info.:	Harcourt Brace Jovanovich, Publishers 1250 Sixth Avenue San Diego, CA 92101

Title: *Into Our Lives: A Guidebook to the IFSP Process for Families Raising Children with Developmental Disabilities*
Authors: Mimi Hunt, Pam Cornelius, Patti Leventhal, Peggy Miller, Tina Murray, and Georgie Stoner
Date: 1991
Ordering Info.: Family Child Learning Center 90 West Overdale Drive Tallmadge, OH 44278 (216) 633-2055; FAX: (216) 633-2658

Developing and Writing IFSPs

Title: *Guidelines and Recommended Practices for the Individualized Family Service Plan, 2nd Edition*
Author(s):   Mary McGonigel, Roxane Kaufmann, & Beverly Johnson (Editors)
Date: 1991
Ordering Info.: Association for the Care of Children's Health 7910 Woodmont Ave. #300 Bethesda, MD 20814
Cost: $15 (#NT-3097-1); $12 each when ordering 10 or more copies (#NT-3097T)

Title: *The Family-Centered Intervention Plan: A Routines-Based Approach*
Author: R.A. McWilliam
Ordering Info.: Communication Skill Builders P.O. Box 42050 Tucson, AZ 85733

Title: *Handbook for the Development of a Family-Friendly Individualized Family Service Plan (IFSP)*
Authors: Vicki Turbiville, Ilene Lee, Ann Turnbull, & Douglas Murphy
Ordering Info.: Order Department Beach Center on Families and Disability 3111 Haworth Hall University of Kansas Lawrence, KS 66045-7516 (913) 864-7600; FAX (913) 64-5323
Cost: $20 (package includes handbook, rating scales, & articles)

CHAPTER 7

Day-to-Day Service Provision

In previous chapters we have stressed that relationships between parents and professionals take time to develop. Over time, parents are more likely to trust the professionals who are working with them and feel more comfortable talking about their thoughts, feelings, hopes, and expectations (Kaufmann & McGonigel, 1991; McGonigel & Garland, 1988; McWilliam et al., 1995; Summers et al., 1990). In turn, professionals become more familiar with families over time and gain a clearer understanding of the family and what is important to them. As pointed out by Kaufmann & McGonigel (1991), "As families and professionals work together over time, the shared joys of success and the disappointments of failure provide a rich arena for the continuing identification of family concerns, priorities, and resources" (p. 55).

Thus, the longer and more frequently we work with a family, the easier it should become to provide services that are truly meaningful to the family. The degree to which this will occur, however, will depend on what transpires between parent and professional in the course of day-to-day or week-to-week service delivery. Whether services are home-based, classroom-based, or clinic-based, continual application of family-centered principles is of paramount importance if we are to achieve the desired outcomes of this approach. In exploring this topic, we will begin this chapter with a brief overview of what professionals should hope to accomplish in their daily work with children and families.

■ OUTCOMES OF DAY-TO-DAY SERVICES

Unlike first encounters, child assessment, and intervention planning, which have some semblance of a beginning and end point and are of relatively short duration, ongoing service delivery can cover a period of anywhere from a few months to several years. As a result, the outcomes of day-to-day services are more complex. Perhaps it is best to consider two types of outcomes—long-term and short-term. Long-term outcomes are what we hope families will have accomplished at the conclusion of their participation in services from our program. Short-term outcomes are what we hope to accomplish on an ongoing basis, throughout the course of our relationship with each child and family we serve. The achievement of short-term outcomes will determine, in large part, the extent to which long-term outcomes are realized.

At the conclusion of our services, a family should be as prepared as possible to meet the challenges they face as they enter the next phase of life with their child. The next phase may be the child's entry into a preschool program or enrollment in kindergarten, and may involve any level of participation in the mainstream, from full inclusion to a self-contained preschool or public school classroom. In addition to changes in the child's educational placement, the family will face continuous challenges in adapting to the changing needs of the child at home, in maintaining relationships with extended family and friends, and in interacting with professionals and institutions they encounter in their quest for services. Finally, as the family life cycle progresses, each family member will encounter numerous challenges and choices associated with the successive phases of individual growth and development.

Obviously, the type and severity of a child's disability will to some extent determine the types of situations parents and other family members will face as the child grows older and enters new service delivery systems. The characteristics of a child may, likewise, affect the nature of family life at home. If, for example, a child is multiply disabled or has significant cognitive delays, the family will be confronted with the issues and difficulties related to having a child in special education services. This will include educational placement decisions, individual education plans (IEPs), transportation, and ensuring that the child receives the related services and therapies they need. At home, the child may remain at a level of dependency on the parents far in excess of what a typically developing child of the same age would require. Feeding, grooming, walking, toileting, bathing, and entertaining the child may continue to fill the parents' hours at home long beyond what would normally be expected. The potential for stress on parents in such a situation is readily apparent, as is the potential restriction on the parents' personal growth and change that typically occurs as children get older and become more independent.

Looking at it this way, we might assume that the severity of a child's disability, alone, would predict the well-being of other family members, but this relationship has not been borne out by research. Instead, the ability of parents to cope with the additional stresses of a child with disabilities and their overall sense of well-being has been shown to be mediated by the quality of support they receive from their formal and informal support networks (Dunst, Trivette, & Cross, 1988; Dunst, Trivette, & Hamby, 1994). Furthermore, it is not the amount of support they have available to them, but rather the degree to which parents perceive the support they receive as meeting the needs they have identified for themselves and their child (Dunst & Leet, 1987).

What are the overall or long-term outcomes we hope to achieve as a consequence of the months or years of services we provide to a child and family? First, we hope to ameliorate the impacts of the child's disability—to facilitate the child's development so that he or she will be as prepared as possible to participate in the mainstream of society. Second, we hope parents will be as prepared as possible to effectively handle the many situations they may encounter in moving beyond our program of services, and that family members may lead as normal a lifestyle as is possible in light of their child's special needs. To accomplish this, parents would ideally leave our services with knowledge of the resources and supports available in the community, and they would have the skills and confidence necessary to secure the assistance they want from others. They would also have the skills and confidence to effectively handle potentially difficult or stressful situations related to their child at home and that home life would be as enjoyable as possible for all family members.

These long-term outcomes cannot be accomplished in a single meeting with professionals, by attending a workshop for parents, or even through extensive discussions and training in the last few weeks or months of service provision. Rather, these outcomes are the cumulative effect of service provision from start to finish—a consequence of the continual achievement of short-term outcomes. And what are these short-term outcomes? The first is that child interventions focus on the development of skills that are important to parents and do not impose unnecessary stresses on the family. Second, that parents are to be provided with the information they need to make informed decisions about their child and to secure the support they need. And third, that parents become increasingly competent and confident in their ability to solve problems as they arise in daily living. Of course, these are similar to the long-term outcomes described earlier; but, remember, it is the cumulative effect of these short-term outcomes that produce our end results. Knowledge, skills, confidence, and pride are not achieved overnight.

Table 7–1 provides a brief summary of what it is that interventionists might strive to do in providing day-to-day services to accomplish the short-term and long-term outcomes for families just described. Let us turn now to what direct service providers can do to facilitate the accomplishment of the outcomes we have identified.

■ GUIDELINES FOR PRACTICE

In the sections that follow, we offer some general principles for providing ongoing services to children and their families. Within these general guidelines, some specific examples of practices are provided to illustrate our points; however, it should be kept in mind that there are no tried and true recipes for providing direct services. Rather, practitioners must continual-

TABLE 7–1. Day-to-day service provision: Outcomes for working with families.

♦ To encourage and support families to independently mobilize resources to meet their needs

♦ To assist and support families in solving problems and meeting challenges as they arise in daily living

♦ To ensure that interventions fit comfortably into the daily lives of families

♦ To revise intervention goals and strategies to reflect changes in families' needs and desires

♦ To facilitate linkages between the family and support systems (community services, friends, neighbors, national associations, extended family, social or civic groups)

ly adapt their strategies to accommodate the unique values, priorities, preferences, and abilities of each family they serve. To the extent possible, we will try to demonstrate the application of these principles to the variety of direct service models available in early intervention. This will include home-based, classroom-based, and clinic-based services.

Translating the Intervention Plan Into Daily Action

Even the best made intervention plan can seem overwhelming to parents and professionals, alike. This is not surprising, however, because an intervention plan typically lays out guidelines for an extended period of time— anywhere from 3 months to a year. One of the responsibilities of direct service providers is to work along with parents in translating the intervention plan into manageable chunks—to decide what to do first and then work out specific details for how the plan will be implemented on a day-to-day basis. Although parents will make the final decisions, service providers are responsible for facilitating the process by providing information, asking questions, and suggesting options from which parents may choose.

Reviewing the intervention plan with the parent at the outset of services and at frequent intervals thereafter is often helpful in facilitating the process. For example, with the intervention plan in hand, the professional might begin the conversation with, "I was looking at the intervention plan yesterday and realized that there certainly were a lot of things that you wanted to accomplish or change. I'm a little unsure of what we need to tackle first/next. I know we agreed that all of the goals listed here were important, but I think it would help me to know where you want to start/go next. Perhaps we could spend a little time talking about the things you want to accomplish and pick a few things to concentrate on over the next few weeks. After all, you know what is most important for your child and your family, and I want to make sure that we spend our time together doing those things that will make the biggest difference to you."

Once priorities are selected, the next step is to come to an agreement on the exact nature of the intervention strategies for accomplishing these goals. Although the intervention plan provides guidance on intervention strategies, rarely have all the details been worked out—the "ifs," "ands," and "buts." In arriving at a specific course of action to follow, a guiding principle should be to preserve the integrity of the family's lifestyle. In other words, the strategies for accomplishing goals should be aimed at relieving the stresses on the family rather than adding more. Interventions should be planned to fit into the family's lifestyle or enhance their ability to live a lifestyle they prefer rather than disrupting their current routines. This sounds obvious, and yet we often make suggestions for parents to "spend just 5 or 10 minutes a day" working with their child on a specific skill, with little awareness of how multiple requests to "spend just 5 minutes a day" can accumulate and how difficult it can be for parents to find those 5-minute periods in an already tight schedule. As one mother put it, "Sometimes I have a difficult time finding 5 minutes a day to brush my teeth and comb my hair. . . . I know doing those things with Rachel are important, and 5 minutes a day seems like so little. Even so, the day just slips through my hands and I never get around to it. It makes me feel so guilty."

Offering parents a variety of intervention strategies to choose from is always a wise idea, but it is perhaps best to start by asking the parents what strategies *they* think might help to accomplish a goal. After fully exploring the parent's ideas, you may or may not choose to expand on their options by adding some of your own ideas to the pool of possibilities. Together, the parent and professional should weigh the pros and cons of the most promising options. This is a good time to ask parents questions such as, "It sounds as though this might be a strategy you want to take, but how will this affect you [your spouse, siblings] on a daily basis? I know that your day is already pretty busy. Will this really fit into your schedule?" By letting parents know that you are sensitive to the needs of the entire family, they are less likely to agree to or select interventions just because they think it is what they should do and to prove that they are "good parents." Openly acknowledging the possibility of competing priorities may allow parents to be more honest about what they perceive as being "do-able."

Flexibility and Responsiveness to Change

As mentioned in the chapter on intervention planning, the priorities and concerns of families may change frequently and unpredictably. This is no more and no less true for all of us. What seems important or urgent to us one week may change the next as a result of unexpected crises in our own lives, competing demands placed upon us by others, opportunities presented to us unexpectedly, or merely as a function of a change in our attitude or thinking. Changes in priorities will be reflected in our actions, that is, in how we choose to spend our time. If we are to be responsive to the priorities of families, we must first be aware of the changes parents experience and, second, be flexible enough to adjust our services and interventions according to families' revised priorities and situations.

Providing opportunities for parents to talk about the changes in their lives and listening carefully to what they say will usually supply professionals with information about changes in family priorities. When conducting home visits this can be accomplished by allocating some time on each visit for relaxed, informal conversation. Open-ended questions often set the stage for parents to talk about what is on their mind. For example, parents might be asked how their week went, how things are going at work, what a sibling has been up to lately, how their latest family vacation or trip to the grandparents turned out, or whether they got a chance to go outside and enjoy the warm weather over the weekend. The better the professional knows the family, the easier it will be to know what types of questions to ask. Follow-up questions may be asked if a parent indicates any new concerns or changes in priorities, and a revision in intervention priorities and strategies may be made if it seems necessary. Similar strategies may be used by professionals providing clinic-based or classroom-based services.

When providing clinic-based services, however, we often feel rushed for time. Services are usually provided on an hourly or half-hour basis, billed accordingly, and there is frequently another client waiting at the close of a session. We may not feel justified in using clinic time for chit-chat with parents. Looked at another way, if we don't use clinic time to work on child skills that are a priority for the family, there is little chance for follow-through at home, and one may also question whether the parent's time and money is being put to good use.

Suppose, for example, that you are providing speech-language services to a 3-year-old child in a clinic setting. Recently, three events occurred or are about to occur in the family's life. First, the family is going to visit the child's grandmother next month, and the grandmother has not seen the child for over a year. Second, new neighbors moved next door to the family. The new neighbors have a little boy named Sammy who has shown some interest in playing with the child—the possibility of a first friendship? Third, mealtime at home has become a bit of a hassle over the past few weeks, in that the child has been throwing minor temper tantrums when the parents can't understand what the child wants. All three of these situations have arisen since the last intervention plan was developed 2 months ago. Wouldn't it be nice if you knew about these events? Perhaps it would mean the world to the family if the child could call the grandmother by name on arrival or learn to say "Sammy." And think how meaningful it would be if you knew about the difficulties at mealtime and could provide some options to alleviate the family's growing frustrations.

Keeping in touch with changing family priorities really doesn't require lengthy meetings or formal interviews. A few minutes of friendly conversation at the beginning or end of a session can provide a great deal of information—especially when it is done on a regular basis so parents are comfortable in talking about their affairs. If the parent is an active participant in clinic sessions it is even easier, in that informal conversation almost automatically takes place while working with the child. At the very least, parents can be encouraged to write down any new skills they would like their child to learn or any additional concerns they have and provide this information when they bring their child to the clinic.

When providing classroom-based services, we may not have frequent contact with families. In many cases, children are transported in a van or bus provided by the program. Even if parents bring their children to the classroom, the protocol may be that parents drop their children off and quickly leave. Often, it is assumed that the child's goals in the classroom would be affected very little by what occurs at home. But, this need not be the case. The situation of the speech-language pathologist described above would hold true for classroom-based services as well. In short, anything that can be worked on in the classroom that would make home life more enjoyable or produce child skills that are meaningful and important to the parent, is well worth undertaking. This can only be done, however, if we are constantly aware of changes in the family's concerns, priorities, and situations.

Again, keeping track of family changes is often best done in an informal manner. Flexibility in arrival and departure times is one way of staying informed. Invite parents to come into the classroom in the morning and be available to engage in conversation while the children play or are supervised by another staff member. Ask them how things are going at home and what their child is doing. The same can be done in the afternoon when the children are being picked up. Walking with a parent out to his or her car can result in some informative and rewarding conversations. Providing opportunities for informal chats with parents may mean delaying the start time of your classroom schedule, but the payoff for lost instruction time is feeling that you have a better handle on what you should be working toward, which are those things that are important to the family.

If parents do not transport their child or need to hurry off each morning because of work schedules, other methods are available. One program had a rather creative and effective method. The teacher in the classroom rode in the van with the children on Friday afternoons, escorted the children to their doors, and talked with one or two of the parents for just a few minutes. She said she learned a lot about the families by doing this and it made the parents more comfortable talking with her at other times when the occasion was more formal.

Making an occasional telephone call or home visit in the evening may also help to keep abreast of families' priorities. This can be done whether or not the parents transport the child to the classroom. Scheduling phone calls has the advantage of ensuring that parents will be available to talk and they can think ahead of time about any questions or issues they may want to talk about. Impromptu calls to parents, however, can also be effective. They can be kept quite informal by an opening line such as, "It's been a while since we've had a chance to talk together, and I just thought I'd give you a quick call to tell you about some of the nice things that [child's name] has been doing at school." When making unscheduled phone calls, however, ask parents if it's a good time for them to talk or if you should call back at another time. Doing so conveys respect for the parents' time and their family routines.

Adjusting goals and strategies are just one way that we can meet the changing needs of families. Sometimes what is needed is a change in the structure or scheduling of services. Parents may need a different service, an additional service, or a change in the amount or scheduling of the services they are already receiving. There are also times when other family priorities take precedence and families may even need a "vacation" from early intervention services. Only through continuous and open communication between direct service providers and parents can this be known to professionals, and only through flexibility on the part of programs and individual professionals will it be accomplished.

Joint Problem Solving

Like all families, the families we work with in early intervention will encounter numerous unexpected events throughout the weeks and months between intervention planning updates. Some may be major events, such as the hospitalization of a family member, a new pregnancy, a financial loss, or a new diagnosis of the child. Others may be relatively minor, such as an extended visit from out-of-state relatives, an argument or disagreement with another professional, a change in babysitters, a change in a parent's work schedule, or a change in a child's behavior that disrupts normal routines or is worrisome for the parent.

When these concerns are communicated by parents, a natural reaction for the professional is to make recommendations or offer advice—to "fix things" and "make it all better." After all, we have been taught that our job is to help people, that we are the experts and have a responsibility to come up with answers and solutions. Even when we are uncertain as to the best course of action to take, we often feel an obligation to come up with something to offer families. Changing perspectives on parent-professional partnerships, however, relieve us of some of these feelings of obligation.

From a family-centered perspective, problem solving is not the sole responsibility of the professional, but rather a joint venture between the parent and the professional. If parents are to become effective decision makers, they will need to acquire problem-solving skills. This may not happen if professionals always assume full responsibility for coming up with solutions. When a new event, concern, problem, or opportunity arises, professionals can guide the parent(s) through the process of decision making. This will include analyzing the factors contributing to the situation, discussing the impacts on various family members, exploring the various options and resources available for addressing the issue, weighing the pros and cons of each option, and finally arriving at a decision and a plan of action. Encouraging parents' active participation in the process will allow them the opportunity to practice their problem-solving and decision making skills. Modeling problem-solving skills, providing information to parents to assist in decision-making, and recognizing the credibility of parents' contributions to the process will enhance their confidence and ability to take a more active role in each successive problem-solving or decision-making situation they encounter.

Parents will vary greatly in their ability, desire, and confidence to take an active role in problem solving and decision making. Some parents are well-equipped to take an active role from the outset. With only a minimal amount of information from professionals, they seem to sprout wings and fly. These are the parents who will scare the pants off the school system in later years with their knowledge of the law, their ability to mobilize the resources available in the community, and their assertiveness and persistence in advocating for the services they want. Other parents may have the same level of knowledge, but do not have the demeanor to enlist their knowledge in the face of intimidating professionals. Still others may be very limited in their ability to fully understand the information we present or to acquire the skills necessary for effective problem solving or negotiating the service system.

We cannot expect all parents to achieve the same level of independence in problem solving or participation in decision making. Even when parents are fully capable of doing so, our role is not to coerce them. We are, however, responsible for providing all parents with opportunities to participate in decision making, encouraging them to do so by recognizing their existing levels of knowledge and skills, and reassuring them about their status as executive decision makers. Every parent has the ability to make some progress in this area if they are provided ongoing opportunities, information, guidance, and support from professionals.

Emphasizing the Positive

Many parents have recounted their feelings of inadequacy in providing their children with everything they needed to reach their potential. Some parents expend enormous amounts of time and effort doing all that they can, sometimes to the point of mental and physical exhaustion, and still feel it isn't enough. Self-esteem is often sacrificed and energy is sapped from other interests and relationships. One mother said she got to the point where she dreaded any upcoming home visit or other appointment with professionals because, "I didn't want to be told yet another thing that I would have to feel guilty about not doing. As it was," she continued, "I would sit on the sofa staring blankly at the television screen at 1:00 or 2:00 in the morning, because I was too tired to get myself ready for bed, and felt as though I hadn't done everything I should have with my tiny daughter who was peacefully asleep in her crib. . . . I felt tortured by my own guilt. . . . As a mother, I was never quite good enough." Stories such as this are a reminder to us all of the potential harm that we can unknowingly inflict, despite the good intentions that drive our actions.

Placing an emphasis on the positive can help counter the blows to self-esteem that parents may suffer. One way to do this is through compliments. Compliments can have far-reaching effects, providing the recipient perceives the compliment as sincere and it is given by someone who is respected. There isn't one among us who does not appreciate a compliment from someone we like or admire, even if we are a bit uncomfortable in responding to it. Making it a personal policy to say something positive about a parent every time we see them can do much to enhance the parent-professional relationship and to bolster the parent's self-esteem or self-confidence.

This does not mean, however, that gushy overtures of admiration have to be delivered on every occasion. In fact, overdone compliments will probably be perceived as unauthentic and perhaps even condescending, thus having just the opposite effect of the intent behind them. "Your garden looks great. . . . You really have a green thumb," "I like your haircut," "That's a perfect toy for Kristy. Where did you ever find it?" "Scotty sure likes the way you feed him—he looks so relaxed and content," are the types of comments that can be appreciated by parents. Compliments may relate to the parent alone, the child, or the parent's interactions with the child. They may also be implicit or explicit. For example, a comment such as "The blue in this dress certainly brings out Anna's blue eyes," is an indirect way of complimenting the child (Anna) and the parent's choice of clothing for the child.

Regardless of the setting in which services are delivered, compliments can be routinely made by the professional providing services. Ten seconds is often all that is needed or desired. It can be done even in classroom programs where teachers and therapists do not have daily contact with parents. A quick note can be written on a scrap of paper and thrown into a diaper bag , backpack, or lunch box saying, "We all loved Jenny's new tennis shoes today. . . . What a trendsetter!" "We're all dying to know where you found the book on trucks that Johnny brought today. We want to get a copy for the classroom," "Sammy sat up by himself for over 3 minutes during circle time. Whatever you're doing, keep it up!" or "Cherie loved her lunch. . . ate like a pig. Good choice Mom!" The few minutes it takes to write the note should not be viewed as detracting from service provision, but rather as enhancing it.

Opportunities for Reciprocity

The notion of reciprocity is often overlooked in our work with families in early intervention. If, however, we want to raise the status of parents from passive service recipients, to full participating team members, and on to executive partners, reciprocity between parents and professionals should be incorporated into our daily work. Parents are often truly appreciative of the help they receive from professionals, but prolonged, one-way helping relationships may give rise to parents feeling indebted to professionals. Such relationships also do little in the way of enhancing parents' feelings of self-confidence and self-worth. It is difficult to feel like an executive partner if you have little to contribute to the partnership. Many parents prefer to give something back in return for the help they receive— some way to equalize the relationship. Even if professionals do not provide opportunities for reciprocity, parents will create their own. This is readily apparent in parents' offers of a glass of iced tea on a home visit, a Christmas present for a teacher or therapist, or a clipping off a houseplant that a professional admired on his or her last home visit.

Thankful acceptance of the small offerings made by parents is one way of allowing reciprocity. Drink the glass of iced tea or coffee and accept the chocolate cookies to take home to your own children. So long as the gifts aren't outrageous or offered with the implication of providing special treatment, it is perfectly acceptable. A special educator working in a rural area once told a wonderful story about such gifts. The father of a child for whom she provided home-based services raised mushrooms on his farm. On her way out the door at the close of each home visit, the father always handed her a brown lunchbag full of mushrooms which she gratefully accepted. In fact, the mushrooms she received were the envy of other team members. Over the course of services, it was determined that the child would begin receiving additional home-based services from the team's speech-language pathologist. The speech-language pathologist accompanied the special educator on a home visit to be introduced to the family. At the end of this visit, the father brought out the customary bag of mushrooms and handed them to the special educator. The father then turned to the speech-language pathologist and grinned saying, "And you'll get yours after you prove yourself!" They all had a good laugh and, after several visits, the speech-language pathologist received the promised gift.

Gifts are certainly not the only way for parents to reciprocate, nor are they necessarily the best way. What professionals have to offer families is largely in the form of information, strategies, or ideas. Parents can offer these as well, although they may not be aware of their potential for doing so. Some of the strategies described in the section above on compliments is equally applicable to reciprocity. For example, asking a parent where they bought a new toy or children's book is asking the parent for information that they have. Saying that you want to purchase one for the classroom or to tell another parent where they are available acknowledges the value of the information they have to share. In fact, parents have many creative strategies and ideas to share with professionals and other parents. They may have come up with a clever idea for administering a child's medication, a nutritious snack that is palatable for picky eaters, an adaptation of a trendy toy that enables a child who is physically challenged to take part in the trend, or a little-known source of financial assistance.

Many parents appreciate the opportunity to share their knowledge with other parents and to assist them in dealing with the ordeals and emotional upsets that they themselves have had to work through. Once again, it is the ability to give rather than always take. Recognizing the benefits of parent-to-parent support, one program embarked on a project to develop a parent-to-parent support network. This project involved training a group of veteran parents in various methods of providing emotional support and sharing information with other parents who would call the project for assistance. Much to the surprise of the staff, there was an overwhelming number of parents who volunteered to participate in the training and be on call to help other parents. Even more surprising, however, was the relative dearth of calls from parents requesting the services of the project. It seemed as though more parents felt a desire to help than to be helped.

Caring and Listening

The ability to convey to parents that you honestly like them and their children means a great deal in the development of parent-professional partnerships. To accomplish this, you must have an honest appreciation of the parents and the children with whom you work. If you do not, it is extremely difficult to portray convincingly otherwise. This doesn't mean that you would necessarily choose the parents you work with to be your best friends, but rather that you can see them in their best light. You recognize the admirable qualities they possess, have a reasonable understanding of the forces and values that guide their lives, and appreciate the efforts they make to accomplish what they deem important for their children, themselves, and their families.

No doubt, parents appreciate the knowledge and skills a professional can offer to assist their children in accomplishing developmental tasks. Many parents, however, appreciate even more the professional's demonstrations of sincere caring for their children. This may, in fact, override the level of expertise demonstrated by a professional. Friends, neighbors, and even extended family members may feel uncomfortable with or frightened by the child's differences and unable to offer the normal, caring interactions with the child that most infants, toddlers, and preschoolers elicit from adults. Parents may also have experienced rather cold and business-like interactions with other professionals, leaving them feeling as though their child was perceived as just another "case." Consequently, a professional who demonstrates an appreciation for the child and offers the normal, friendly interactions with the child that other children receive may be highly valued by parents. Looking at it from the perspective of partnerships, the well-being and development of the child is the common focus or product of the parent's and professional's activities. If the professional does not demonstrate a sincere commitment to and caring about the outcome, the partnership may be weakened.

Parents' perceptions of a professional's caring for their child arise from repeated observations of the interactions between professional and child as well as from the little things the professional says about the child during the day-to-day conversations between parent and professional. Stroking a child's brow while talking with a parent, giving a good-bye hug, a friendly tickle, telling a funny story about something the child did in the classroom that day, using a cute nickname or term of endearment—these are the little things that let parents know professionals like their children.

A mother of a young child with severe and multiple disabilities once told an interventionist how much she appreciated something that the interventionist did consistently but was completely unaware of doing, "You are the only one who actually talks *to* Michael," the mother said. "Most people talk *about* Michael to me—they talk around him. But you treat him like a real person by talking directly to him. That means a lot." Another mother still cherishes a rather gaudy plate that was painted by the children and teacher in her child's classroom and delivered to the hospital when her child was admitted for heart surgery 3 years ago.

Demonstrating that you care about the parents you work with can be equally important. Again, it is the accumulation of small, caring gestures over time that eventually leads to the development of trust on the parents' part and enhancement of the partnership in general. Perhaps the most effective gesture of caring we have to offer parents is taking the time to listen to them when they want to talk. The impact of listening is reflected in a young mother's story about a caring pediatrician. After repeated bouts of ear infections, bronchitis, and two hospitalizations for pneumonia, the mother was again in the pediatrician's office explaining the child's latest symptoms of illness. In closing, the mother sighed deeply and waited for the pediatrician's diagnosis and instructions. The pediatrician looked directly into the mother's eyes and asked, "And how are *you* doing?" The mother explained that she was exhausted and that she was afraid her boss' patience for her absences from work might run out. They briefly discussed these issues and some possibilities for additional support, but no real solutions came out of the conversation. For the most part, he just sympathized with her situation and listened and that, alone, meant a lot. Had it not, this story would never have been told.

Parents do not automatically talk to professionals about their feelings, concerns, and recent family events. Most are far too polite to take up our time with such things, unless we let them know in some way that we are available for listening. Just as the pediatrician did in the story related above, we may have to issue an invitation for them to talk. Also comparable to the story about the pediatrician, we don't have to have an answer for the problems that families may talk to us about. Sometimes it is enough to show that you care by taking the time to listen. So, ask how parents are doing, be sympathetic, maintain a nonjudgmental stance, and provide assistance if you can—and if it is wanted. Furthermore, listening need not be restricted to problems. You can also show an interest in parents' careers or hobbies to let them know that you are interested in and appreciate them as people and not just as parents of a child with disabilities.

In addition to listening, you can do an unlimited number of little things to show parents you care about them. We can clip out coupons for baby food or disposable diapers and offer them to parents, share a magazine article on a topic we know is of interest to a parent, or let a parent know where there is a sale on children's shoes or clothing. On occasion, we can also offer to make exceptions in our work schedules or duties to help out a parent in a difficult situation. For example, we can offer to keep a child for an extra 20 minutes at the end of the school day if we know the parents have a meeting out of town and will have a difficult time picking up their child at the scheduled closing time.

Building Support Networks

During the time that we provide direct services to children and their families, we are a part of their support network. Especially in the case of weekly home-based services and daily classroom-based services, parents may not only rely on us to support them in facilitating the development of their children, but also depend on us to help them access other community resources. This is our job. In providing our support, however, we should keep in mind that most families had other sources of support before we came on the scene. They probably continue to have other sources of support during the time we work with them. And they will, in all likelihood, need support in one form or another after our services come to an end. Therefore, we should be mindful not to supplant existing sources of support, not to make families overly dependent on us, and not to allow a situation to occur in which a family leaves our services without a system of support in place and the skills and knowledge to use the resources available to them.

Each of us has a support network we rely on in carrying out our daily tasks and in working toward our dreams for the future. We may rely upon state, federal, or private funds for our own or another family member's tuition for college. We may rely on the city's or county's public school system for the education of our young children. We may also rely on state or local governments to provide our families with locations and programs to enjoy our leisure time, whether it be a public beach or park, a Little League baseball program, or wooded trails for a Sunday hike or picnic. On a more personal level, we may rely on a child care center to provide daily nurturance to our infant or toddler while we are at the office, a grandmother or other babysitter one evening a month to allow us to nurture our marriage or social relationships. And we may depend on a good friend, a close neighbor, or a colleague to listen to our tales of joy, frustration, and sorrow. Although we all differ in the amount and type of support we need from others, our knowledge of the resources available to us, and our willingness to ask for help, there is none among us who is without a network of support. No one is completely self-reliant.

When parents talk to us about a problem that has arisen or a new concern they have about their family or their child, our first instinct is usually to tell them about resources or services in the community that may be helpful. This is, indeed, one of our responsibilities, but often we neglect to explore alternatives outside of the formal network of human service agencies. Suppose, for example, we learn through our conversations with a parent that they are under a lot of stress, that they are feeling tired or worn out, or that they are having a difficult time adjusting emotionally to their child's diagnosis or special needs. We may very well inform them of the availability of respite care programs in the community, ongoing parent-to-parent support groups, or qualified counselors in the community. Although this is all well and good, before we make these suggestions, a few well-posed questions can enlighten us as to the availability of existing support systems that may serve the same purpose. The parent may be asked something like, "Is there anyone you know who you feel comfortable talking to about these things?" and "Do you think it would be helpful to talk to them about these things?"

Taking a slightly different tact, you might begin with, "You seem to be feeling pretty down and exhausted by all you've had to deal with. What do you think it would take to help restore your energy?" Taking this latter approach, you have not made assumptions about what it is that the parent needs. They may say they would like a day or evening of relief from child care responsibilities, or they may say they would like someone to talk to who would understand their situation. Then, you can follow up by exploring the available options.

The major point to be made here is that we shouldn't overlook the use of existing informal support systems to meet family-identified needs and the only way we will know of their existence and potential for effectiveness is by asking families. Support that is potentially available from grandparents, spouses, siblings, aunts, uncles, friends, neighbors, church members, colleagues, civic groups, and social clubs often goes untapped. Furthermore, if support can be enlisted from these sources, it may prove to be more long-lasting than the limited terms and eligibility criteria for support from our own and other community programs (Dunst, Trivette, & Deal, 1994; Vincent, 1988). In other words, informal sources of support may be available to the family long after our services have come to an end.

Although parents may opt to use informal sources of support to meet some of their needs and accomplish their goals, many will still have need of the expert knowledge and skills of human service professionals. The network of services available in communities to very young children with special needs and their families is oftentimes complex and confusing for parents. Services may be fragmented and scattered across a multitude of agencies, each with their own peculiarities in paper work, eligibility, and avenues of entry. Even seasoned professionals can have a difficult time negotiating the mazes of the network.

Part of our job is to know what community resources are available to children and families. Another part of our job is to share our knowledge about available resources with families and to help them develop skills for accessing needed resources on their own. This does not mean that we shouldn't take an active role in securing resources from other agencies, for indeed we should. What it does mean is that we should encourage families to become increasingly more skilled, independent, and confident in negotiating the maze on their own. For most families, this will not happen overnight. It will happen only with the accumulation of information about resources over time, encouragement and practice in accessing resources on their own, and the resultant enhancement of self-confidence as parents experience success in exercising their abilities.

Remembering What Is Normal

As a result of our professional training and experience, we can lose sight of what is normal for children and families during the early years of childhood. Although we are focusing on developmental progressions, assessment tools and strategies, intervention techniques, and the latest technology in our respective fields, parents may be thinking about those aspects of childhood that most parents think about, such as birthday parties, bedtime stories, playing in the park, trips to the zoo, and important "firsts." If these are the types of things that are important to parents, can we address them in our day-to-day services?

Professionals who conduct home visits may be in the best position to address such issues. They have a chance to see the environment in which a child and family lives and can have regular conversations with the parents to discover what is important to them—what their dreams were or are for their child and family. Perhaps they are "outdoor people" and would like to go hiking or fishing at the lake for their summer outings and are unsure how to care for or incorporate their child on these outings. Joint problem solving between the parents and the professional might result in a way for them to do what they may have originally thought was impossible. Suppose another family is very involved with their church. The parents may consider their child's participation in religious education and his or her ability to sing spiritual songs as normal and important developmental milestones. Can we address these priorities in our interventions? Of course we can. Some parents may even consider the first time their child sits on Santa Claus's lap to be an important milestone of early childhood. If the child is hearing impaired, can we help the family find a Santa who knows sign language? If the child is on a ventilator, can we assist the family in locating a Santa who makes home visits?

We have already discussed some of the ways that family priorities for the child at home can be addressed in classroom settings, but there are also other strategies for "normalizing" the classroom. Making corny Mother's Day cards, learning nursery rhymes, singing "Sesame Street" songs, planting a classroom garden, or having a real fire engine visit the children are among the many things that classroom programs do to incorporate the "normal" aspects of early childhood. Although most preschools do such things, perhaps they don't realize the significance they can have for some parents.

One preschool teacher described an experience she had that made her realize the importance of doing "regular kid things." The teacher had been responsible for developing a series of once-a-month evening parent meetings for families whose children were in the classroom program. She had talked to parents about the types of information they wanted and had arranged for guest speakers from the community to address the topics the parents had identified. She had even arranged childcare for the children and their siblings to make it easier for parents to come. The teacher was extremely disappointed, however, when meeting after meeting was poorly attended. In fact, there were rarely more than three or four parents who had attended any of the meetings.

About 6 months later, the teacher planned a Friday night Halloween costume party for the children, their parents, and their siblings. Nearly every parent attended and everyone had a great time. The teacher then realized that her emphasis on parent education and topics related to disabilities may not have been what the parents really wanted. They preferred spending their leisure time participating in "regular" parent-child activities. Realizing this, the teacher planned more activities like the Halloween party. They had a Saturday expedition to the zoo, one evening a week they had a parent-child swim group at the local YMCA, and they had several after-work Kentucky Fried Chicken picnics at a nearby community park. Although all the parents did not participate in every event, attendance was far greater than was ever achieved at the previous parent meetings. At the end of the school year, the children put on a play about Goldilocks and the Three Bears. It was definitely an amateur production, but the children were adorable and, in addition to all of the parents attending, the families were accompanied by grandparents, aunts, uncles, siblings, and even a few close friends.

Incorporating regular kid things into the clinic setting may seem more difficult, but it can be done. Making a Mother's Day or Father's Day card, having a teddy bear tea party, playing dress-up, or making a city out of building blocks, toy houses, and miniature cars are excellent activities for conducting speech-language therapy. Physical therapy or occupational therapy can be conducted within the context of similar early childhood activities or by walking outside the building to a nearby children's park. In addition to "normalizing" therapy and making it more fun for the children, conducting therapy within the context of everyday early childhood activities, can help parents translate what is done in therapy to the home environment and incorporate therapeutic activities into their daily routines.

Honoring Confidentiality

Throughout this book we have talked about the importance of the developing relationship between parents and professionals. We have said that parents' trust in us is not automatic, but rather builds over time as we repeatedly demonstrate through our words and actions that we are responsive, dependable, and caring professionals. What we have not mentioned, however, is that the trust we engender in parents comes with a huge responsibility—the responsibility to respect families' rights to privacy and to honor the confidentiality of information that they share with us.

As human service professionals, we are well-attuned to the importance of keeping children's records confidential and obtaining informed consent for the sharing of information between agencies. But as pointed out in Kaufmann & McGonigel (1991), we may be somewhat careless within our own agencies and teams:

> Professionals are often less careful, however, about sharing family information with colleagues in casual settings, such as the lunchroom or hallway. Many families can give examples of overhearing conversations about themselves or about other families that left them feeling embarrassed and angry over the violation of their privacy. Careful attention to what family information can be shared with other team members and to where such discussions occur are necessary to true confidentiality of family information. (pp. 50–51)

The personal nature of the relationships we develop with parents will often result in their sharing information with us that they would not want divulged to others. Keep in mind, too, that what is considered private or personal information will vary considerably from one family to another. For example, one parent may be very open about being recently separated from his or her spouse or having marital problems, whereas another parent might be devastated if such information were made public. So, be careful about what you tell other team members and about what you write in progress notes, reports, or other permanent records. A good rule of thumb to follow is not to share family information with others unless it is deemed absolutely necessary. Even then, it is wise to openly discuss with the family how the information they have given you might be useful to other team members or professionals outside your agency, and either ask the family for permission to share the information or encourage them to share the information with others on their own.

In conclusion, the degree to which a family-centered approach is realized will, in large part, be determined by the quality and nature of ongoing interactions between parents and individual professionals. As we have seen, it is often the little things we say and do that can have a big impact on parents. A kind gesture, a sincere compliment, asking for the parent's ideas, joining in their celebration of small successes, and just plain listening are ways in which we demonstrate respect and understanding. Respect and understanding should, in turn, lead to interventions that are more meaningful to families and parents who feel more confident in their ability to identify what they want for their children and themselves. In addition, continually sharing information with parents about available resources and encouraging them to advocate for themselves should result in families who are more capable of accessing resources for both themselves and their children. In other words, the power of the individual professional is great. Through their ongoing interactions with families, individual professionals can achieve the outcomes of a family-centered approach even within the context of programs, agencies, institutions, and service delivery systems that are not family-centered.

Let us end this section by pointing out the revised roles of parents and professionals when a family-centered approach is taken. These revised roles are probably best summarized by Wright, Granger, and Sameroff (1984) as they write, "The role of the family is not an educational extension of the intervention program. Rather, the opposite is true, the intervention program should be an extension of the family" (p. 86). These revised roles stand in stark contrast to our old notions about the importance of parent involvement. We used to think it was important for families to be "involved," which usually meant that they would help us do our jobs. Consequently, we provided "parent training" to share our expertise and make parents better teachers of their children. We also encouraged parents to learn our educational and therapeutic techniques so that they might implement these with their children in their homes. In contrast, a family-centered approach upholds that professionals should help parents do *their* jobs—that we become "involved" in what they are trying to accomplish for their children and their entire family. Parents are in the driver's seat, and our job is to assist them in ways that help them get where they want to go and that are consistent with their values and lifestyles.

■ CHALLENGING SITUATIONS

Even for professionals who firmly believe in a family-centered approach and who sincerely attempt to apply the principles and practices described in this book in their daily interactions with children and families, there will be situations that tax their abilities to do so. There will be families that make unreasonable demands on our time and services, families who are angry or openly hostile toward us, families who engage in child rearing practices that border on neglect or abuse, families who say they want our services but then don't keep appointments or fail to follow through with interventions, and families wherein the parents themselves are intellectually limited or whose competence is otherwise questionable such that their ability to identify appropriate goals, implement interventions, or make reasonable decisions about their children is doubtful. We would be remiss in writing this book not to at least acknowledge that such challenging situations exist and to discuss how they might be handled from a family-centered perspective. Although we cannot address in detail all of the many types of difficult situations that interventionists may encounter, we will present here a few of the more common challenges that interventionists face in working with children and families.

Families Who Don't Follow Through With Interventions

Perhaps the most common challenge interventionists face are those situations in which families appear not to be meeting the needs of their children. It can, indeed, be frustrating for interventionists when they perceive a clear need for intervention with a child but the family does not provide the intervention or allow others to provide it to the child. For example, perhaps a child has been diagnosed as having a severe hearing impairment, but the parents won't purchase aids, neglect to put aids that they have on the child, do not provide a signing environment for the child, or neglect to have the child regularly attend a center-based program where a signing environment is available. Or perhaps there is a child who has severe cerebral palsy and does not speak. The professionals perceive the child to be of normal or near normal intelligence and have recommended the use of an augmentative communication system, but the parents do not want the child to use one either at home or in the classroom. Or maybe the parents have agreed to the child's using an augmentative communication system and have purchased one, but the device is never used at home and seldom, if ever, is sent to the classroom for use there. In still another situation there may be a child with cerebral palsy who clearly needs special positioning and other intervention to prevent contractures. The physical therapist has explained the child's condition and special intervention needs to the parents, provided them with a prone stander and special seating equipment with appropriate supports. Even so, the interventionist is aware that the special equipment is never used at home. Nearly every time the interventionist arrives at the family's home, the child is found slumped over in a regular baby walker or propped up with pillows on the living room sofa.

How do we approach such situations from a family-centered perspective? Perhaps the first step is remembering that it is ultimately the family's decision whether or not the child will receive the prescribed or recommended interventions, and that we should respect and support their decisions. When looked at this way, the professional's goal is not to come up with ways to convince or cajole the family into implementing the interventions, but rather to find out what their decision *really* is. The interventionist might open a conversation with the family by saying something like, "I've noticed that Joey's augmentative communication system hasn't been coming to school with him over the past few weeks. I know we all agreed it would be a good idea a few months ago, but I was wondering how it was really working out for you now that he's had it for a while. Do you still think it's worth using, or should we try to come up with something else?" By asking questions such as this, we are not implying that the family *should* be using the augmentative communication system, and this nonjudgmental stance, may result in the family's being comfortable in expressing their honest opinions about the usefulness of the board and their reasons for not using it with their son, Joey.

Maybe the family thought the augmentative communication system was a good idea when it was first discussed, but when they actually got it they found that it didn't work out like they thought it would. Perhaps they don't have the skills or confidence to use the system with Joey and it has, therefore, been a frustrating experience that they have come to avoid. Or maybe Joey has not been responsive to their attempts to get him to use the system or has actively resisted using it. It may also be that using the system interferes with the family's daily routines, such as making mealtimes with Joey more chaotic or difficult than they already were. In other words, the hassles involved in using the augmentative communication system might far outweigh any immediate benefits. It may also be that extended family (e.g., Joey's grandparents) do not approve of Joey's using the augmentative communication system and have dissuaded the family from using it. Then again, perhaps the family didn't really see a need for or want the device in the first place, but only agreed to getting the system because it was suggested by professionals and so they thought they should.

No matter what the reason is for not implementing interventions, by taking a nonjudgmental stance, you will have a better chance of finding out why the family is not following through with interventions. This will prove to be far more productive than assuming that the family doesn't understand the importance of the intervention or doesn't really care about their child's progress and making repeated attempts to get the family to implement the intervention. Once you understand why the family isn't following through, frank discussions about more appropriate or useful interventions can take place. Maybe the family needs more information, maybe they need more intensive assistance to learn the skills they need to implement interventions, maybe alternative methods to meet the same priority/goal are called for, or maybe the intervention needs to be postponed until more pressing family priorities are taken care of. The family knows best what will work for them, but they may need our help in identifying alternative strategies and resources from which they may choose.

Families Who Have Been Coerced Into Services

Perhaps the most difficult situations among parents who don't follow through with interventions are those families who are angry or hostile in response to our attempts to help. More often than not, these are the families who would prefer that we not be involved in their lives, but who have been coerced by another agency into receiving our services. The most common example of this are families who have been told that they risk losing custody of their children if they do not participate in our services. These are the families who, when we conduct a home visit or when they bring their child to the clinic for therapy, make it very clear that they do not want our involvement. They may be passively aggressive, sitting as far away from us as they can and making no attempt to communicate or otherwise be involved in the situation, or they may be quite open about the fact that they are only coming because they have been told that they must.

Working with families like this is usually an uphill battle from the very start. Chances are that they have had numerous unpleasant encounters with other professionals and agencies before they ever came to us. They have probably been told over and over again what they should, shouldn't, and have to do with their children. From the very beginning we will, in all likelihood, be perceived by these families as yet another interference in their lives. Perhaps the most important thing for us to remember is not to become immediately defensive or to counter the anger of these families with admonitions. Sometimes the best approach is to be straightforward—to acknowledge the fact that they have little choice about participating in your services. You might even sympathize with their position by saying that you can understand how they might be angry about being told that they have to come to you for services or risk having their child taken away. Then you might say, "If you have decided to accept my services so your child won't be taken away, maybe we can figure out something to work on that would actually be helpful to you and worth the time you are going to have to spend with me." The family may still not be excited about having to spend time with you, but by acknowledging their situation and showing respect for them, perhaps an amicable agreement can be achieved. Deciding on priorities and developing and implementing interventions would involve the same principles and practices that have been described throughout this and the preceding chapters.

The chances are high that these families will never come to fully trust us or be open with us. Likewise, we probably can't expect that we will promote any significant or lasting changes in their parenting practices. Nevertheless, small changes may be achieved and, in demonstrating our respect for them, they may perceive us as someone they can return to if, at a later time, they want assistance. This is probably more than could be achieved if we took a confrontative approach.

Families With Multiple or Complex Needs

Also among those families who are perceived as not meeting the needs of their children are those families who have so many needs that we, ourselves, may feel completely overwhelmed at the prospect of providing services that would make a difference. Some families' lives are complicated by drugs, violence, and crime. Some families may live in such impoverished conditions that having a roof over their heads, food on the table, or heat in the winter are a real struggle, and the top priority for these families may be mere survival. In still other families, the child may not be the only family member with disabilities. Parents with mental retardation or mental illness may not only have difficulty understanding their children's special needs and providing them with appropriate learning experiences and interventions, but they are also frequently among those families with scarce resources.

In situations such as these, the family circumstances, alone, may place the child at risk for developmental delays and be the reason for the child's referral to an early intervention program. And in some instances, the family situation may be even further complicated by the child's having a clearly defined disability such as Down's syndrome, cerebral palsy, or a sensory impairment. But how can an early intervention professional or program be expected to meet the complex needs of families like these? And what can an interventionist do to ensure that the identified children in these families get the interventions they need?

As pointed out, the educational, developmental, or therapeutic needs of their children may be the least pressing need these families face. They may not have the motivation, skills, or resources to provide for their children's special needs. In some situations, starting off with small child goals that are important to the family, and ensuring that intervention strategies do not impose an additional burden (i.e., fit easily into existing daily routines) may ensure that at least some of the children's needs are being met. In other situations, even these tactics may prove fruitless. Another option may be to offer an arrangement wherein the child's needs would be met by someone else and in a location outside of the home (e.g., classroom program, childcare center). Although this solution may not meet all of the child's needs, it may be of some benefit to the child, and the respite afforded to the family may provide opportunities for them to meet some of their other more pressing needs (e.g., securing food stamps, obtaining therapy or other care for themselves, looking for alternative housing). But in some communities, such an offer may not be possible due to limited resources and, even in communities where such services are available, some families may not accept them. Furthermore, options that focus only on the needs of the child will do little to meet the needs of the family and may, thus, have limited—and perhaps only temporary—effects on the child's developmental progress.

It should be remembered that, from a family-centered perspective, the goals of services are not just to enhance child development, but rather to strengthen and support families. Therefore, the responsibility of early interventionists includes attending to the needs of the family as a whole. This means providing families with the support, skills, information, and resources they need to meet their own needs. Remember too, that the manner in which this is accomplished is critical. It should be done with respect for the family and in accordance with their values and priorities. This is not to say that doing so will be easy, for indeed, it usually isn't when working with families whose needs are so complex.

Two excellent case examples of how a family-centered approach can be applied when working with parents who have mental retardation and families with extremely limited resources are recommended: *An Orange Raincoat* by Marilyn Espe-Sherwindt (1993) and *The Blooming of Rose* by Eileen Ziesler (1993). In both of these touching accounts of real life, it is pointed out that the families were coerced by other agencies to enroll in early intervention services and were reluctant to engage in conversations with the professionals or to participate in therapeutic activities with their children. For example, the following excerpt from Espe-Sherwindt's story describes the initial impressions of program staff to a mother named Pearl who had mental retardation:

> In person, Pearl was as intimidating as her referral. . . . Her responses to questions were curt and brief. She never smiled or started a conversation with us or any of the other parents. . . . Agencies were concerned about her

ability to care for [her baby]. There never seemed to be enough baby food in the apartment. Safety hazards abounded. We were told that Pearl often failed to respond to visitors' knocks on the door. It was also painfully clear that she did not want to be part of our program.

What were we supposed to do? We felt dumped on—early intervention to the rescue again because all other attempts to improve Pearl's caregiving skills had allegedly failed. We were the program of last resort. . . . She came to us only because she had been ordered to come—or lose her baby. (pp. 87–88)

Perhaps the most important message offered by these stories is that the development of trusting and productive relationships with the families took a long time (a year or more). Rather than "pushing" the families, the interventionists allowed them to become involved with services in the manner they chose for themselves and to proceed at their own pace. The pace of the parents in both cases was extremely slow and there were frequent backslides as the families encountered new crises (e.g., abuse of the mother by her husband, the birth of a second child with disabilities, severe illness). The forging of relationships between the professionals and the parents were also achieved, in part, by recognizing and appreciating the small steps that were accomplished by the child and parent. Sometimes this included setting up specific opportunities for the parent to succeed and, subsequently, build self-esteem (e.g., asking the parent to volunteer in the classroom). Another ingredient found in both cases was helping the families to access resources from other agencies and advocating on behalf of the families for them to get what they needed.

This is not to say , however, that the professionals in these cases were perceived by others as being heroes or saints in the approach they took with these families. In fact, in some instances they were sharply criticized by other professionals (even within the same program) for not taking a more directive approach with the parents. Take for example the following situation described in Eileen Ziesler's (1993) case example about a mother named Rose:

Rose lived across the street from the elementary school where our program operated. She brought Anna to school every day, stood near the door, and she stayed. Subtle hints did not dissuade Rose from her position at the door. She couldn't be encouraged to join in the children's play, nor would she accept offers of a chair. Little Anna stood with Rose each morning until Rose would finally tell her, "Go play." In my mind, I nicknamed her "Stand-Around Rose." While I practiced serenity in accepting the things I could not change, my teammates tried to instill in me the courage to change the things they felt I should change.

I felt very alone in this dilemma. My firm belief in parent involvement supported Rose's constant presence in the classroom. Needless to say, I won no popularity votes for my decision to leave Rose alone. Anna's second school year [also] began with Rose as permanent a fixture as the doorway in which she stood. (pp. 160–161)

In both Espe-Sherwindt's (1993) and Ziesler's (1993) case examples, the interventionists frequently found themselves "sticking up," not only for the family, but also for their approach in working with the family. Sometimes the criticism and resistance of other professionals resulted in the interventionists' questioning themselves about their adherence to family-centered principles. In fact, feelings of uncertainty on the part of the interventionists are described throughout both of these case examples, and this uncertainty frequently gave rise to the need for self-examination about their philosophy in working with families and the influence of their own personal values on how they felt about families and the decisions they made.

Another message offered by these two case examples is that we can't expect a family-centered approach to result in miracles. In neither of these cases did the parents' mental retardation go away, nor did they become rich or independent of the need for assistance from others. Even so, a respectful approach that included an emphasis on family strengths resulted in the development of a trusting relationship between parents and professionals. In addition, the parents developed new skills, improved self-esteem, and gained confidence in their abilities to parent their children and more effectively handle their own affairs. And a final message offered by these case examples is that a single professional or program can't necessarily meet all of the many needs that families may have. Advocating for additional resources, enlisting the assistance of others, and building support networks were critical ingredients for success in both of these stories about working with families that had multiple needs. For example, the following excerpt from Espe-Sherwindt's (1993) story about Pearl describes the classroom staff's efforts to enlist the help of others to assist Pearl in regaining custody of her baby:

> In our team meeting, we talked about how Robert [Pearl's baby] had been placed in a unique foster home. The foster mother was willing to let Pearl visit in the foster home and went out of her way to make Pearl feel comfortable. Because Pearl spoke so highly of her, we began to view the foster mother as a sort of mentor to Pearl. Pearl's support network was expanding. Our staff, the foster mother, and the workers and drivers from the protective services agency were all part of the same trusted network, working with and on behalf of Pearl and her son.
>
> Keeping in touch with the "network" took some time and effort on our part. Pearl knew how frequently we talked with the other people involved because we always asked for her permission. She became an increasingly active member in the communication loop and began to assume control in other ways as well. (pp. 90–91)

Families Who Want More Than We Have To Offer

On the opposite end of the continuum are those families who appear to want *everything* for their child. These are the families who want as much and as many kinds of therapy as they can get for their child. They may "shop around" for diagnoses and treatment methods, and they may be willing to travel long distances and pay a lot of money for extremely controversial therapies. The amount of energy such families expend in getting services for their children and implementing interventions, and all that their children may be subjected to as the targets of intervention, may make us want to scream, "STOP!" Perhaps even harder for us to deal with are those families who want and demand more services from us than we are able to or prepared to provide. And when we can't provide them with all they want for their child, they may become angry and hostile toward us.

What does a family-centered approach have to offer in the way of advice for handling these types of situations? Again, we must remind ourselves that it is the family who has ultimate authority in deciding what they want for their child and themselves—and how they choose to expend their resources. It is not our place to judge them or to convince them that they need to handle their situation in a different way. We do, however, have a certain obligation to ensure that the family is aware of alternative perspectives and methods of intervention. Perhaps the first step is to accept and respect how they are handling the situation. If we can join them in where they are, perhaps we can intersperse alternative perspectives in our conversations with the family—making sure that our intent is simply to provide information and not to convince them to think or act in a different way. Offering printed materials and opportunities to talk with other parents or professionals are other strategies for providing such information. Some families may eventually come around to a different perspective on how to meet their children's needs, but many will continue their fast-paced search for more and more services for a long time. If, however, we have been respectful of their decisions they may be able to seek our assistance if they should ever tire of the pace, question its effectiveness, or change their minds for other reasons.

But what do we do when families who want more and more services want them to be provided by us? These are the families who may be eventually labeled by some professionals as "chronically dissatisfied," and it is little wonder that this happens when what these families are basically doing is questioning the quality of the services being provided. A first reaction for some professionals is to become defensive and retaliate by saying that the parent's expectations are unrealistic or unreasonable. If, however, this posture is assumed by the program or the individual professional, it can quickly spiral downward into a rather sordid conflict that may never be resolved. Avoiding a defensive reaction is the first step toward resolving any conflict between families and professionals. Then, rather than convincing parents that a child doesn't need more therapy, we should acknowledge their desire for additional time or services. By showing respect for the family's opinion about what their child needs, they may be more open to discussing available options. Before examining options, however, it may be a good idea to begin the discussion by exploring what it is the family hopes additional time or services will accomplish for the child or themselves—what is the hoped for outcome or goal? By returning to what the family wants to accomplish, options other than additional services may be explored that might be equally effective in achieving the goals the family identified. The identification of options, however, may require considerable creativity and some compromise on the part of the professionals.

Some families may not be willing to budge from their original position of wanting more therapy time or additional services for their children. When this happens, we should still be respectful of their desire for additional services—even if we do not have the resources to provide them. In such situations we might say to the family, "I understand that you want more therapy time for [child's name] and I wish we had the resources to provide her with it, but I'm sorry to say that we don't. What we can do, however, is help you explore ways that you might get the additional therapy that you want [child's name] to have. Would you like to spend some time doing this?" If the family says yes, then the next step is to provide the family with information. This information may include the names, addresses, and telephone numbers of people in the system who control the purse strings. It might also include information about other programs (public and private) that might be able to provide additional therapy and information about financial assistance to pay for therapy the family might secure from outside your own agency.

Some families may still be dissatisfied and angry for your not providing their children with what they think their child needs. This may result in a temporarily or permanently strained relationship between the family and the program, the family's deciding to discontinue services from your program and/or enroll in another program, or the family's filing a grievance or a law suit. If such situations should arise, it is more important than ever to remain nonjudgmental and not to become defensive. The importance of doing so is exemplified in one true story. In this case, a family wanted more services for their child than a classroom-based program could offer. As a result, the family became critical of the program and increasingly angry with the staff. In turn, the teachers and therapists became highly critical of the family, talking frequently among themselves about how unreasonable the family was being. In the end, the family took the child out of the program and enrolled him in another classroom program that offered a more structured setting combined with more one-on-one therapy. After a year, the family had become disenchanted with the new classroom. They felt that their child had been happier in his original classroom and requested that he be readmitted. Unfortunately, the staff had taken the family's criticism and anger personally and, in the end, the family's request for their child's readmission was denied.

Obviously, we have only skimmed the surface in terms of the many and varied types of challenging situations that early interventionists may encounter in their work with children and families. We hope, however, that the above discussion of some of the more common challenges has demonstrated how family-centered principles can be used by interventionists to guide problem solving and decision making in their daily work. Perhaps the most important thing to remember from this chapter and the rest of this book is that every situation an interventionist encounters in working with families will be unique and will, therefore, require a unique or individualized solution. There are no pat answers or recipes for success, but rather we must use the basic principles of a family-centered approach to individually analyze each situation and decide upon a course of action that is consistent with these basic principles. In doing so, we must consistently ask ourselves the following types of questions:

- What is important to this family?
- Have I sincerely tried to understand the family's perspective? Have I really listened to what they have to say about their child and themselves?
- Have I recognized and acknowledged child and family strengths?
- Am I being respectful of the family?
- Am I being judgmental of the family?
- Are my own personal values influencing my decisions and actions? And if so, how?
- Have I considered both the short-term and long-term needs of the child and family?
- Will my decisions and actions be instrumental in preparing the child and family for the future?
- Have I provided the family with the information they need to make decisions and access resources?
- Have I allowed the family to make their own decisions?
- Have I demonstrated my support for the family's priorities and decisions?

■ REFERENCES

Dunst, C. J., & Leet, H. (1987). Measuring the adequacy of resources in households with young children. *Child: Care Health and Development, 13,* 111–125.

Dunst, C. J., Trivette, C. M., & Cross, A. H. (1988). Social support networks of families with handicapped children. In S. E. Keefe (Ed.), *Appalachian mental health* (pp. 102–121). Lexington: University of Kentucky Press.

Dunst, C. J., Trivette, C. M., & Deal, A. G. (1994). Resource-based family-centered intervention practices. In C. Dunst, C. Trivette, & A. Deal (Eds.), *Supporting and strengthening families: Vol. 1. Methods, strategies and practices* (pp. 140–151). Cambridge, MA: Brookline Books.

Dunst, C. J., Trivette, C. M., & Hamby, D. W. (1994). Measuring social support to families with young children with disabilities. In C. Dunst, C. Trivette, & A. Deal (Eds.), *Supporting and strengthening families: Vol. 1. Methods, strategies and practices* (pp. 152–160). Cambridge, MA: Brookline Books.

Espe-Sherwindt, M. (1993). An orange raincoat. In P. J. McWilliam & D. B. Bailey (Eds.), *Working together with children and families: Case studies in early intervention* (pp. 87–98). Baltimore: Paul H. Brookes.

McGonigel, M. J., & Garland, C. (1988). The individualized family service plan and the early intervention team: Team and family issues and recommended practices. *Infants and Young Children, 1*(1), 10–21.

Kaufmann, R. K., & McGonigel, M. J. (1991). Identifying family concerns, priorities, and resources. In M. J. McGonigel, R. K. Kaufmann, & B. H. Johnson, (Eds.), *Guidelines and recommended practices for the individualized family service plan* (2nd ed.) (pp. 47–55). Bethesda, MD: Association for the Care of Children's Health.

McWilliam, R. A., Lang, L., Vandivere, P., Angell, R., Collins, L., & Underdown, G. (1995). Satisfaction and struggles: Family perceptions of early intervention services. *Journal of Early Intervention, 19*(1), 43–60.

Summers, J. A., Dell'Oliver, C., Turnbull, A. P., Benson, H., Santelli, E., Campbell, M., & Siegel-Causey, E. (1990). Examining the individualized family service plan: What are family and practitioner preferences? *Topics in Early Childhood Special Education, 10*(1), 78–99.

Vincent, L. (1988). What we have learned from families. *OSERS News in Print, 1*(4), 3.

Wright, J. S., Granger, R. D., & Sameroff, A. J. (1984). Parental acceptance and developmental handicap. In J. Blacher (Ed.), *Severely handicapped young children and their families: Research in review* (pp. 51–90). Orlando, FL: Academic Press.

Ziesler, E. (1993). The blooming of rose. In P. J. McWilliam & D. B. Bailey (Eds.), *Working together with children and families: Case studies in early intervention* (pp. 155–166). Baltimore: Paul H. Brookes.

PAMELA J. WINTON AND ELIZABETH R. CRAIS ■

■ CHAPTER 8

Moving Towards A Family-Centered Approach

As you have read through this book, you have probably had a range of reactions to the ideas presented. Some ideas are probably similar to your current practices; whereas others may be new, but promising, relevant, and worth trying. Still others may seem impractical and unrelated to your particular situation. One of the underlying premises of this book is that there is no one way or method for effectively implementing a family-centered approach. What might be an effective service delivery system in Harlem, KY, might be very different from an effective system in Harlem, NY. Community traditions, values, and resources all contribute to defining what constitutes an effective early intervention system. Our attempt has been to provide an array of possible strategies and ideas, some of which may be helpful as you consider your particular community, agency, and the families you serve.

The purpose of this chapter is to provide additional ideas for making changes that you are interested in making and will include changes at the individual, agency, community, and policy levels. For each of these levels, strategies are provided that will assist you in figuring out where you are, where you want to be, and in developing and implementing a plan to accomplish desired changes in practices. At various points in the chapter, resources related to making changes are briefly described. A resource section at the end of the chapter provides availability and ordering information related to each resource mentioned.

■ THE INDIVIDUAL PRACTITIONER

Each of us has the capacity to make a difference in the lives of children and families through our individual relationships and interactions. Again and again, families tell us about the little things that professionals have said or done that have "made a difference." Parents will often describe a conversation, a letter, or a phone call with a professional that they will never forget because of its positive impact. Sally Sloop, a parent we know who conducts early intervention training, always shares with students a handwritten letter she received from a physician many years ago that accompanied a diagnostic examination of her child (personal communication, October 1995). The letter (see Figure 8–1) is a compassionate and honest summary of the physician's diagnosis and is provided here to illustrate one strategy for conveying difficult information. In addition to the diagnostic information, the words used by the professional convey a feeling of genuine caring about the family and the child, an appreciation for child and family strengths, acknowledgment that diagnosis during the early years is imprecise, and recognition and compassion for what the family has experienced in their search for information.

Figuring Out Where You Are

One of the most challenging aspects of making changes is that the practices and behaviors of a family-centered approach have not been defined

---

Dear Sally and David,

I greatly enjoyed meeting both of you <u>and</u> Peter! He is a charming, huggable fellow and I know how much you love him ....and worry about him.

I hope my enclosed report will help but it is always hard to see your child in "print"—it is too inflexible. I only saw Peter once and he is still so young, but he does appear to have a global developmental delay. However, he <u>will</u> be just as happy about his accomplishments as another child.

Although he does "tune out" at times, it appears that it is when he is overwhelmed or in a two year old negative frame of mind. I do feel we need to withhold descriptive "labels"....such as autistic....until Peter has been around a little longer. I felt that Peter did try to communicate and interact.

I was pleased about my conversation with [<u>name</u>] and hope that therapy will continue.

I do want to hear how Peter <u>and</u> both of you are doing. I also have some books, some from a Religion & Medicine series, which you might find useful.

My very best wishes to you <u>and</u> a hug for Peter.

Sincerely,
Joanna S. Dalldorf, M.D.

Figure 8–1. Letter accompanying the first diagnostic report sent to the parents of a young child. (Reprinted with permission from Sally Sloop and Joanna Dalldorf.)

in terms of specific procedures and techniques. There is no early intervention "cookbook" with step-by-step instructions for what one should do to be family-centered. The approaches you take and the words you use will need to be carefully individualized depending on each family's situation. This means that, in many ways, it is up to each of us to develop our own flexible "style" and a variety of ways to be family-centered. The best place to start in developing these skills is with existing strengths—that is, recognizing those behaviors and practices you already engage in that are family-centered and building on those. This requires conducting some sort of self-assessment of current practices.

In this time of change, with new roles and skills being emphasized that may be vaguely defined or defined by different people in different ways, our powers of self-observation may be challenged. What does it mean to "empower parents"? How do I know if I am doing it? If I am candid with parents, am I being insensitive? Can I be sensitive without being less than candid? These are the kinds of questions that are often raised as professionals struggle to redefine practices in light of the new directions. One means of analyzing "where you are" is through self-assessment. There are three aspects of self-assessment that might be considered if change is your desired outcome: (a) conducting an honest appraisal of current strengths and weaknesses, (b) identifying specific skills and behaviors you want to master, and (c) selecting small, manageable behavioral changes that you think are possible within a relatively brief time span. The major resources for conducting a self-assessment are yourself, your peers, and families who are consumers of early intervention services. Self-assessment strategies related to each of these three resources are presented in the following sections.

Reflection and Self-Observation

Reflection involves stepping outside of the immediate day-to-day routine and trying to look objectively at practices and interactions. Reflection is probably best accomplished within the context of a mentoring or supervisory relationship; because trying to identify personal strengths and areas in which change is desired without feedback from others can be very difficult (Fenichel, 1991). Unfortunately, many early intervention professionals do not have regular mechanisms for self-reflection or reflective supervision and mentoring (Fenichel, 1991). Without an existing structure, asking for this kind of feedback from others can be threatening and risky, so we start with some strategies that you might use on your own without enlisting help from others.

There are a small number of self-assessment tools that provide concrete examples of behaviors or practices related to a family-centered approach that might be helpful. One such tool is *Moving Toward Cultural Competency* (Taylor, 1993). This checklist is intended to heighten the sensitivity of personnel to the importance of cultural congruence between home and early intervention settings. It gives concrete examples of the kinds of practices that enhance congruence across three domains: (a) physical environment, materials, and resources, (b) communication styles, and (c) values and attitudes. Individuals rate themselves in terms of the frequency with which they engage in these practices.

Another example is the *Personal Values Self-Reflection Tool* (Moore & Beatty, (1995). This tool consists of five questions designed to encourage individuals to explore the cultural traditions and values they bring to the intervention process, and the manner in which these cultural variables may affect outcomes with families.

A third example is *Brass Tacks: A Self-Rating of Family-Centered Practices in Early Intervention, Part II—Individual Interactions with Families* (McWilliam & Winton, 1990a). This tool was designed to provide some specific examples of practices and behaviors related to being family-centered. The instrument consists of a series of questions related to interactions with parents. Professionals who have direct contact with families are asked to consider their current practices in light of each question. The questions are related to four areas of practice: (a) first encounters with families, (b) identifying goals for intervention (child and family assessment), (c) intervention planning for children and families, and (d) day-to-day service provision. The questions on the *Brass Tacks* instrument are not meant to represent a set of directives about what it means to be family-centered; rather they are designed to stimulate a process of thoughtful self-reflection. A sample page from this instrument is provided in Figure 8–2.

A speech-language pathologist in a university-based clinic describes how her movement towards a more family-centered approach resulted from a reflective process that was partially inspired by the *Brass Tacks* instruments.

> After attending a few conferences about family-centered practices and reading further on the topic, I was still having difficulty transferring the ideas into my own clinical practice. It was around this time that I became aware of the *Brass Tacks* instruments and decided it might be useful to just read through it as a way to prompt my thinking about my own practices. Indeed, that is exactly what happened. I found it very useful as a starting place in helping me identify areas where I might want to make some changes. And as I was quite involved in conducting assessments, I decided that within this broad area there might be a few practices that I could target. Before approaching my colleagues about any of these ideas, however, I thought I might try a few of them myself. At the time, our clinic was still conducting individual disciplinary assessments of each child. So I set out to try the new ideas in my own sessions with children and families.
>
> A few simple steps seemed easy to accomplish, such as asking the family what questions about their child they would like answered by the assessment; explaining the purpose, content, and scoring of all the assessment

Area #1: First Encounters with Families (referral & program entry)

Policy or Practice	How Often?					How Important is This Practice?					Change Needed?	
	Never	Seldom	Some-times	Usually	Always	Not Important	Somewhat Important	Important	Very Important	Critical		
1. Do you give parents enough information to allow them to plan or prepare for the first meeting with professionals from your program?	1	2	3	4	5	1	2	3	4	5	Yes	No
2. Do you give parents the opportunity to determine at least a portion of the agenda of the first meeting(s) with program staff?	1	2	3	4	5	1	2	3	4	5	Yes	No
3. Do you ask parents what they want before telling them what the program does?	1	2	3	4	5	1	2	3	4	5	Yes	No
4. Do you convey to the family your admiration or recognition of what they have accomplished to date (in a sincere and convincing manner)?	1	2	3	4	5	1	2	3	4	5	Yes	No
5. Do you comment to the parent(s) about the strengths, accomplishments, or positive aspects of the child?	1	2	3	4	5	1	2	3	4	5	Yes	No
6. Do you ask questions and provide information using language that is readily understood by the family?	1	2	3	4	5	1	2	3	4	5	Yes	No
7. Do you convey to parents a sincere choice regarding the release of information from other agencies or professionals?	1	2	3	4	5	1	2	3	4	5	Yes	No
8. Do you answer parents' questions in an open and honest manner?	1	2	3	4	5	1	2	3	4	5	Yes	No

Figure 8–2. Example of a self-assessment tool for clinicians in first encounters with families. (From *Brass-Tacks: A Self-Rating of Family-Centered Practices in Early Intervention, Part II—Individual Interactions with Families* by P. J. Williams and P. Winton, 1990. Chapel Hill, Frank Porter Graham Child Development Center, University of North Carolina. Reprinted with permission.)

tools before they were used; and talking with the parents throughout the assessment about how the child was performing. Although parents had always been positive about the assessment process in the past, after trying some of these changes, I felt parents seemed more a part of process and less like "bystanders." After trying some of these ideas and beginning to feel a positive impact from using them, I decided to expand and try several more of the ideas generated from *Brass Tacks*.

I soon began asking parents to validate the results of the evaluation immediately following the testing, and made certain to include their perceptions in the follow-up report. I also began offering parents the opportunity to review the report before it was finalized. In addition, I tried to focus throughout the assessment and in the discussion that followed on the child's strengths rather than only on his/her needs or weak areas. These little changes began to encourage me to look for other ways that I might make my assessment practices more family-centered. Over time, I continued to return to the Brass Tacks instrument to identify other practices I might want to change and to try them out with children and families. In this way, without trying to change everything at once, I began to implement the ideas in a way that matched both my personal style and my beliefs that one individual can make a difference.

For those who conduct child assessments or evaluations, a helpful tool that focuses on family-centered practices within the assessment process is *The Role of Parents in Child Assessment* (Crais & Wilson, 1993). This tool is an adaptation and expansion of the "Child Assessment" portion of the *Brass Tacks* instruments (McWilliam & Winton, 1990a, 1990b) and covers three broad topics within assessment: (a) preparing for assessment, (b) performing assessment, and (c) sharing assessment results. For each area, a series of questions is posed in a checklist format to help identify the ways that families take part in the assessment process. As indicated by the work of Crais & Wilson (1996), just reading and answering the questions prompted some individuals to consider making changes in their procedures for conducting child assessments.

The speech-language pathologist working in a university-based clinic, who we mentioned earlier, also told about how she and the graduate students she supervised began to make modifications in their practices using the Crais and Wilson (1993) adaptation of *Brass Tacks*.

First, I asked the students to read over the tool and pinpoint practices that they usually performed in the assessments in which they had taken part. The students indicated several "family-centered" practices as quite routine, such as gaining information on family concerns and priorities, offering a choice as to the time of the assessment, making comments as to the strengths of the child, asking family members to interpret the child's behaviors and to describe family routines, summing up the assessment findings, and asking the family's reactions to the assessment results. Other practices were reported by the students to happen rarely, such as asking families to identify strategies to use in assessment, offering the choice of where the assessment will take place, asking family members if they would like to record their observations during the assessment, providing ways for family members to organize their observations before the sharing meeting, or reviewing the report before it is finalized.

I then asked the students to choose a few of the practices least (or never) performed and to identify ways that they might facilitate their use in an upcoming assessment. In this way, I was helping the students identify practices that they might like to try and helping them develop plans for implementing the practices.

Asking Peers and Supervisors for Feedback

The supervisory process just described for helping students reflect on their assessment practices is one that should ideally extend into the workplace; and, in fact, peer and supervisory feedback are standard practices in some programs and agencies. Fenichel (1991) once described supervision or mentorship in early intervention as comparable to "having a friend on a difficult journey." Thinking about ways that you can create or improve opportunities for feedback from your colleagues and supervisors is one strategy for self-assessment. For example, it may be helpful to identify a colleague whose skills you admire and begin creating opportunities for interactions. You might observe your colleague with families, have your colleague observe you with families, discuss challenging situations, identify specific behaviors or practices that you want to try, and ask your colleague to serve as a sounding board, a mentor, or a model as you learn these new skills. One of the self-assessment tools just mentioned might provide you and a colleague with a mechanism for providing each other with feedback. You might agree to rate yourselves and discuss ideas for change, or you could rate each other and discuss similarities and differences in approaches.

A specific strategy that involves the use of colleagues in facilitating or sustaining professional growth is peer coaching. Peer coaching has been described in the literature as an interactive partnership between peers that provides a safe environment for developing and practicing new skills (Gallacher, 1995; Hudson, Miller, Salzberg, & Morgan, 1994). In a recent review article, Hudson et al. (1994) describe peer coaching as having two components: peer observation and peer support groups. Peer observation has three stages. First, peer and coach meet to identify specific behaviors that have been targeted for change. Second, the coach observes the peer on the job to collect information on the targeted behaviors. Third, peer and coach meet so that feedback is provided and new goals can be established. The other component, peer support groups, occurs when small groups of practitioners meet to share ideas about target behaviors and problem solve together about changes they want to make. Gallacher

(1995) has developed a six-step peer coaching model for early interventionists. A manual describing the model provides (a) details to help early intervention coaching partners engage in the process, (b) information regarding different techniques that coaching partners might use in the process, and (c) strategies to embed the coaching process into organizational structures (Gallacher, 1995).

Asking Parents for Feedback on Behaviors and Practices

Asking families for feedback is probably one of the most effective ways of determining your strengths and weaknesses. How to do this in a way that truly invites honest feedback, however, is a challenge and requires consideration of several issues outlined below.

TIPS FOR ASKING PARENTS FOR FEEDBACK

♦ Make sure if you ask, that you have the time to listen.
♦ Ask for feedback about specific events (e.g., an assessment, a planning meeting, a particular home visit, a diagnostic procedure). This will probably yield more information than asking for feedback in general.
♦ Let parents know why you are asking for feedback. Doing this in a way that convinces families that you want candid and practical suggestions to help you make changes is more likely to result in helpful information being shared.
♦ Ask parents what you are doing that they like. This is always a good starting point.
♦ Use some of the questioning techniques outlined in "Tips for Eliciting Feedback from Families." (See Table 3–1 in Chapter 3.)

Here are some questions you might consider asking to elicit information from parents:

- If you could change one thing about [my visits, this assessment, this meeting, etc.], what would it be?
- If you could always count on one thing happening [when I visit, during these kinds of assessment, etc.], what would that be?
- If I could improve one thing about the way I work with you and other families, what would you choose?
- If you could give me one piece of advice about how I might improve [my home visits, my assessment procedures, etc.], what would it be?

The simple act of asking parents for feedback can be powerful in establishing equal partnerships and empowering families. It conveys the message that you care about parents' opinions, feel they have valuable information that can help you in your job, and that you are willing to make changes based on their feedback. But not all parents will feel comfortable in this role, especially without some explanation about what you are trying to accomplish, and some parents may not have time to provide this type of assistance. Prior to asking for in-depth feedback, it may be important to ask parents for their help and explain what you are doing. It may also be important to consider which families you ask for feedback. It is probably least threatening to start with families with whom you feel successful and effective, but you might want to expand your requests to families with whom you have had challenging relationships. You might also consider requesting feedback from families whose backgrounds and ethnicity are varied and different from yours. Lastly, you may want to enlist the assistance of families who are no longer being served by you. These families will have the additional advantage of dealing with different approaches, if they are now working with other professionals.

One professional working in a center-based program described how he had contacted a few parents with whom he had worked and asked them for their feedback on the services he and other professionals had provided to them.

With each of these parents, I had had the opportunity to establish a good working relationship with them and so felt comfortable asking for their advice. By way of introduction, I told them that we were taking a look at our program practices and wanted some expert advice on how we might make our services more responsive to families. At the beginning of the meeting, I asked them to just tell me about their feelings about the services they had received from our program, specifically what practices were helpful and which ones were not helpful. All of the families talked about the positive personalities of the professionals with whom they had worked and appreciated that the professionals listened to what they had to say.

Although the parents agreed on what was helpful, they all had different ideas about what was not helpful. One mother suggested that she did not appreciate the fact that the first thing she was asked to do was complete the program's case history form that asked for detailed and intimate information. In asking what may have been preferred, she suggested that she would have rather sat down and just talked about what she thought would be useful information to us. Another parent noted that she did not always feel welcome in the classroom her child attended nor did she feel the team was very accommodating in trying suggestions made to them by the family. A third parent related that across all the services their family had received (the child was now eight years old), he felt there was too much focus on assessment and not enough on intervention.

Across the parents, several ideas were generated that I felt could help me modify my own practices and that could be shared with my colleagues about the ways that family members perceive our services. In addition, I suggested to my colleagues that we may want to try this type of information gathering with parents currently receiving services from our program.

Making and Implementing a Plan for Change

Whatever means you choose for conducting self-assessment, it is important to also have a means for developing a vision and some concrete ideas about how you want to change. Whether that comes from reading articles, using checklists that describe new ways of practicing, talking to families about their preferences, or observing colleagues you believe have outstanding skills and success with families, it is important to have some clear idea about the skills you are hoping to develop and the new practices that you want to try. This leads to the next steps which are setting priorities and developing an action plan.

Setting Priorities

Think about the times in your life when you have decided to instigate a new approach or change a particular habit or behavior. Were you successful, and, if so, what contributed to your success? Common characteristics of successful plans for change include:

- Identified goals are small, manageable, and can be accomplished in a fairly short time frame.
- Identified goals can be accomplished within the framework of existing conditions (e.g., major changes in environmental context are not required).
- Outcomes are clear. You know if and when you have succeeded in accomplishing what you set out to do, and you are, thus, able to celebrate your success.

The same guidelines apply when making personal action plans for becoming more family-centered. It is important to select goals that you are truly excited about and feel are possible within the context of your work situation. It is also important to consider the amount of resources, support, and time you will have available to enact your plan. If you choose too many goals, goals that require resources that are not in place, or goals that require a time commitment beyond what is possible, you may find yourself frustrated and disheartened.

The following are examples of some individual goals identified by early intervention practitioners who used the *Brass Tacks* instrument for individual professionals (*Brass Tacks: Part II—Individual Interactions with Families*) as a catalyst for identifying needed changes. These goals were generated within the area of practice related to "First Encounters with Families."

- To listen to families' needs during a phone referral before I explain our program services, during a phone referral
- To look at the whole family and ask questions about what is important to them, even if it is not in the scope of our program activities and services

- To become more acquainted with the cultural differences in the population we serve
- To offer sincere praise for what the family has already accomplished
- To listen more and talk less
- To practice effective questioning techniques to obtain desired information from family

Making an Action Plan

Once you have identified the specific practices that you want to develop or enhance, the next step is to develop a plan of action for accomplishing your goals. A "plan" may be a set of informal ideas that you keep in your head, or it can be a more formal written document. Whatever approach you take, it is important to think about specific strategies and activities for accomplishing what you want to do. A good rule of thumb for developing your plan is to include activities that you can put into action immediately. It has been estimated that if you do not try out a new idea that is inspired by a specific event (e.g., a workshop, presentation, journal article, book, etc.) within 4–6 days of thinking of it, the idea will probably never be implemented. This information reinforces the importance of developing a plan that can be implemented almost immediately.

Plans need not be complicated, as is demonstrated by the following goal and related activities that one practitioner wrote for herself at the conclusion of a workshop on family-centered practices.

Goal: To step back and listen to the parent before rushing in and talking myself.

Activities
1. Wait at least 1 minute after broaching a subject with parents to allow them the opportunity to respond
2. Practice asking more open-ended questions

Two activities were identified within this practitioner's goal. The first activity, "wait at least 1 minute after broaching a subject with parents to allow them the opportunity to respond," focused on a concrete, measurable behavior. Because this practitioner had daily contacts with parents, it is quite likely that she could try this behavior within 4 to 6 days of identifying the goal. The other activity, "practice asking more open-ended questions," is also a behavior that could be implemented immediately. This activity, however, is less precisely defined than the activity related to waiting 1 minute to encourage parent contributions to a conversation. Without baseline data or feedback from a colleague, the practitioner might have a harder time knowing if she was succeeding. Even so, the activities she selected seem quite "doable," and there is a good chance that a plan such as this will be put into action.

Identifying Criteria for Success

A critical component to any plan for change is some mechanism for measuring or noting that positive changes in the directions expected have occurred. Given that each person reading this book who is inspired to develop a plan will have a different set of priorities and goals, how can success be evaluated? Again, there is no one agreed upon evaluation tool that can be used to measure "family-centeredness" across all contexts. This is the same challenge practitioners face as they attempt to evaluate progress towards accomplishing the individualized goals listed on intervention plans for children and families. Strategies for monitoring progress must be flexible, informal, and capable of addressing individualized outcomes.

One strategy that might work for some behaviors or practices is the use of an informal rating scale. For example, if you wanted to spend more time trying to listen to families' concerns or interests at the beginning of each home visit, you might rate where you are now in terms of the amount of time you currently spend or your success at eliciting their comments using a 1–10 scale. You might want to elicit help from a colleague or even from the family in making this informal judgment of your baseline behavior. Using your beginning rating as a pretest point, you could ask for periodic feedback using this scaling process. If you have videotaped or audiotaped an interaction with a family, this could provide the basis for evaluating baseline behavior for any number of practices or behaviors.

The most important thing to remember is that success breeds success. Figuring out strategies for recognizing progress and changes in desired directions is important in sustaining your energy and interest in pursuing your goals. Another method that is quite simple and yet often effective is the use of homemade checklists. Suppose, for example, you provided therapy in a clinic setting and wanted to become more family-centered. You decided on several things you could do that would help you achieve this and wrote these activities in a question format. Your checklist might look something like this:

____ Did I say something positive about the child to the parents?

____ Did I ask how things were going at home?

____ Did I ask the parent(s) if there were any changes in how we spent our time together or what our efforts should be focused on?

____ Did I welcome parents to stay during therapy?

____ Were the therapy activities "normalized"(combining regular kid things with therapy)?

___ Did I offer the parents choices re: day/time of next appointment?

A checklist such as this can be used both as a reminder of your goals and activities and as a barometer of how well you are doing in accomplishing your goal. You could make multiple copies of the checklist (perhaps on 3" × 5" index cards or small sheets of paper) and fill in the blanks at the close of each therapy session or home visit. You could simply check off the items you completed, or you could use a rating scale of some sort to indicate how well you thought you did on each item.

Figure 8–3 provides another format that might be helpful in monitoring your progress. *The Brass Tacks Report of Progress & Barriers* is designed to be used on a less frequent basis (e.g., once every 3 months) than other measures of success we have described. Measures such as this can be used separately or in combination with more frequent measurement systems.

Resources for Building Skills

The strategies you choose will naturally depend on the individual goals you identified for yourself. In our experience, many practitioners identify communication skills as an area needing self-improvement. Throughout this book we have referred to the communication skills and conversations that convey to families acknowledgment and validation of their past experiences, that convey to families that they are heard and believed, and that provide families with opportunities to consider possibilities and solutions that address their unique priorities. The resource section of this chapter includes articles, chapters, books, and other training resources and materials related to communication skills. The self-instructional materials on communication skills might be of particular interest to individual practitioners. They include:

Essential Interviewing, a Programmed Approach to Effective Communication by D. Evans, M. Hearn, M. Uhlemann, & A. Ivey (4th ed., 1993). A programmed text that defines and demonstrates how to use a group of core communication skills.

Effective Communication for Parents and Professionals by S. Duff, S. Phillips, S. Davis, T. Maloney, J. Stromnes, B. Miller, & K. Larson (1995). A set of audiotapes with a manual that is ideal for home-based interventionists who spend a lot of time in the car.

Culture and the Clinical Encounter: An intercultural sensitizer for the health professions by R. Gropper (1996). This monograph presents a series of critical incidents in which communication between a health professional and a patient or client breaks down due to a lack of knowledge about cultural differences. Four possible explanations are offered; information on best choices is presented in a separate section.

Increasing Family Participation in the Assessment of Children Birth to Five by E. Crais (1994). Audiotapes and a manual focused on providing theoretical and practical information for helping practitioners increase family participation in the assessment process.

Program Goal: _____

1. Level of Progress—Please check the statement that best describes the extent to which this goal was achieved. (Check one):
   ☐   NO PROGRESS TOWARD ACCOMPLISHING THIS GOAL
   ☐   A LITTLE PROGRESS TOWARD ACCOMPLISHING THIS GOAL
   ☐   A MODERATE AMOUNT OF PROGRESS TOWARD THIS GOAL
   ☐   GOAL COMPLETELY ACCOMPLISHED

2. How satisfied are you with the amount of **progress** you have made toward accomplishing this goal? (Circle one number)

1	2	3	4	5
NOT AT ALL SATISFIED		SOMEWHAT SATISFIED		COMPLETELY SATISFIED

3. Have you encountered any **barriers or difficulties** in working toward accomplishing this goal? (Check one)
   ☐   YES
   ☐   NO
       If yes, then go to #4

4. Put a check beside **the barriers or difficulties** you have encountered in working toward this goal. (Check all that apply)
Yourself
☐ NEED ADDITIONAL SKILLS, KNOWLEDGE OR INFORMATION
☐ NEED MORE TIME AVAILABLE TO ACCOMPLISH CHANGES
☐ OTHER (SELF): _____

The Program
☐   FUNDS NEEDED BUT NOT AVAILABLE
☐   ADMINISTRATION DOES NOT AGREE WITH OR SUPPORT CHANGES
☐   STRUCTURE OR SCHEDULING OF SERVICES INTERFERES WITH CHANGE
☐   CHANGES CONFLICT WITH RULES AND REGULATIONS OF PROGRAM OR REGULATING AGENCIES
☐   OTHER (PROGRAM): _____

Other Team Members
☐   DO NOT AGREE WITH OR SUPPORT CHANGES
☐   DO NOT HAVE TIME AVAILABLE TO ASSIST WITH CHANGES
☐   NEED ADDITIONAL SKILLS, KNOWLEDGE, OR INFORMATION TO MAKE CHANGES
☐   OTHER (TEAM): _____

Families
☐   DO NOT HAVE THE NECESSARY SKILLS OR ABILITIES
☐   DO NOT WANT THE CHANGES
☐   DO NOT HAVE ENOUGH TIME AVAILABLE TO TAKE ADVANTAGE OF OR SUPPORT CHANGES
☐   OTHER (FAMILY): _____

Goal
☐   DECIDED THAT CHANGE WAS NOT NEEDED AFTER ALL
☐   OTHER GOALS WERE DEVELOPED THAT WERE MORE IMPORTANT
☐   THERE HAS BEEN NO OPPORTUNITY TO TRY OUT NEW METHODS
☐   ACTIVITIES RELATED TO CHANGES ARE TAKING MORE TIME THAN ORIGINALLY ANTICIPATED

Additional Barriers or Comments _____

Figure 8–3. Report of progress and barriers in working with families. (From *Brass-Tacks: A Self-Rating of Family-Centered Practices in Early Intervention, Part II— Individual Interactions with Families* by P. J. Williams and P. Winton, 1990, p. 2. Chapel Hill, Frank Porter Graham Child Development Center, University of North Carolina. Reprinted with permission.)

In certain areas, such as intercultural communication and team building, developing self-awareness and building skills might best be promoted through small group activities that focus on examining and respecting individual differences. Especially given the emphasis in early intervention on collaborative problem-solving skills and the ability to function effectively in a group, it makes sense that group activities might be an important means for developing collaborative skills. "The act of sharing ideas, of having to put one's own views clearly to others, of finding defensible compromises and conclusions, is in itself educative" (Sizer, 1992, p. 89). Training resources that are particularly valuable in this regard are compilations of group exercises by O'Malley & Davis (1994) and Seelye (1996) that include activities focusing on the areas of: uncovering stereotypes and biases, intercultural and individual differences in terms of disclosure, communication styles, conflict resolution, team player style, and so on. It may be that a small group of colleagues and families would be willing to devote their time and energy to engaging in exercises designed to build more collaborative practices; however, this would not likely happen without leadership and initiative from some direction. In a later section on making changes at the agency level, more information is provided about strategies for building skills and promoting family-centered practices with an entire team or agency.

Other potential resources for skill development are workshops or courses sponsored by universities, state agencies, or professional organizations. Strategies for locating such opportunities include contacting the Part H agency or allied agencies that provide early intervention services in your state, local interagency coordinating councils (LICCs), community colleges and universities, and state-level professional organizations. Many of the behaviors described in this book include process skills (e.g., communication skills, group process skills, understanding family and organizational systems) that are not easily taught through traditional means (e.g., lectures and readings). This challenges you to look for innovative opportunities to learn and develop your skills. You may have to carefully scrutinize course and workshop offerings and even get in touch with the organizers and presenters to ask them about the format and activities planned. A checklist of quality indicators related to early intervention inservice training has been developed by Winton (1993). Included in this checklist are some of the following questions:

____ Will there be an interdisciplinary focus?

____ Will families be present as participants or presenters?

____ Have families been involved in planning the workshop or course?

____ What formats will be used for conveying information? For instance, will experiential activities be included? To what extent?

___ Will there be opportunities to practice skills and get feedback?

___ Is there a follow-up component to the workshop that will provide continued opportunities for skill-building and feedback?

So, perhaps now is the best time for you to develop your action plan. Identify some short-term objectives and stick them on your refrigerator, your bulletin board, your office wall, or some other visible place. Make sure you pick small things that can be accomplished and checked off when done, so you have the satisfaction of knowing that progress is being made. Constantly update your plan with new objectives and ideas. Celebrate your successes. Share your plan with friends and colleagues. Some parent advocacy groups talk about "candle power"—the impact that one small light can have on the way things are. Remember your own "candle power." In 20 years, a parent may still be recounting the small thing you did or said that made the difference.

■ MAKING CHANGES AT THE AGENCY LEVEL

It is important to recognize that new or innovative ideas brought in by individuals to institutional structures enter an existing ecology. Each community and agency has its own unique history, tradition, models, and structures for providing services to young children. These things compose the ecology within which change takes place. Unfortunately, institutional structures tend to be characterized by inertia. Unless the new ideas fill an existing gap, or meet a universally agreed upon need within that ecology, or are truly capable of being implemented by an individual in their individual interactions, the ideas are likely to wither on the vine.

Why are changes at the program level so difficult to accomplish? The reasons are multiple. Numerous agency factors play a role in how services are provided to children and families and what changes might be possible. These include (a) agency size, (b) agency structure, (c) the extent to which that structure is flexible and responsive to the needs and diversity of the community, (d) history and philosophy in terms of working with families and children and in terms of past expectations of service providers, (e) methods of evaluation and supervision, and (f) type and extent of staff development opportunities.

Many of those factors are interactive. For instance, large agencies might have greater resources, meaning that broad-based support to families might be easier to achieve within a single agency. However, large agencies might also have more rigid bureaucratic structures as compared to small agencies. This might make adoption of new practices more difficult.

Innovative ideas impact people and systems on many levels of the ecology. They may require changes in policies and programs structures, as well as changes in interactions between people. Without the participation and agreement of all people affected by an innovation, it is unlikely they will be able or willing to make the accommodations necessary for the innovation to succeed (Winton, 1990). Even if the ideas seem to address an agreed upon need, if they are introduced by just one person they are unlikely to be implemented by an entire team or agency.

A study carried out in Great Britain (Georgiades & Phillimore, 1975), entitled "The Myth of the Hero-Innovator and Alternative Strategies for Organized Change," documented the failure of the training strategy that had one staff person in a mental health center sent to a training event to take an innovation back that the rest of the staff would implement. The study suggested that one of the reasons for the failure was that staff members did not share the same knowledge or values about the innovation. The authors speculated that if the entire agency had received the training together, the desired changes might have occurred. The issues and concerns that each individual had about the innovation could have been effectively addressed within the training context, but they could not be addressed by the lone individual. If you have ever attended a course or a workshop during your professional career, returned to work eager to try out new ideas and felt disappointed in the outcome, then you have experienced the powerful influence of the "status quo" and the frustrations of being a "hero innovator."

This information on the change process is quite relevant to many of the ideas presented in this book. In fact, some recent research has documented the extent to which early interventionists recognize the complexity of making desired changes in their practices with children and families (Bailey, Buysee, Edmondson, & Smith, 1992). Early interventionists in this study were asked to identify the barriers that prevented them from being as family-centered in their practices as they wanted to be. The largest number of barriers they identified were related to systems and program structures. These barriers included the monitoring and reimbursement procedures that dictated their practices, the size of their caseloads, and other factors that could be considered beyond an individual's power to control, the second largest number related to families. Interventionists who mentioned this type of barrier indicated that families did not have the time, interest, or skills to participate in a family-centered approach. Only a small percentage of the barriers identified by interventionists related to their own knowledge and skill. Therefore, it is important to consider the ecology of the system of services in your community, the perceptions of your co-workers, and the ways that the ideas you want to try might affect and be affected by that ecology.

Deciding Where Your Agency or Program Is

If you are interested in making changes in your agency or program, you might begin by asking yourself the following questions:

- Is my supervisor/administrator/board of directors familiar with and/or interested in the ideas presented in this book?
- Are my colleagues familiar with and interested in the ideas presented in this book?
- Do these ideas mesh or fit with other priorities of my agency?
- What strategies can I use to introduce this information to supervisors and peers?

These questions are designed to assist you in finding and mobilizing support and interest for the ideas presented in this book within the agency where you work. Perhaps you could interest others in creating a task force or authorizing an existing group to develop a plan for assessing the family-centered aspects of your program. Maybe you could enlist a small group of staff who routinely work together to examine one aspect of your program (e.g., first contacts, waiting list). The bottom line is how can you share your enthusiasm and interest—your "candle power"—with others in a way that inspires the larger group effort that is necessary for making program changes.

Inspiring others is, indeed, a significant challenge. One strategy that has proven effective is for an individual to provide a model for family-centered practices that eventually gets noticed. If you can generate group interest within your program through your own example or through other methods, the resources described below may be helpful in examining program practices and deciding which practices should be targeted for change.

■ PROGRAMMATIC ASSESSMENT TOOLS AND MATERIALS

Brass Tacks: A Self-Rating of Family-Centered Practices in Early Intervention, Part I—Program Policies and Practices by P. McWilliam & P. Winton (1990b).

> This instrument is designed to assess the degree to which program policies and practices are in line with a family-centered approach. Five areas of program practices are addressed: (1) initial contacts, (2) identifying first encounters with families, goals for intervention (child and family assessment), (3) intervention planning, and (4) day-to-day service provision. A number of questions related to specific program practices are posed within each area. Respondents rate the degree to which the program engages in each practice and identify practices that

they want to change. Additional forms for developing action plans and evaluating progress towards goals are included. This instrument is ideal for obtaining group consensus when used with teams or entire agencies.

Brass Tacks: The Family Report by P. McWilliam (1991).

This instrument is designed to obtain parent input regarding the degree to which programs and individual professionals engage in family-centered practices. The instrument is divided into the same four areas of program practices as the Brass Tacks instruments (see description above) and uses a comparable rating format. The questions used for rating, however, are worded to reflect the family's perception of how they were treated during each phase of service delivery.

Brass Tacks: Neonatal Intensive Care Units by P. McWilliam (1993).

This instrument is designed to assess the degree to which NICUs engage in practices that are family-centered. Like the other Brass Tacks instruments, the NICU version uses a question and rating scale format. The instrument, however, is much briefer than the other Brass Tacks instruments, consisting of only 28 characteristics of family-centered care in NICUs.

Infusing Family-Centered Practices into Agency Administration by P. Parham & P. McMahon (1994).

This manual focuses on the application of family-centered principles to agency administration issues. The format used is that information is provided about an aspect of agency administration, such as governing boards; and questions are posed that ask how families are (or could be) involved in that aspect of administration. Illustrative examples from the authors' own agency are provided throughout. These questions could provide the basis for developing a plan of action for changing administrative policies and procedures.

Family-Centered Program Rating Scale (Provider and Parent Scale—Spanish versions available) by D. Murphy, I. Lee, V. Turbiville, A. Turnbull, & J. Summers (1991).

This scale consists of 59 questions related to family-centered practices. Respondents are asked to rank the personal importance of each item as well as rate how well the program is doing in that area. This tool does not include a format for actually developing a plan of action for making changes.

Hospitals: Moving Forward with Family-Centered Care by J. Hanson, B. Johnson, E. Jeppson, J. Thomas, & J. Hall (1994).

This publication is designed to encourage hospital staff, advisory boards, and families to examine their environment, policies, and practices related to family-centered care. There are several checklists and questionnaires included in the publication that relate to: family-to-family support , hospital design, linking families with communities, and education of professionals.

Family Orientation of Community and Agency Services (FOCAS) by D. Bailey (1991).

This scale consists of 12 items designed to give practitioners an opportunity to assess typical and ideal practices across five dimensions of family involvement in early intervention programs: family-centered philosophy, family participation in decisions about the child assessment process, family participation in child assessment, family participation in team meetings and decision making, and provision of family services.

Family Support Principles: Checklists for Program Builders and Practitioners by C. Dunst (1990).

This tool is designed to give program developers and practitioners an opportunity to assess whether or not policies and practices are consistent with the aims of family resource programs. Six principles are addressed: enhancing a sense of community, mobilizing resources and supports, shared responsibility and collaboration, protecting family integrity, strengthening family functioning, and proactive human service practices.

Workbook for Developing Culturally Competent Programs for Families of Children with Special Needs by R. Roberts (1990).

This tool (self-study workbook and accompanying monograph) is designed for two target audiences: (1) programs and (2) larger state organizations or interagency groups. The focus is on both policy and practices that promote sensitivity to individual family variations. The practice section is divided into the areas of: assessment, outreach, staffing, client load, and training. A summary section provides a framework for developing an action plan for change.

Understanding Family Uniqueness Through Cultural Diversity by M. Luera (1994).

These materials are designed to be used in a 4-day workshop sequence. Self-awareness, cultural exclusiveness, and consciousness raising are completed in the first workshop; heightened awareness in the second workshop; overemphasis in the third workshop; and integration and balance in the fourth and final workshop. Each component builds on the previous component.

Cultural Competence Tool for Self-Reflection by S. Moore and J. Beatty (1995).

This tool serves to provide a guide for teams in identifying cultural variables that may serve as barriers to conducting unbiased child assessments, and in identifying a plan for making changes.

Asking Parents for Feedback on Program Practices

Some programs have parent advisory boards or parent representatives on their advisory boards. Parents who serve in this capacity might be willing to talk with program staff and administration about areas of program practice that they feel need changing. Guidelines for effectively promoting family participation in advisory and professional development activities may be found in Jeppson & Thomas (1995) and Winton & DiVenere (1995). These authors make the point that often a small number of parents are continually asked to represent the "parent perspective." Ideally, feedback should be solicited from a larger group of families and one that is sociologically and culturally diverse. Strategies to enlist parents include: (a) recruiting families through community-based advocacy organizations, community centers or churches; (b) translating materials into the native languages of parents being recruited; (c) providing childcare, transportation, financial stipends, and other incentives for participation; (d) planning meetings and events for times when working parents can participate; and (e) developing networks of families who are willing to participate in advisory and training capacities.

Another way to obtain more family input for evaluation and feedback purposes is to conduct a family focus group that addresses specific questions about program policies and practices. The advantage of a focus group is that families are stimulated by each other's comments and may, therefore, contribute more information than they might if asked the same questions on a one-to-one basis. Parents are also likely to build on each other's ideas and generate strategies for making positive changes. More information on how to effectively use focus groups for conducting evaluations is available in Krueger (1994).

Paper and pencil methods of obtaining parent feedback are another option. The family version of the Brass Tacks instruments, *Brass Tacks:*

The Family Report (McWilliam, 1991), has now been used by numerous programs and several states in an attempt to solicit parent input and evaluation regarding the degree to which early intervention services are family-centered. In choosing a survey or developing your own, keep in mind that the more specific your questions are, the more useful they will be in identifying areas of practice that should be changed. Global satisfaction measures usually result in overall positive ratings and provide little information that can actually be used in planning for change.

Surveys such as *Brass Tacks: The Family Report* can be mailed to parents with return envelopes or service providers can hand deliver them. You can ask a selected sample of parents to complete ratings of the program or you can ask all parents to participate. A program in Canada used an interesting variation in their attempt to make services more family-centered. The program decided to concentrate on changes in one aspect of the program at a time (e.g., referral and intake, child assessment, intervention planning) and they solicited parent input by mailing out only the area of *Brass Tacks: The Family Report* that corresponded with the aspect of the program they were attempting to improve. One advantage of this method was that the surveys were shorter and thus reduced the amount of time that parents were asked to contribute.

A problem in using written surveys sent by mail is that many families will not respond, especially if the survey is not written in their native language or in language that they can understand. The literacy levels of the families being surveyed must be considered. Translating surveys into the native language of the families whose opinions are being sought is a strategy that also must be considered if programs desire to effectively serve all families. Another way to collect survey information is to conduct face-to-face or telephone interviews with families using a standard set of topics and related questions. Again, using the native language of the families being surveyed is important, meaning that interpreters will be needed in situations in which the staff is not bilingual. As mentioned in Chapter 3 issues and guidelines for effectively using interpreters are available in Jeppson and Thomas (1995), Lynch and Hanson (1992), and Randall-David (1989).

When talking with families for evaluation or feedback purposes or collecting this information by mail, there are several things to keep in mind. First, provide clear explanations as to why parent input is being requested and how it will be used. Second, make sure parents know whether their ratings or comments will be kept confidential and, if so, how confidentiality will be ensured. Anonymous feedback tends to be more honest. Third, whenever possible, offer parents options for providing feedback. Even when using existing paper-and-pencil surveys, you might think about offering parents the option of having a staff member sit down with them to complete the forms. You never know when a parent may have difficulty reading, but would still like to offer their assistance. Finally, let parents know the results of any survey that is conducted and how the information was or will be used. If you ask parents for their input, they are provided with the results, and they see change as a result of their efforts, they are more likely to offer their time and assistance in the future.

Developing and Implementing a Plan for Change

As mentioned earlier, skill-building and awareness-raising activities related to improving the effectiveness of early intervention are often most effective when carried out with a group of individuals who must work together in a collaborative fashion to best serve families. A team-based, decision-making model for assisting programs, agencies, and teams in developing concrete plans for moving toward family-centered practices was developed at the Frank Porter Graham Child Development Center and has been described in the literature (Bailey, McWilliam, & Winton, 1992; Winton, 1990; Winton, McWilliam, Harrison, Owen, & Bailey, 1992). The model consists of a series of workshops that are designed to give key players in an early intervention program (e.g., administrators, teachers, therapists, families) an opportunity to identify existing practices in light of family-centered principles, to identify areas in which change is desired, and to develop concrete strategies for moving in the desired directions. A training curriculum for the model that includes handouts and overhead transparencies has been developed and is available (Bailey, McWilliam, Winton, & Simeonsson, 1992). The *FOCAS* and *Brass Tacks* instruments described previously were developed within the context of the model as tools for assisting the team-based, decision-making aspects of the model, but other tools could be used within the general framework of the model.

One of the essential aspects of the model is family participation. The decision-oriented format provides families with a structured opportunity for sharing their perspectives and providing feedback to practitioners. Research conducted on the model has documented the central role of family participation (Bailey, Buysse, Smith, & Elam, 1992). Six teams from one large agency participated in the research study in which three of teams (experimental group) were instructed to invite families to participate in the series of workshops, and three teams (control group) did not invite families. Those teams with family participants differed from those teams without families in that they identified more areas of practice in which change was desired. Anecdotal evidence substantiated the contribution of families. The workshops for the two groups (experimental and control) were conducted in separate rooms in the same large facility. During the workshop breaks, teams without families started asking the teams with families if they could "borrow" parents. They complained that decisions about how to change their program practices were difficult to make without family input.

The team-based model and *Brass Tacks* instruments were success-fully used for promoting family-centered practices by a large agency in Southern California serving many Latino families. The agency translated the *Brass Tacks* into Spanish and hired Spanish interpreters so that the workshop portion of the training event could be understood by all partic-ipants. One of the unexpected outcomes of this approach was that the bilingual staff at the agency, who had primary responsibility for serving the Spanish-speaking families, felt that the agency's commitment to involve Latino families in the staff development effort validated and affirmed their staff role in the agency. Giving the families they served a "voice" and an opportunity to speak that everyone, including administra-tors, could hear, created a greater sense of belonging and importance in the agency for the bilingual staff, as well as for the families.

The team-based model for change and the *Brass Tacks* instruments have also been used for creating changes in a university-based clinic and practicum site. The colleagues of the university-based speech-language pathologist we introduced earlier who had begun trying various family-centered practices on her own noticed the changes in her practices and asked her to share some of her ideas. Her department chair and dean were supportive of the ideas and the interest they generated, and therefore, funded a 2-day training session on family-centered practices for the facul-ty and clinical supervisors associated with their university department. The following description outlines how the planning and implementation of the training session evolved.

I was pleased when my colleagues first approached me about sharing with them some of the family-centered techniques that I, and some of the students I supervised, had been trying with children and families. In discussing the idea of information sharing, we agreed on two goals. First, we wanted to make our clinic practices more in-sync with the theory and ideas discussed in our acad-emic courses; and second, we hoped to provide students with multiple mod-els of family-centered practices. In thinking about how best to "share" this information with our academic and clinical faculty, we agreed that a small group of faculty representing the disciplines of our clinic (speech-language pathologists, audiologists) and who served different populations (e.g., chil-dren, adults) would plan a series of training events. The first event would be a 1-day workshop geared to presenting family-centered principles and prac-tices across the lifespan. To encourage the use of family-centered practices within our clinic and in our many off-campus practicum placements, both our faculty and all our area supervisors were invited. In addition, to provide us with consumer perspectives, several family members (e.g., parents, spouses, adult children) of those receiving services in our clinic were invited. Two area professionals who, themselves, were advocates of family-centered practices, were asked to help facilitate the workshop activities.

The 1-day event was recently held and was attended by 40 individuals representing facilities surrounding the university community and a variety of family members. The topics presented included first contacts with families, identifying priorities and concerns, assessment practices, and intervention planning, and were provided through mini-presentations and application activities.

A second event planned for the day following the workshop was a smaller retreat designed to provide the faculty an opportunity to review overall and individual clinic practices. The focus during the retreat was on using the *Brass Tacks* tool (*Part I: Program Practices*) to get faculty to examine their own clinical practices (and policies of our clinic), to identify those policies and practices in need of change, and to develop strategies for addressing the changes. The day was spent working through three of the areas of practice identified on *Brass Tacks* (first encounters, identifying goals for intervention, and intervention planning) and a variety of ideas and plans for change were developed. The faculty agreed to a second meeting at a later time to take up issues not addressed and to assess the extent to which changes identified were made.

A few days following the workshop, one of the participant supervisors who works in a neonatal intensive care unit called to ask if she could cite some of the materials used during the workshop. She was planning an in-service event in her hospital and wanted to share some of the ideas and handouts with her colleagues. Of course, I was pleased to share the materials with her and suggested a few others that she might wish to use. In addition, she noted her frustrations at times in working with families and went on to say, "The hardest thing for me is when I can make the baby feed and I hand him over to the mom and as she is doing it, the baby falls apart. And she says to me 'You can feed my baby and I can't.' I hate that part of my job because I know that at that moment, the mom thinks of herself as a failure." She went on to say that she was planning to try some ideas from the workshop in working with families. In particular, she wanted to work toward encouraging families to use their own knowledge and skills, and investing more of her time in helping them feel more competent. She said, "Maybe if I build on their skills by suggesting small things, and don't come off as the expert who can instantly make the baby feed, they will feel better about their own parenting skills."

It was exciting to think that not only had the workshop impacted this one professional, but was likely through her in-service training efforts to impact her colleagues as well. Thus the workshop information was like a small stone skipping across the water, causing a rippling effect here and another there. Clearly, one small stone tossed in the water did cause ripples, but only because someone took the time to toss it.

Our experience suggests that there may be certain critical agency characteristics that sustain changes at the program or agency level (Winton et al., 1992). These include:

- An on-site supervisor who is supportive of a family-centered approach and who is able and willing to provide support and feedback to staff who are trying out new ideas related to being more family-centered

- Making time available for team meetings, discussions, and ongoing staff development related to family-centered practices
- An agency administrator who is able and willing to support staff and supervisors as they try new practices and able to advocate for these approaches with bureaucrats and decision makers at higher levels, such as state monitors
- A willingness to continue to include families in decision making and monitoring roles so that family perspectives are included in decisions about how programs should be structured

Because some of the ideas associated with family-centered early intervention are new, the extent to which an agency can respond to change and disruptions of the status quo is an important factor to consider. Questions that you may want to consider in regard to sustaining the new ideas include: (1) Are there rewards and incentives for staff who are willing and open to trying new ideas? and (2) Do the evaluation systems in place reward a family-centered approach or the new ideas I want to try? For example, in a later section of this chapter, information is provided from two states (Alaska and Kansas) that have implemented a state-wide "family-centered" approach to program monitoring and review. If you feel that your agency is responding to state guidelines or monitoring procedures that do not support the practices that your agency wants to implement, you might want to look at what Alaska and Kansas have done.

■ THE BIGGER PICTURE

Changes in individual or program practices are likely to affect professionals in other community agencies. Likewise, the influence of other community agencies frequently affects our own ability to succeed in making changes. For instance, how children are referred for early intervention services is one of those issues that cuts across agencies. In one community, the early intervention program was frustrated because the county health department referral process was deterring rather than encouraging families from seeking services. Another community-based issue is the quality and presence of inclusive settings. Philosophically, providers might support the concept of inclusion, but they might be reluctant to make this recommendation if they do not feel quality early childhood programs are available that accept children with disabilities. Transitions between programs (hospital to home; infant to preschool, and preschool to kindergarten) are often points at which services to children and families suffer unless there are interagency efforts to ensure that needs are being met. Unfortunately, there are numerous barriers that impede collaboration across agencies (Blank & Melaville, 1991; Harbin, 1996; Harrison, Lynch, Rosander, & Borton, 1990).

One factor that makes collaboration challenging is that agencies have different regulations that affect services. For instance, in some states the eligibility criteria for infant–toddler services (birth–3 years) is different from the eligibility criteria for preschoolers (3–5 years). As a result, some children receiving infant–toddler services will not be eligible for services after their third birthday. There are also important philosophical differences in how agencies approach families. A family may find that their home-based service provider is supportive and helpful, but that visits to the follow-up clinic in the hospital only increase their stress; or vice versa. Other potential barriers include inadequate knowledge of each other's service, lack of collaboration skills, and competition for scarce resources.

Families probably suffer the most from these discrepancies in agency philosophies and regulations because the services and support they need are often spread across a number of different agencies. If providing broad-based community support to families is an underlying theme of the practices you would like to implement, you will need the cooperation and resources of your colleagues in other agencies.

Deciding Where to Start

In some communities, local interagency coordinating councils (LICCs) serve as a mechanism for community collaboration. A good resource related to initiating and sustaining an effective LICC is a book by Swan and Morgan (1993). This practical book includes sample letters, contracts, and charts related to the organization and structure of an LICC, tips for involving family members, strategies for financing interagency efforts and for effective service coordination.

Questions that you might want to ask yourself in terms of how you can personally increase your effectiveness in the area of community service systems are:

- Are you familiar with existing community programs and resources that might serve young children with disabilities and their families?
- Do you share information about other resources with families?
- Do you actively work with generic early childhood programs (YMCA, community centers, parks and recreation programs) to ensure access to these programs for children with disabilities?
- Do you participate in formal or informal activities that promote greater coordination of services?
- Would you be a good representative to your local interagency coordinating council (LICC)?

In addition, there are checklists and tools that have been developed to assist communities in looking at present policies and practices with a focus on making changes. These include:

Do You Need to Collaborate? **In W. Swan & J. Morgan (1993),** *Collaborating for Comprehensive Services for Young Children and their Families.*

This is a simple one-page "yes/no" checklist of statements pertaining to community-based service delivery models and problems within that system.

Process for Crafting a Profamily System of Education and Human Services. **In A. Melaville, M. Blank, & G. Asayesh (1993),** *Together We Can: A Guide for Creating a Profamily System of Education and Human Services.*

This checklist was developed for the purpose of assisting interagency community-based agencies develop an effective, collaborative team that can make positive changes in community services and programs for families. The checklist addresses the stages of team development: (1) getting together, (2) building trust and ownership, (3) developing a strategic plan, (4) taking action, (5) going to scale.

Guidelines for Community and Societal Supports. **In S. Epstein & A. Taylor (1989),** *Enhancing Quality: Standards and Indicators of Quality Care for Children with Special Health Care Needs.*

The focus of this document is society's responsibility to empower the child with special needs. Checklists are provided for evaluating quality within 3 major areas: (1) public awareness, (2) family support, and (3) integration of service and ease of access.

Colorado Child Identification Process (Birth–Five Years): Effectiveness Indicators. **Colorado Department of Education.**

This tool is designed to help interagency and community groups develop strategies related to the process of child identification. The tool is process-oriented and focuses on action planning related to making positive changes in the process.

Continuity in early childhood: A framework for home, school, and community linkages. **Regional Educational Laboratories' Early Childhood Collaboration Network (1995).**

This document provides home, school and community partners with an opportunity to examine and rate current policies and practices in eight areas and identify practices in need of change. The eight areas of focus are families as partners, shared leadership, comprehensive and responsive services, culture and home language, communication, knowledge and skill development, appropriate care and education, and evaluation of partnership success.

If collaboration of this sort supports some of the ideas you want to try, you might identify ways to nurture budding relationships within your community and introduce strategies and tools such as those listed above that might lead to greater collaboration. Because one of the underlying assumptions of family-centered early intervention is that families will have access to a comprehensive, coordinated service system, this issue of existing resources and the extent to which they are coordinated is an extremely important one for families.

Making Changes at the Policy Level

Numerous sets of policies (e.g., federal laws, state laws, local policies and regulations, professional licensing and certification requirements, monitoring, and reimbursement procedures) influence how we carry out our professional roles and responsibilities. In fact, we have all experienced situations in which it seemed that meeting these standards and requirements was "the bottom line" in terms of officially doing a "good job." An important factor in how we work with families has, therefore, been our ability to document what we do on paper in ways that meet state or local regulations for service delivery. For example, as we pointed out in the chapter on intervention planning, state monitors who check program practices to see if they are in compliance with state regulations often evaluate IEP and IFSP forms. By emphasizing the form, rather than the process by which families and professionals developed what is included on the form, the monitors perhaps unwittingly have focused efforts on the development of a product rather than a process. In this book, we have continually emphasized the process over the product. We have described an IFSP or IEP product that might be written by parents in their own language and one that might look more like a "To Do" list tacked up on the refrigerator than a formal and official document. You might find these ideas appealing but totally unlike what is currently acceptable in your agency or community for monitoring purposes. Our experience suggests that in at least some situations state monitors are receptive and open to modifying procedures for documenting compliance with regulations if efforts are made to explain the rationale for the process being followed and the subsequent product that results (Winton et al., 1992).

Another set of policies and procedures that influence professional practices and affect our ability to make changes are those related to reimbursement procedures. We have continually described in this book the importance of establishing a relationship with families and understanding their perspectives, values, and priorities. Building rapport and developing good relationships with families takes time, yet some of the activities associated with this process may not mesh readily into existing reimbursement categories. You may like the idea of spending more time with families but may be wondering how this fits with the need to account for your time under your current reimbursement system.

It is important to point out that at this time of change and restructuring, there are opportunities for you to have an influence on early intervention policies. As mentioned earlier, the local and state interagency coordinating councils that were mandated through P.L. 99-457 have provided opportunities for professionals and consumers working in direct service to have a role in policymaking. This information suggests some questions related to policies that you might want to consider when developing a strategy for implementing the ideas you want to try:

- Do existing policies and regulations support the ideas I want to try?
- To what extent are policies flexible and subject to varying interpretations?
- Do opportunities exist for discussing interpretations of policies and regulations with policymakers in light of a family-centered approach?
- Are there opportunities for administrators, service providers, and families to work collaboratively in ways that influence policies in positive ways?
- What strategies might work to create such opportunities for discussion and collaboration?

Some states have addressed the need for family-centered principles to be embedded in state policy by developing program review and monitoring systems that support a family-centered approach. The monitoring systems developed by Alaska and Kansas serve as models that might be duplicated in other states.

Alaska has developed a process and a tool for monitoring their state early intervention programs that is quite extensive and uses family and peer feedback as integral to the process (Alaska Infant Learning Program, 1994). The process consists of a 4-day site review conducted by a review team that is guided by a 42-page program assessment tool. Unique features to this approach are:

- Families receiving services play a major role in the monitoring process. Three of the five members on the program review team are from the community (parents of children with disabilities and a representative from a primary referral source such as Head Start), and one member is a "peer" representative (a provider from another early intervention program).
- The standards assessed during the review process include both program indicators and family outcomes, which serves to enhance the participation of families in the review process.

- One of the outcomes of the review process is that a technical assistance plan is developed and will be supported by the state early intervention program staff. This increases the likelihood that positive changes will result from the monitoring process.

The program review process in Kansas (Kansas Infant-Toddler Services, 1993) was developed through a collaborative effort undertaken by the Part H agency and the Beach Center on Families and Disability at the University of Kansas. The first step in the development process was to hold focus groups with service providers and families throughout the state, asking them to identify what elements should be included in an effective review process that would promote family-centered principles. The information generated through the focus groups was used to develop the community-based process that is now in place. The process includes three phases: preliminary data collection and planning with communities about the upcoming review; on-site visitation by a 5-member review team; and development of a plan for addressing areas of concern identified during the process. Unique features of the review process developed by Kansas include:

- Two of the five members of the site visit team are parents; a parent is invited to serve as the team leader.
- In advance of the site visit, self-assessment tools are sent to the community. The tools are tailored to gather information from: all parents whose children are served through Part H, all service providers who provide Part H services, and a network self-assessment that is filled out by the local interagency coordinating council. The self-assessment information is summarized and provides a framework for the site visit.
- Additional information that guides the visit is collected through a conference between the site review team and key members of the community being reviewed. During this call, community members are asked: What should our review team examine and observe? What is going well that you want us to see? In what areas would you like assistance? During this call an agenda for the visit is created.
- The 1–2 day observation visit by the site team is shaped by the self-assessment information and the conference call. Therefore, each visit is unique to each community. A final activity during the site visit is a synthesizing meeting or exit interview during which a summary of effective and less effective practices and policies is shared by the site team with the community.
- A follow-up written report is sent to the community summarizing the site visit, and the community is invited to provide any additional input by submitting written comments. This summary is also sent to the Infant-Toddler Services (ITS) staff at the state agency.

■ The Infant-Toddler Services staff uses this summary and other information (e.g., semi-annual reports) to develop a report addressing areas where changes are needed. These changes may have been identified by the community, the ITS staff or the site visit team. The report also suggests sources of technical assistance that may be appropriate or other remedies or solutions.

In concluding this chapter, we want to return to the important role that individuals play in creating and sustaining changes. In an article on school reform, Weatherly and Lipsky (1977) called each of us who work directly with people a "street level bureaucrat." By this definition they meant that we all have certain demands placed on us from "above." These include changes in policies and procedures, monitoring and review protocols, and so on. These directives are often vague, sometimes contradictory, and often difficult to monitor from above. All of us have a certain level of freedom to translate and carry out our jobs in ways that suit our styles, beliefs, and attitudes. Weatherly and Lipsky's point is that we are all policymakers in our own work arenas with a substantial amount of power to make decisions, behave, and perform in ways that match our values. From this perspective, each one of us has a personal responsibility and opportunity to make a positive difference for each family that we serve. We hope that this book has provided you with information and resources that will serve you well in your journey towards identifying the early intervention practices that work best for you and the families you serve.

■ REFERENCES

Alaska Infant Learning Program (1994). *Alaska Early Intervention/Infant Learning Program Monitoring Tool.* Anchorage: Alaska Department of Health and Social Services, Division of Public Health, Section of Maternal, Child, and Family Health.

Bailey, D., Buysse, V., Edmondson, R., & Smith, T. (1992). Creating family-centered services in early intervention: Perceptions of professionals in four states. *Exceptional Children, 58,* 298–309.

Bailey, D., Buysse, V., Smith, T., & Elam, J. (1992). The effects and perceptions of family involvement in program decisions about family-centered practices. *Evaluation and Program Planning, 15,* 23–32.

Bailey, D., McWilliam, P., & Winton, P. (1992). Building family-centered practices in early intervention: A team-based model of change. *Infants and Young Children, 5*(1), 73–82.

Bailey, D., McWilliam, P., Winton, P., & Simeonsson, R. (1992). *Implementing family-centered services in early intervention: A team-based model for change.* Cambridge MA: Brookline Publishing Co.

Blank, M., & Melaville, A. (1991). *What it takes: Structuring interagency partnerships to connect children and families with comprehensive services.* Washington, DC: Education and Human Services Consortium.

Crais E., & Wilson, L. (1993). *The Role of Parents in Child Assessment*. Division of Speech & Hearing Sciences, CB #7190, University of North Carolina at Chapel Hill, Chapel Hill, North Carolina, 27599.

Crais, E., & Wilson, L. (1996). The role of parents in child assessment: Self-evaluation by practicing professionals. *Infant-Toddler Intervention* 6(2), 125–143.

Fenichel, E. (1991). Learning through supervision and mentoring to support the development of infants, toddlers, and their families. *Zero to Three: Bulletin of the National Center for Clinical Infant Programs, 8*(2), 1–9.

Gallacher, K. (1995). *Coaching partnerships: Refining early intervention practices*. Missoula: Montana University Affiliated Rural Institute on Disabilities.

Georgiades, N., & Phillimore, L. (1975). The myth of the hero-innovator and alternative strategies for organized change. In C. Kernan & F. Woodford (Eds.), *Behavior modification with the severely mentally retarded* (pp. 313–319). Amsterdam, NY: Elsevier.

Gropper, R. (1996). *Cultural and clinical encounter: An intercultural sensitizer for the health professions*. Yarmouth, MA: Intercultural Press, Inc.

Guskey, T. (1986, May). Staff development and the process of teacher change. *Educational Researcher,* 5–12.

Harbin, G. (1996). The challenge of collaboration. *Infants and Young Children, 8*(3), 68–76.

Harrison, P., Lynch, E., Rosander, K., & Borton, W. (1990). Determining success in interagency collaboration: An evaluation of processes and behaviors. *Infants and Young Children, 3*(1), 69–78.

Hudson, P., Miller, S., Salzberg, C., & Morgan, R. (1994). The role of peer coaching in teacher education programs. *Teacher Education and Special Education, 17*(4), 224–235.

Jeppson, E. & Thomas, J. (1995). *Essential allies: Families as advisors*. Bethesda, MD: Institute for Family-Centered Care.

Kansas Infant-Toddler Services. (1993). *Community network program review*, Topeka: Kansas Department of Health and Environment.

Krueger, R. (1994). *Focus groups: A practical guide for applied research* (2nd ed.). Thousand Oaks, CA: Sage.

Lynch, E., & Hanson, M. (1992). *Developing cross-cultural competence*. Baltimore: Paul H. Brookes.

McWilliam, P. (1991). *Brass tacks: The family report*. Chapel Hill: Frank Porter Graham Child Development Center, University of North Carolina.

McWilliam, P. (1993). *Brass tacks: Neonatal intensive care units*. Chapel Hill: Frank Porter Graham Child Development Center, University of North Carolina.

McWilliam, P., & Winton, P. (1990a). *Brass tacks: A self-rating of family-centered practices in early intervention, Part 2—Individual interactions with families*. Chapel Hill: Frank Porter Graham Child Development Center, University of North Carolina.

McWilliam, P., & Winton, P. (1990b). *Brass tacks: A self-rating of family-centered practices in early intervention, Part 1—Program policies and practices*. Chapel Hill: Frank Porter Graham Child Development Center, University of North Carolina.

Moore, S., & Beatty, J. (1995). *Developing cultural competence in early childhood assessment*. Boulder, CO: University of Colorado.

O'Malley, M., & Davis, T. (1994). *Dealing with differences*. Carrboro, NC: Center for Peace Education.

Pearl, L., Brown, W., & Myers, M. (1990). Transition from neonatal intensive care unit: Putting it all together in the community. *Infants and Young Children*, *3*(1), 41–50.

Roberts, R. (1990). *Developing culturally competent programs for families of children with special needs*. Washington, DC: Georgetown University Child Development Center.

Randall-David, E. (1989). *Strategies for working with culturally diverse communities and clients*. Bethesda, MD: Association for the Care of Children's Health.

Regional Educational Laboratories' Early Childhood Collaboration Network. (1995). *Continuity in early childhood: A framework for home, school, and community linkages*. Tallahassee, FL: SERVE.

Seelye, N. (Ed.). (1996). *Experiential activities for intercultural learning* (Vol. 1). Yarmouth, ME: Intercultural Press.

Sizer, T. (1992). *Horace's school: Redesigning the American high school*. Boston, MA: Houghton Mifflin.

Swan, W., & Morgan, J. (1993). *Collaborating for comprehensive services for young children and their families: The local interagency coordinating council*. Baltimore: Paul H. Brookes.

Taylor, T. (1993). *Moving toward cultural competence: A self-assessment checklist*. Washington, DC: Georgetown University Child Development Center.

Weatherly, R., & Lipsky, M. (1977). Street-level bureaucrats and institutional innovation: Implementing special education reform. *Harvard Educational Review*, *47*(2), 171–197.

Winton, P. (1990). A systemic approach for planning inservice training related to Public Law 99-457. *Infants and Young Children*, *3*(1), 51–60.

Winton, P., & Bailey, D. (1993). Communicating with families: Examining practices and facilitating change. In J. Paul & R. Simeonsson (Eds.), *Understanding and working with parents of children with special needs* (2nd ed.) (pp. 212–233). New York: Holt, Rinehart, & Winston.

Winton, P. (1993). Early intervention personnel preparation: The past guides the future. *Early Childhood Report*, *5*(5), 4–6.

Winton, P., & DiVenere (1995). Family-professional partnerships in early intervention personnel preparation: Guidelines and strategies. *Topics in Early Childhood Special Education*, *15* (3), 296–313.

Winton, P., McWilliam, P., Harrison, T., Owens, A., & Bailey, D. (1992). Lessons learned from implementing a team-based model of change. *Infants and Young Children*, *5*(1), 49–57.

■ RESOURCES

Mentoring and Coaching

Title: *Learning Through Supervision and Mentorship to Support the Development of Infants, Toddlers and Their Families: A Source Book*

Authors:	Fenichel, E.
Date:	1992
Ordering Info.:	ZERO TO THREE/National Center for Clinical Infant Programs 2000 14th Street, North, Suite 380 Arlington, VA 22201-2500 (703) 528-4300 FAX (703) 528-6848 (800) 899-4301 (ordering information only)
Cost:	$18.95 plus $4 shipping and handling

Title:	*Coaching Partnerships: Refining Early Intervention Practices*
Authors:	Gallacher, K.
Date:	1995
Ordering Info.:	Montana University Affiliated Rural Institute on Disabilities, 52 Corbin Hall, University of Montana, Missoula, MT 59812, (406)243-2427
Cost:	Free while available

Interagency Collaboration

Title:	*Together We Can: A Guide for Crafting a Profamily System of Education and Human Services*
Authors:	Melaville, A.I., Blank, M.J., & Asayesh, G.
Date:	1993
Ordering Info.:	Call Susan Talley at (202) 219-2129.
Cost:	Free

Title:	*Colorado Child Identification Process*
Authors:	Colorado Department of Education
Date:	1994
Ordering Info.:	Colorado Department of Education, 201 East Colfax, Denver, CO 80203, (303) 866-6694
Cost:	Free

Title:	*Enhancing Quality: Standards and Indicators of Quality Care for Children with Special Health Care Needs*
Authors:	New England SERVE
Date:	1989
Ordering Info.:	New England SERVE , 101 Tremont Street, Suite 812, Boston, MA 02018 (617) 574-9493
Cost:	$5.00

Title:	*Collaborating for comprehensive services for young children and their families: The local interagency coordinating council*
Authors:	Swan, W. & Morgan, J.

Date: 1993
Ordering Info.:   Paul H. Brookes Publishing Company, P.O. Box 10624,
                    Baltimore, MD 21285-0624 , 1-800-638-3775
Cost: $37.00 plus shipping and handling

Cultural Diversity

Title: *Moving Toward Cultural Competence: A Self-Assess-
                    ment Checklist*
Authors: Taylor, T.
Date: 1993
Ordering Info.:   Georgetown University Child Development Center,
                    3800 Reservoir Road, NW, Washington, DC 20007 (202)
                    687-8635
Cost: Free upon request

Title: *Developing Culturally Competent Programs for Fa-
                    milies of Children with Special Needs*
Authors: Roberts, R.
Date: 1990
Ordering Info.:   Georgetown University Child Development Center,
                    3800 Reservoir Road, NW, Washington, DC 20007
                    (202) 687-8803
Cost: monograph - $6.00; workbook - $4.00

Family-Centered Practices

Title: *Alaska Early Intervention/Infant Learning Program
                    Monitoring Tool*
Authors: Alaska Infant Learning Program
Date: 1995
Ordering Info.:   Pam Muth, Alaska Infant Learning Program Alaska
                    Department of Health and Social Services Division of
                    Public Health, Section of Maternal, Child, and Family
                    Health, 1231 Gambell Street, Anchorage, AK 99501-4627
                    (907) 274-2542
Cost: One free copy will be sent to you upon request.
                    Subsequent copies can be made from this original at
                    no charge.

Title: *Brass Tacks: Part I - Program Policies and Practices,
                    Part II - Individual Interactions with
                    Families*
Authors: McWilliam, P. J., & Winton, P. J.
Date: 1990
Ordering Info.:   FPG Child Development Center, CB #8185, The
                    University of North Carolina, Chapel Hill, NC 27599
                    (919) 966-4221 FAX (919) 966-0862

Cost: $10.00

Title: *Family-Centered Program Rating Scale Provider's Scale (available in Spanish) Parent's Scale (available in Spanish)*
Authors: Turnbull. A.P.
Date: 1991
Ordering Info.:   Ann P. Turnbull, Beach Center on Families and Disability, The University of Kansas Institute for Lifespan Studies, 3111 Haworth Hall, Lawrence, KS 66045 (913) 864-7600 FAX (913) 864-5323
Cost: $1.30 per scale

Title: *Family Orientation of Community and Agency Services* (FOCAS)
Authors: Bailey, D.
Date: 1992
Ordering Info.:   Don Bailey, Ph.D., Frank Porter Graham Child, Development Center, Campus Box #8180, University of North Carolina, Chapel Hill, NC 27599-8180 (919) 966-4221
Cost: $1.00

Title: *Family Support Principles: Checklists for Program Builders and Practitioners*
                      (Family Systems Intervention Monograph Series, vol. 2, no. 5.)
Authors: Dunst, C.
Date: 1990
Ordering Info.:   Family, Infant and Preschool Program, Western Carolina Center, 300 Enola Road, Morganton, NC 28655 (704) 433-2661

Title: *Hospitals Moving Forward with Family-Centered Care*
Authors: Hanson, J. L. et al.
Date: 1994
Ordering Info.:   Institute for Family Centered Care, 5715 Bent Branch Road, Bethesda, MD 20816 (301) 652-0281 FAX (301) 320-0048
Cost: $10.00 prepaid

Title: *Increasing Family Participation in the Assessment of Children Birth to Five*
Author: Crais, E. R.
Date: 1994

Ordering Info.:   Applied Symbolix, 8420 Bryn Mawr Avenue,Chicago, IL 60631
1-800-676-7551
Cost: $59.00 includes workbook and 6 audio cassettes
Title: Infusing Family-Centered Concepts Into Agency Administration
Authors: Parham, P., & McMahon, P.
Date: 1994
Ordering Info.:   Project Ta-kos, Alta Mira Specialized Family Services, Inc., 3201 Fourth Street, NW Albuquerque, NM 87107 (505) 842-9948
Cost: $45.00

Title: *Implementing Family-Centered Services in Early Intervention: A Team-Based Model for Change*
Authors   Bailey, D. et. al.
Date: 1992
Ordering Info.:   Brookline Books, P.O. Box 1046, Cambridge, MA 02238-1046 1-800-666-2665
Cost: $19.95

Communication Skills

Title: *Communicating with Families in Early Intervention: A Training Module*
Authors: Winton, P.
Date: 1991
Ordering Info.:   FPG Child Development Center, CB #8185, The University of North Carolina, Chapel Hill, NC 27599-8185 (919) 966-4221
Cost: $15.00

Title: *Effective Communication for Parents and Professionals*
Authors: Duffy, S. et al.
Date:
Ordering Info.:   Sandy Davis, Dynamic Communication Process Project, Rural Institute on Disabilities, The University of Montana, 52 Corbin Hall, Missoula, MT 59812 (406) 243-2446
Cost: Request from source

Title: *Essential Interviewing, A Programmed Approach to Effective Communication*
Authors: Evans, D., et. al.
Date: 1993 (4th edition)

Ordering Info.:   For multiple copies: Wadsworth, Inc., 7625 Empire Drive, Florence, KY 41642 (606) 525-2230 For single copies: Van Nostrand/Reinhok (800) 842-3636
Cost: $27 plus 6% shipping and handling

Family Participation

Title: *Essential Allies: Families as Advisors*
Authors: Jeppson, E. & Thomas, J.
Date: 1995
Ordering Info.:   Institute For Family Centered Care, 7900 Wisconsin Avenue, Suite 405, Bethesda, MD 20814 (301) 652-0281
Cost: $10.00

Index